FROM LINEAGE TO STATE

Lethbridge

FROM LINEAGE TO STATE

Social Formations in the Mid-First Millennium B.C. *in the Ganga Valley*

ROMILA THAPAR

DELHI
OXFORD UNIVERSITY PRESS
BOMBAY CALCUTTA MADRAS

Oxford University Press, Walton Street, Oxford OX2 6DP

Oxford New York
Athens Auckland Bangkok Bombay
Calcutta Cape Town Dar es Salaam Delhi
Florence Hong Kong Istanbul Karachi
Kuala Lumpur Madras Madrid Melbourne
Mexico City Nairobi Paris Singapore
Taipei Tokyo Toronto

and associates in
Berlin Ibadan

First published 1984
Oxford India Paperback 1990
Fifth impression 1996

ISBN 0 19 562675 3

Printed at Rekha Printers Pvt. Ltd., New Delhi 110020
and published by Manzar Khan, Oxford University Press
YMCA Library Building, Jai Singh Road, New Delhi 110001

FOR KAUSHALYA

The Heras Memorial Lectures honour the memory of the Reverend Henry Heras, S.J., who came to India from Spain in 1922 to be Professor of Indian Historical Research Institute, now renamed the Heras Institute of Indian History and Culture. He died in Bombay in 1955, after spending more than half his life digging up India's past in order to display to the world the history and culture of the land he made his own and whose citizen he became. Sponsored by the Heras Society and organized by the Heras Institute, the 1980 Heras Memorial Lectures, seventeenth in the series, were delivered by Professor Romila Thapar, a scholar of the history of ancient India.

PREFACE

This is an expanded version of the Heras Memorial Lectures on the subject of lineage and state systems in early India, delivered at St. Xavier's College, Bombay in February 1980. I am grateful to Father John Correia-Afonso and the authorities of the Heras Institute and the Heras Society for inviting me to deliver these lectures.

An attempt has been made in these lectures to define the nature of early Indian society during the mid-first millennium B.C. and relate it to the ancient Indian historical tradition in its earliest forms. I have also sought to indicate the particular character of social formations, their genesis and continuity as part of the later Indian social landscape. The data for this book was collected whilst I was on a Jawaharlal Nehru Fellowship during the years 1976 and 1977.

I would like to express my gratitude to my colleagues in the Centre for Historical Studies of the Jawaharlal Nehru University and in particular to Neeladri Bhattacharya, Bipan Chandra, B.D. Chattopadhyaya and Satish Saberwal for their helpful comments on an earlier draft. I would also like to thank Leslie Gunawardana and Sirima Kiribamune at the University of Peradeniya for discussions on the Ceylon Chronicles.

Romila Thapar

ABBREVIATIONS

AISH.	Romila Thapar, *Ancient Indian Social History : Some Interpretations*, New Delhi, 1978
Ait.	*Aitareya*
Aṅg.	*Aṅguttara*
Āpa.	*Āpastamba*
Brāh.	*Brāhmaṇa*
D.S.	*Dharma-sūtra*
D.Śā.	*Dharma-śāstra*
DED.	T. Burrow and M.B. Emeneau, *A Dravidian Etymological Dictionary*, Oxford, 1961
Dīp.	*Dīpavamsa*
G.S.	*Gṛhya-sūtra*
H.O.S.	Harvard Oriental Series
IHR	*Indian Historical Review*
IRRI	International Rice Research Institute, Philippines
JAOS	*Journal of the American Oriental Society*
JESHO	*Journal of the Social and Economic History of the Orient*
Maj.	*Majjhima*
Manu	*Mānava Dharma-śāstra*
Nik.	*Nikāya*
PED	T.W. Rhys Davids and W. Stede, *Pali-English Dictionary*, P.T.S., London, 1966
PIHC	*Proceedings of the Indian History Congress*
P.T.S.	Pali Text Society
Ṛg. V.	*Ṛg Veda*
Śat.	*Śatapatha*
Sam.	*Saṁhitā*
SBE	Sacred Books of the East
Sm.	*Smṛti*
Tait.	*Taittirīya*
Up.	*Upaniṣad*
Vedic Index.	A.A. Macdonell and A.B. Keith, *Vedic Index of Names and Subjects*, Delhi, 1967 (reprint)

CONTENTS

FROM LINEAGE TO STATE

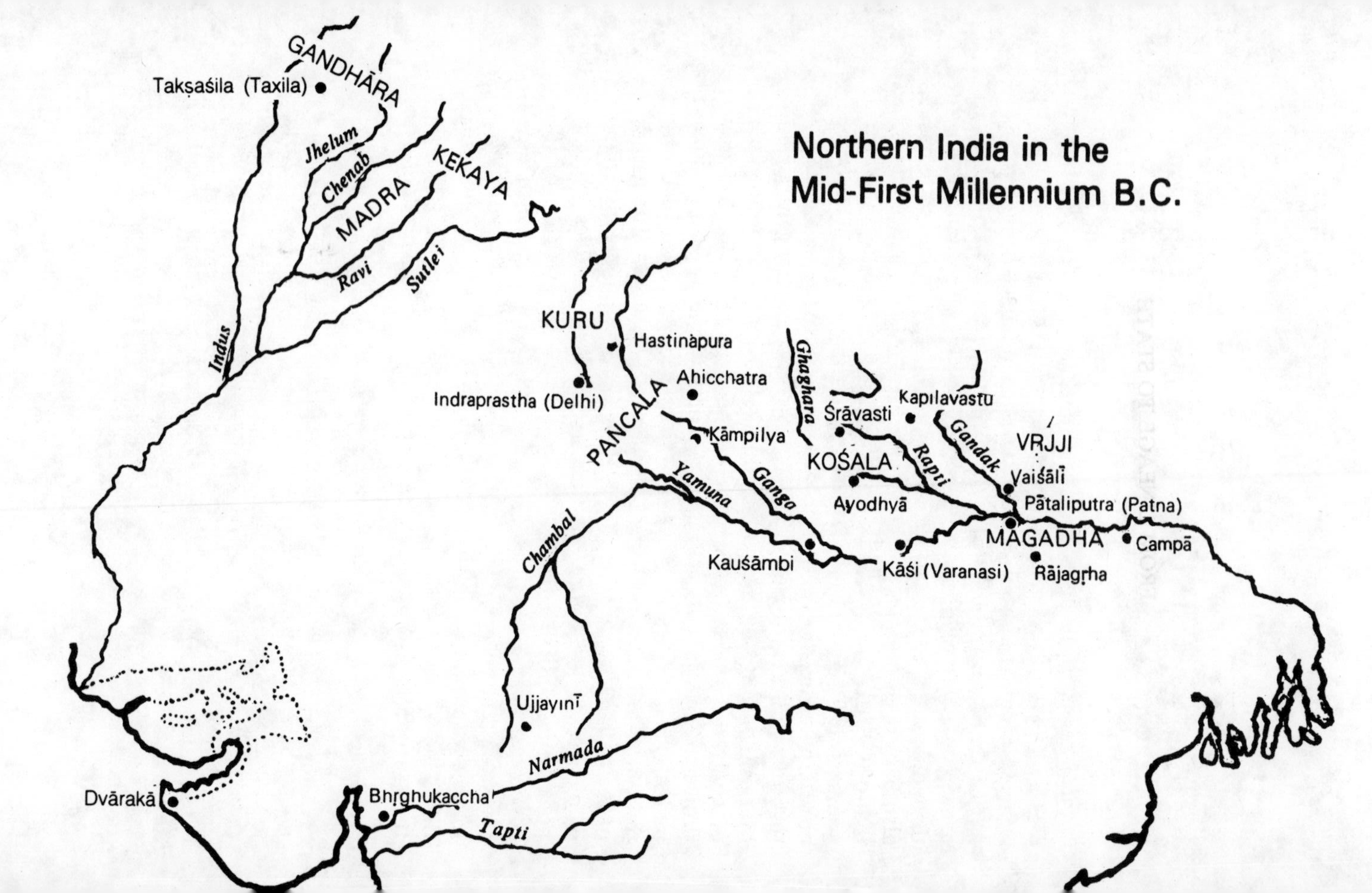
Northern India in the
Mid-First Millennium B.C.
GANDHĀRA
Takṣaśila (Taxila)
Jhelum
Chenab
MADRA
KEKAYA
Ravi
Sutlej
Indus
KURU
Hastināpura
Indraprastha (Delhi)
PANCALA
Ahicchatra
Kāmpilya
Ghaghara
Śrāvasti
Kapilavastu
KOŚALA
Rapti
Gandak
VṚJJI
Vaiśālī
Pātaliputra (Patna)
Ayodhyā
Yamuna
Ganga
Chambal
Kauśāmbi
Kāśi (Varanasi)
MAGADHA
Campā
Rājagṛha
Ujjayinī
Narmada
Dvārakā
Bhṛghukaccha
Tapti

I PRELIMINARIES

Theories on the earliest formation of states in India have been few and generally simplistic. There is none of the conceptual richness which characterizes the discussion on state formation in Africa or Meso-America, partly perhaps because the latter have drawn on ideas relating to the early state among political anthropologists. This poverty of theory on the early Indian state has also been in part due to an abiding obsession with a single image, that of Oriental Despotism: an image projected initially by British administrators and historians and which did not even find its counterpoint, as did many other images from the same source, in the more radical writings of this century.[1] The equally generalized Marxist concern with the Asiatic Mode of Production,[2] in the face of contrary empirical evidence, continued to be enthusiastically projected. The labours of Indian Marxists who have tried to show its inapplicability[3] have often been brushed aside, particularly by those who are interested in it as a theoretical concept. The nature of the Indian state became a favourite subject with those historians who were influenced by Indian nationalism. Studies on the political institutions of early India assumed the existence of the concept of the state but rarely analysed the process by which state formation came about. The concern was substantially with proving the importance of republics, democratic forms and constitutional monarchy or with projecting a monolithic, unitary state virtually from its inception,[4] thereby providing ammunition for the

[1] Romila Thapar, *The Past and Prejudice*, New Delhi, 1975.

[2] Lawrance Krader, *The Asiatic Mode of Production*, Assen, 1975.

[3] Such as the papers by Irfan Habib and S. Naqvi in *Science and Human Progress*, Bombay, 1974. See also, Bipan Chandra, 'Karl Marx: his theories of Asian societies and colonial rule' in Marion O'Callaghan (ed.), *Sociological Theories: Race and Colonialism*, UNESCO 1980, p. 383 ff; cf. P. Anderson, *Lineages of the Absolutist State*, London, 1974.

[4] N. N. Law, *Aspects of Ancient Indian Polity*, Oxford, 1921; U.N. Ghoshal, *A History of Hindu Political Theories*, Calcutta, 1923; K. P. Jayaswal, *Hindu Polity*, Bangalore, 1943 (first edition 1924); A. S. Altekar, *State and Government in Ancient India*, Banaras, 1949.

nationalist ideology. In the last couple of decades a few attempts have been made to describe the difference between the non-state situation and the emergence of the state.[5] These studies can be followed up with a more detailed analysis of the formation of the state. That the latter would have a bearing on even the late forms of the state in India is evident from the most recent studies of some Indian states.[6]

The emergence of a state marks a qualitative change in the history of a society since it arises out of and initiates a series of interrelated changes at many levels. The transition from an absence of states to state systems in the mid-first millennium B.C (the earliest historical period for which there is sufficient literary evidence), has generally been treated as a sudden change. Ṛg Vedic society has been described as a tribal society and that of the later Vedic period as one of state-based kingdoms, the transition having occurred during the period from the late second to the early first millennium B.C. This has sometimes been assumed on the basis of the conquest theory[7] of the rise of the state, which argues that after the supposed conquest of the area by the Aryans when they gained control over the indigenous society, the state almost automatically came into existence. Where the theory of internal stratification[8] and diversification has been applied in preference to the conquest theory, it has been argued that class stratification is reflected in the caste structure with the *kṣatriya*s forming the ruling class and the *viś* constituting the peasantry. In this situation the increasing power of the former led to the emergence of states.

One of the problems in examining the nature of social stratification in early India has been the rather casual and imprecise translations of indigenous terms into English. The influence of European history on nineteenth century Indologists has generated a tendency to use parallels from European society and particularly feudal England, in translating terms relating to socio-economic forms even in literature as early as that of Vedic times, as for example the

[5] R. S. Sharma, *Aspects of Political Ideas and Institutions in Ancient India,* Delhi, 1968 (first edition 1959); C. Drekmeier, *Kingship and Community in Early India,* Berkeley, 1962.

[6] H. Kulke, *Jagannātha-Kult und Gajapati Königtum,* Wiesbaden, 1979; B. Stein, *Peasant State and Society in Medieval South India,* Delhi, 1980.

[7] F. Oppenheimer, *The State,* New York, 1914.

[8] R. H. Lowie, *Primitive Society,* New York, 1920, p. 380 ff.; H. H. Gerth and C. W. Mills, *From Max Weber,* London, 1947, p. 252 ff.

uniform translation of *viś* as peasantry and *śūdra* as serf.[9] The assumption was that *rājanya*s/*kṣatriya*s were nobles and barons and *śūdra*s were serfs.[10] This has resulted in some confusion in attempts at defining exactly when a peasant economy came into existence in northern India. If the *viś* represented the peasantry in Vedic times then various other features which co-exist with a peasant economy should also be present, but this as we shall see, is not the case. The establishment of a peasant economy is also crucial to many theories regarding the origins of the state and the prime movers towards state formation.

Stratification has been viewed as a precondition to the emergence of the state since stratified groups become involved in internal conflicts, require contracts for agreements or result in the evolution of a powerful élite. The prerequisites for stratification are however under debate.[11]

Thus, the theory of stratification is applied in the concept of the Asiatic Mode of Production by arguing that village communities consisting of peasant agriculturalists in the main had a communal land tenure and the state intervened and appropriated the surplus. Here despotism and the irrigation system are secondary traits. Where it is argued that the state owned the land and organized agriculture through settlements of cultivators, there class opposition would be absent.[12]

The most influential theory on the nature of the early Indian state and one which has held the field for many decades is that of Oriental Despotism with its variants and among these the Asiatic Mode of Production. Briefly summarized, the discussion on the state in pre-modern India assumes a static situation until the colonial period, the only change being from clan systems to the socie-

[9] A. A. Macdonell and A. B. Keith, *Vedic Index of Names and Subjects,* vol. II, Delhi, 1967, pp. 389 ff., 202 ff. (fst. ed. 1912).

[10] This is a major weakness even in the recent and otherwise excellent translation of the Critical Edition of the *Mahābhārata* by J. A. van Buitenen (Chicago, 1973). The translator states that he took the terms from the *Vedic Index* and confesses that 'the choice probably was a mistake'. *Journal of Asian Studies,* XXXV, May 1976, no. 3, p. 471.

[11] E. R. Service, 'Classical and Modern Theories of the Origin of Government', in R. Cohen and E. Service (eds.), *Origins of the State,* Philadelphia, 1978. Also H. T. Wright, 'Towards an Explanation of the Origin of the State', in the same publication.

[12] H. J. M. Claessen and P. Skalnik, 'The Early State: Theories and Hypotheses', in H. J. M. Claessen and P. Skalnik, *The Early State*, The Hague, 1978, p. 1 ff.

ty being engulfed by the despotic state, a change believed to have occurred in antiquity.[13] The state was characterized by its ownership of the land with an absence of private property in land, by a despotic king extracting revenue from the village communities which were otherwise autonomous and autarchic except that production being purely agricultural was dependent on irrigation facilities controlled by the state through a hierarchy of officials who also collected the revenue. In such a situation towns were administrative centres, there being an absence of commerce. The only commodities produced were for royal or courtly consumption. The village community although autonomous within itself was nevertheless totally subservient to the state.

Recently a variant on the Asiatic Mode of Production has been suggested with data relating to the Inca state in Peru and its environs.[14] The pre-Inca situation was one in which land was owned communally by clans, was redistributed periodically between extended families who worked it but did not own it and labour was in the form of communal labour with the villagers acting in co-operation. The Incas conquered these clans and declared that all land was the property of the state and some of it was declared crown land. The rest of the land was worked by the members of the clan but as forced labour. The clans lost their rights over the land in terms of ownership but continued to have rights of possession and use, and production therefore remained communal in spite of a changed mode of production. The Inca state maintained some of the earlier customs of providing food, drink and seed to the cultivators in a seeming attempt to suggest that the earlier system still prevailed. There was also an administrative organization to control the clans. The operational base to the Inca system was that labour was now involved in conquest and defence, irrigation, enlargement of the area of cultivation and in the cult of the

[13] K. Marx and F. Engels, *On Colonialism,* Moscow, 1968; P. Anderson, *Lineages of the Absolutist State,* London, 1974; R.A.L.H. Gunawardana, 'The analysis of pre-colonial social formation in Asia in the writings of Karl Marx', *Indian Historical Review,* 1976, II. no. 2, p. 365 ff.; D. Thorner, 'Marx on India and the Asiatic Mode of Production', in *Contributions to Indian Sociology,* 1966, no. 9; Bipan Chandra, 'Karl Marx; his theories of Asian Societies and Colonial Rule', in Marion O'Callaghan (ed.), *Sociological Theories: Race and Colonialism,* UNESCO, Paris, p. 383 ff.

[14] M. Godelier, *Perspectives in Marxist Anthropology*, Cambridge, 1977, p. 186 ff.

ancestors and construction of monuments. Projects involving large numbers of people as manpower followed after the establishment of the state. The state in such a system was the collective landlord and therefore the superior community. Kinship relations as ties in production were destroyed as was the earlier social formation.

The centrality of irrigation systems has been picked up by other commentators arguing for technology as a major variable.[15] The managerial function behind irrigation systems, particularly in the organization of labour and maintenance of control, is seen as germinal to the idea of the state. Control over irrigation does not necessarily imply despotism[16] but does provide a source of power, although the relationship of irrigation to environment, soil, cropping patterns and calendric foci would have to be considered before a correlation can be established. The managerial functions in such a situation became the pre-conditions to the state.

If irrigation systems are seen as a causative factor then the ecological context has also to be discussed for, apart from managerial functions, those with access to good agricultural land would tend to accumulate power. But the nature of control in early societies would vary, where nomadic groups were sometimes known to overpower sedentary agriculturalists. In a situation of evironmental circumscription where, for instance, prime agricultural land is surrounded by poor quality land, sedentary cultivating groups may prefer to come under the hegemony of the surrounding nomadic groups rather than migrate from good agricultural land.[17] The resulting tension may have led towards the formation of a state. Migration would also become difficult in the proximity of areas unfavourable for resources. The emergence of a proto-state in such ecological relationships has been suggested in the case of nomadic groups in juxtaposition with agriculturalists in Baluchistan, where the leading family of the pastoralists becomes the focus of power and the settled agriculturalists are the source of wealth and labour.[18] Such a symbiotic relationship may have

[15] J.H. Steward, *Theory of Culture Change,* Urbana, 1955.

[16] E. and R. C. Hunt, 'Irrigation, Conflict and Politics: A Mexican Case', in R. Cohen and E. Service (eds.), *Origins of the State.*

[17] R. L. Carneiro, 'A Theory of the Origin of the State', in *Science*, 1970, 169, pp. 733-8. Also, 'Political Expansion as an Expression of the Principle of Competitive Exclusion', in R. Cohen and E. Service, *Origins of the State.*

[18] B. Spooner, 'Politics, Kinship and Ecology in S.E. Persia',*Ethnology,* 1969, i, pp. 139-52; P. C. Salzman, 'The Proto-State in Iranian Baluchistan', in Cohen and Service, *Origins of the State.*

characterized the declining Harappan culture and the advent of the Aryan speaking peoples in north-western India in the second millennium B.C.

Population growth and social circumscription are described as primary factors towards state formation where surplus can only be produced under coercion and population growth creates the need to produce and control surplus.[19] This theory does not however examine the reasons leading to population growth. Some significance has also been given to population pressure creating tensions which become accentuated when there is a conflict between communal and private ownership, particularly in societies undergoing such change.[20] Such tension is sometimes diffused by groups migrating to new settlements. Here authority tends to accrue to the founding groups who become the holders of property with preferential access to resources.[21] The coming about of the state can also be seen as an integrative process in which a variety of factors conducive to conflicts are sought to be settled and controlled.[22] Where there is a possibility of groups in conflict being able to migrate, there this fission would prevent conflict as well as make it unnecessary for the mechanism of a state to control conflict.

Increasing social and cultural heterogeneity can also lead to social stratification and a tendency towards centralized political control. In the process of stratification and the building up of a hierarchy, marriage alliances are of some importance. Endogamous alliances strengthened a small group with potential and actual power. Exogamous marriages were more suitable for the assimilation of new groups. Differentiation in status is then wrapped up in legitimation which often derives sanction from religious beliefs and ritual in early societies. Legitimation increases the distance between those of high status and commoners. Sacral kingship is an aspect of this distance and is in turn tied to beliefs concerning the welfare and prosperity of a society being symbolized in that of the individual regarded as the chief.

[19] K. V. Flannery, 'The Cultural Evolution of Civilisations', in *Annual Review of Ecology and Systematics,* 1972, 3, pp. 399-426.

[20] M. H. Fried, *The Evolution of Political Society,* New York, 1967.

[21] R. Cohen, 'The Political System', in R. Naroll and R. Cohen, *A Handbook of Method in Cultural Anthropology*, New York, 1970, pp. 484-99.

[22] E. R. Service, *Origins of the State and Civilisation*: *The Process of Cultural Evolution*, New York, 1975; R. Cohen, 'The Political System', in R. Naroll and R. Cohen (eds.), *Handbook of Method in Cultural Anthropology*, New York, 1971.

In the elaboration of social stratification as a force in state formation others have emphasized the role of urban centres and trade,[23] where trade is generally confined to, or at least reinforces the status of the wealthy, both in terms of actual wealth as well as in terms of trading in goods which are regarded as special and difficult to come by.

These theories point to the analysis of state formation being a complex process in which a range of factors may be crucial and may apply differentially to varying situations. As such there can be no single factor which causes the change, although certainly some would be more central than others. The logical extension of this argument would also be that the forms taken by the state once it had come into being would vary in accordance with the nature of its origin. This allows of the possibility of a variation in the types of early states. These would in turn influence to some extent the typologies of state systems prevalent in different areas and periods of time. A distinction has also to be maintained between primary state formation with which the present study is concerned and secondary state formation which relates more closely to later typologies of states and their control over lineage or proto-state societies.

The investigation of pre-state forms has been much debated in recent decades. Differences between bands, ranked societies, stratified societies, chiefships and state systems have been elaborated upon, as for instance in the writings of Morton Fried. To this may be added the perceptive work of Karl Polanyi[24] which, even if unacceptable as a total paradigm, does nevertheless provide some insights which are very pertinent to the analysis of early historical societies. There has also been considerable discussion on the concept of what has been called the lineage mode of production, proposed by Emmanuel Terray[25] and Pierre-Philippe Rey,[26]

[23] R. McC. Adams, *The Evolution of Urban Society*, Chicago, 1966.

[24] K. Polanyi, *Dahomey and the Slave Trade*, Seattle, 1966; K. Polyani, *et al.*, *Trade and Market in the Early Empires*, Glencoe, 1957; K. Polanyi, *The Great Transformation*, Boston, 1957.

[25] E. Terray, *Marxism and 'Primitive' Societies*, New York, 1972; M. Bloch (ed.), *Marxist Analyses and Social Anthropology*, ASA Studies 2, London, 1975.

[26] P. P. Rey, 'Class Contradiction in Lineage Societies', in *Critique of Anthropology*, 1979, 4, nos. 13 & 14, pp. 41-60; 'The Lineage Mode of Production', *Critique of Anthropology*, Spring 1975, no 3., pp. 27-79.

and commented upon by Maurice Godelier[27] and Claude Meillesoux.[28] Another useful study of the lineage system relates to data from ancient Polynesia.[29] In attempting to re-examine the process of state formation in northern India in the mid-first millennium B.C. the arguments derive from some of the implicit questions posed in these studies. This does not mean however that the present work is in agreement with the theories put forward by these studies and in fact on some points there is not only divergence but disagreement. Nevertheless, within the broad framework of the discussion on stratification and lineage systems, it was felt that the characteristics of the lineage system do appear to be recognizable in much of what we know of Vedic society.

A lineage has been defined as a corporate group of unilineal kin with a formalized system of authority.[30] It has rights and duties and accepts genealogical relationships as the binding factor. It can be divided into smaller groups or segments. Several unilineal descent groups go to make up a clan which traces its origin to an actual or mythical founding ancestor. The basic unit in such a system is the extended family based on a three or four generation lineage controlled by the eldest male who represents it on both ritual and political occasions. The constituents of the family and its relations with the descent group are based on the system of marriage alliances, involving both the circulation of women and the exchange of wealth associated with it, residence patterns, and rights relating to the wealth produced by the family as an independent unit as well as in its relationship with the clan. Such rights in property are determined by settlements in new territory, inheritance orders and acquisition of wealth. The family has clearly defined rights on pasture-lands, livestock and cultivated land. These are frequently rights of usage determined by rules rather than ownership. The optimum size of the lineage is determined by environment and economy. The jural community takes decisions and is constituted from the dominant authentic lineage segments. Ritual occasions are

[27] M. Godelier, 'The Appropriation of Nature', ibid., *Perspectives in Marxist Anthropology*, Cambridge, 1977.

[28] C. Meillassoux, 'Historical Modalities of the Exploitation and Over-exploitation of Labour', in *Critique of Anthropology*, Summer 1979, vol. 4, nos. 13 and 14, pp. 7-16. 'From Reproduction to Production', *Economy and Society*, 1972, vol. 1, no. 1, pp. 93-105;

[29] I. Goldman, *Ancient Polynesian Society*, Chicago, 1970.

[30] J. Middleton and D. Tait, *Tribes without Rulers*, London, 1964.

marked by sacrifices offered to a cult object where the congregation is often the descent group of the lineage. In the lineage mode of production[31] the jural community has some control over production and its inherent exploitative tendencies differentiate it from the more egalitarian bands and ranked society. Exploitation takes the form of those in authority claiming power on the basis of kin connections and wealth and excluding those who are unrelated. This exclusion could be expressed in non-kin groups labouring for the others. In such a system the produce, whether acquired through labour or from raids, is divided on the basis of redistribution in which voluntary tribute and gift-giving plays a central role. Kinship relations have a genealogical base and at the same time are a unit of production in accordance with lineages, segments and extended families. In a clear separation between élite groups and commoners, kinship constitutes a charter for establishing the authority of the ruling lineage through genealogical connections. Rituals reinforce the system, particularly initiation rituals and the public worship of ancestors.[32] Myths of origin become significant in emphasizing the separate and special nature of the élite. Heterogenous groups are knit together through their dependence on the ruling clan. Political stability often lies in the open frontier which makes migration possible so that tensions within the clans can be eased by the migration of some. Territorial sovereignty or the delineation of boundaries do not play a central role. Lineage becomes the legal sanction and regulates the activities of its members. The chief therefore acts through and in relation to a lineage and not as an individual. Traditional history would also take the form of a history and exposition of the lineages which is essentially a charter of legitimation, often in the form of precedents and guidelines.

In contrast to lineage systems the establishment of a state points to a different kind of society. A state registers the evidence of a political authority functioning within a territorial limit, and delegating its powers to functionaries. This is financed by an income collected by those who contribute regularly on an impersonal basis to its maintenance and acts as an instrument for integrating social segments identified not merely by ritual roles but also by economic functions.[33] These four attributes are essential but their

[31] Terray, *Marxism and 'Primitive' Societies*.

[32] E. V. Winans, *Shambala*, Berkeley, 1962

[33] L. Krader, *Formation of the State*, New Jersey, 1968; 'The State in History', in *Studies in History*, forthcoming.

importance in a particular situation may vary and their application need not be equal in every instance. A state has further been defined as a collection of specialized agencies and institutions both formal and non-formal which help in maintaining an order of stratification. Hierarchy is as acceptable as is differential access to basic resources. The hierarchical groups may be defined as classes in which the opposition lies between those who labour and those who enjoy the fruits of the labour and the resultant surplus. A conflict between these groups would be one condition for the emergence of the state and implies that other forms of authority have become ineffective. Obedience to officials is a necessary characteristic and this is not tied by bonds of kinship. The state has an obligation to defend its citizens and its territory, implying an identification of its citizens over others and a monopoly over the use of force. The jurisdiction of the state is defined in terms of its sovereignty over a fixed territory and membership is therefore determined by residence or birthright in a territory.[34] The state establishes and maintains its sovereignty both externally and internally, the former by protecting the territory from aggression and the latter by the promulgation of laws. The observance of customary rules is gradually formalized, often resulting in the codification of laws. Taxes are regulated and collected, and become a permanent part of the income of the state. Censuses of the population are sought to be maintained since these would be crucial, among other things, to the systematic collection of taxes. The state establishes and maintains sovereignty both in external relations and internally: the former through military strength and the latter through legitimacy, power, the control of groups involved in production and the organization of taxes and a treasury.[35] It has also been argued that the emergence of a civil society, an essential prerequisite for a state, is characterized by a differentiation between public tax and private rent.[36] The maintenance of law and order is preferably to the exclusion of individual actions and is at the effective level in the hands of the ruling groups, who also have preferential access to strategic goods and services.

The state regulates social relations in a society which is divided

[34] S. F. Nadel, *A Black Byzantium*, London, 1942.

[35] Fried, *Evolution of Political Society*, p. 235 ff.

[36] Krader, *Formation of the State*.

into the rulers and the ruled.[37] The main administrative function is to keep the balance between those who hold office and those who aspire to it and is concerned with people as a reference point. The community passes its surplus product to the state through its administrative hierarchy. A distinction is maintained between communal lands and state lands. When necessary, extra economic coercion can be used to obtain the surplus. The state controls succession to high office and provides avenues for upward mobility to a few. In its ideological function it justifies the social divisions, supports powerful religious systems where they are of use to the state, maintains the coherence of heterogeneity, for instance by insisting on a common official language or by trying to inculcate a common cultural idiom.

The state therefore is differentiated from government and also, in turn, from society. The functions of the state are performed through the government in which the process of policy-making is crucial and is the concern of political élites.[38] Policy is usually in support of those interests which stem from privileged groups who have access to rights over land and over ideology in the form of religion, shared interests leading to the formation of an interest group. The privileged group in addition to controlling resources is often one with either the favour of the king or else a following of kinsmen, clients or professionals which makes the group important. The tension between the privileged and the unprivileged can either lead to the overthrow of the former by the latter where the existing political structure would have to be overthrown or more often, to attempts by the latter to enter the ranks of the former. This would result in the new group being accommodated as part of the élite, either directly or through some fictionalized relationship.

Centralization of power depends on the ability of the government to interfere in society. One area where this may be limited is the sphere of law where the prevalence of customary law may restrict the application of a code determined by government. The degree of control exercised by the government over office-holders would also determine the degree of interference. Where appointments are made by the government and holders are liable to

[37] P. Skalnik, 'The Early State as a Process', in Claessen and Skalnik, *The Early State*, p. 597 ff.

[38] P. Lloyd, 'The Political Structure of African Kingdoms: an Exploratory Model', in *Political Systems and the Distribution of Power*, ASA Monographs 2, London, 1965.

transfer, the power of the state would be greater than institutions managed by local patrons and magnates over whom the state has nominal control. This in turn relates to the question of the composition of political élites. In early societies it is rarely open to all. It is conditioned by the power of the royal lineage; the rights in land of privileged groups, particularly rights to waste land; the degree to which the group can manipulate physical force; and the degree to which the individual has any alternative to maladministration other than migration. Factors which can lead to a change in the political system revolve around democratic processes, conquest, extensive trade and the decline of a political élite.

In this study an attempt is made to examine four different situations: the Ṛg Vedic and Later Vedic societies of the Indo-Gangetic watershed and the western Ganga valley as well as the *gaṇa-saṅgha* system and the emergence of monarchies in the middle Gaṅga valley. In both regions there is evidence of a change in the direction towards state formation. In the fomer it tends to be stymied but in the latter it reaches fruition. There is greater similarity in the first two societies than in the second two. The Later Vedic society evolves out of the Ṛg Vedic; but the *gaṇa-saṅgha* and the monarchical states are in a sense political bipolarities. Thus it becomes necessary to investigate the variations in polities rather than to assume that since they belong to an early period they must be similar. In drawing out the dissimilarities the emphasis may inadvertently be placed on sharp contrasts, such as that of the importance of ritual in some pre-state systems and that of contract in a state system. Such counterposing may clarify the argument but it has to be recognized at the same time that in early societies there is a considerable intermeshing and accommodating of contrasts which can often hide the nature of change. In attempting to show the contrast between the lineage and the state system it should not be assumed that this contrast was familiar to contemporary observers, or that it was as sharp as is postulated in a theoretical analysis.

The areas and types of states under discussion were not the only examples of state formation during this period. The territories of Kamboja and Gandhāra (the latter with its capital at Taxila) are mentioned among the early *janapada*s as also those in the Punjab, western India and central India. The western and middle Ganga valley have been selected not merely because there is maximum data on these areas for an analysis of the process of state formation and because they are contiguous areas and therefore useful to a comparative study but also because these areas provide the prelude to the emergence of the complex state system of the Nandas and Mauryas. Not surprisingly this region is also regarded as the most important in the ancient Indian historical tradition. Similarly there was a wide geographical distribution of the *gaṇa-sanghas* or chiefships which were also located in the Punjab and western and central India, and were contemporary with those in the middle Ganga valley. This study is limited to the latter for much the same reasons as those for the territories which were to evolve into kingdoms.

The earliest evidence on social formations locate this activity in north-western India and gradually the major portion of the sources confine themselves to what has come to be called *madhya-deśa,* or the middle region. The Vedic texts which provide this evidence are the *Ṛg Veda* and what is generally termed the Later Vedic Literature (i.e., the *Sāma, Yajur* and *Atharva Veda*s together with their associated texts the *Upaniṣad*s, *Aranyaka*s and *Brāhmaṇa*s). The date of these texts remains somewhat uncertain and controversial. The *Ṛg Veda* is believed to be of earlier origin than the others but even in this the tenth *maṇḍala* (book) is later and some scholars would also include the first *maṇḍala* as of late origin. Similarly, there are parts of the *Atharva Veda* which are believed to be of earlier origin than the rest of the text. The suggested date for the earlier sections of the *Ṛg Veda* would be sometime between the latter part of the second millennium and the early first millennium B.C. The Later Vedic Literature is dated closer to the mid-first millennium B.C. ranging from the eighth to the sixth centuries. The two epics, the *Mahābhārata* and the *Rāmāyaṇa* are quite evidently compiled at various periods and even the Critical Editions of both, admirable as they are, have not been able to prune the texts to the original or approximate epics. They were edited until as late as the mid-first millennium A.D. but sections of the texts would relate to earlier societies, possibly going back to the early first millennium B.C. and perhaps to some even earlier memories.[39]

Subsequent to this, in what may be regarded as the period of the early state, the sources used consist of the *sūtra* literature, especial-

[39] Romila Thapar, 'The Historian and the Epic', in *Annals of the Bhandarkar Oriental Research Institute*, Poona, 1979, LX, pp. 199-213; Romila Thapar, *Exile and the Kingdom: Some Thoughts on the Rāmāyaṇa*, Bangalore, 1978.

ly the *Gṛhya* and *Dharma-sūtras*, the more important among the latter being those of Baudhāyana, Gautama and Āpastamba. The grammar of Pāṇini, the *Aṣṭādhyāyi,* is generally dated to the fifth, though some would prefer the early fourth century B.C. The Buddhist Pāli Canon is widely used for this period in spite of its imprecise chronology although some attempts have been made at a chronological stratification.[40] Among the Buddhist texts, sections of the *Dīgha, Majjhima, Sañyutta* and *Aṅguttara Nikāya*s are early. The *Vinaya Piṭaka* and the *Jātaka*s are later, some parts of which possibly date to the Mauryan period. The *Jātaka* literature is more difficult to date as the verses in it are believed to be of early origin. The above sources which provide the evidence for the *gaṇa-saṅgha* chiefships and the early forms of the state in the kingdoms of Kośala and Magadha relate in the main to the middle Ganga valley and date to the latter half of the first millennium B.C. These sources are therefore later than the corpus of Vedic literature Jaina sources have not been brought into the discussion since, valuable as they are, their chronology remains as yet even more obscure. Attempts to date the *Arthaśāstra* of Kauṭilya remain elusive although its time bracket is that of the Mauryan and post-Mauryan period, i.e. from the fourth century B.C. to the third A.D.[41] The *Viṣṇu Purāṇa* dates to the Gupta period or the mid-first millennium A.D. Purāṇic sources and the *Viṣṇu Purāṇa* in particular are central to the structure of genealogies because although they were composed many centuries after the purported events, they are not only based on an oral tradition but they constitute the core of the early historical tradition. Genealogical data from Vedic sources tends to be very limited. The Purāṇic data, even if deliberately inflated, is nevertheless regarded as the literature which preserves the past. The chronological stratification of literary texts, particularly those which arise out of religious needs or come to serve a religious function and which have been preserved as part of an oral tradition before being edited and recorded in writing, do present multiple problems in providing data on precise points of historical and social change. Because of the difficulty in assigning an exact chronology to the sources it is impossi-

[40] G. C. Pande, *Studies in the Origins of Buddhism*, Delhi, 1957.

[41] R.P. Kangle, *The Kauṭilīya Arthaśāstra*, pt. III, Bombay, 1965; T.R. Trautmann, *Kauṭilya and the Arthaśāstra*, Leiden, 1971

ble to be precise or dogmatic as to when particular changes took place, except in a rather general way. Consequently the major significance of these sources lies more in their indication of the nature of the trends of change which they delineate rather than in a precise dating of the change.

The geographical background to these sources is in some cases a little easier to define than their chronology. Most of the texts included in the category of Later Vedic Literature relate to the western Ganga valley (the Kuru-Pañcāla region) but some among them, such as the *Śatapatha Brāhmaṇa,* seem also to have included north Bihar and others are thought to have been familiar with western India and Gujarat. Pāṇini's grammar probably relates more closely to north-western India but nevertheless has references to the Ganga valley. There is a controversy as to whether the *Dharma-sūtra* of Baudhāyana may not have been written in south India. Buddhist literature is more firmly confined to the middle Ganga valley (eastern Uttar Pradesh and Bihar) with Śrāvasti and Rājagṛha providing the two focal urban centres. However, later interpolations into these texts could have had their provenance in central India or the north-west or even further afield. The archaeological data discussed for these regions covers northern Rajasthan, the Indo-Gangetic watershed extending to present-day Punjab and the northern half of Haryana, the Ganga-Yamuna *doāb* ('the land between two rivers', generally referred to as the Doāb), and its eastern fringe in present-day Uttar Pradesh, as well as the middle Ganga valley, demarcated by a somewhat lower elevation than the western Ganga valley, and consisting of eastern Uttar Pradesh and northern Bihar.

The main theme of this study is to suggest that the Vedic period saw a change from the lineage system (most closely represented by the data of the *Ṛg Veda*) to a combined lineage and householding economy (as suggested by the Later Vedic texts); that in the post-Vedic period the sharper stratification of the chiefdoms of the middle Ganga valley was in part a continuation of the lineage system but in effect also germinal to the tendencies encouraging state formation and therefore these *gaṇa-saṅgha*s were both a contrast to, as well as in some ways the pointers to the kingdoms of Kośala and Magadha which saw the emergence of a peasant economy and subsequently commerce

It is not our intention here to argue that the model of the lineage system developed by anthropologists exactly fits the picture of

Vedic society. It is used more in the nature of a general theory helpful in reconstructing the past and trying to prise from the data something more than just a descriptive narrative. The house-holding economy (a term borrowed from Polanyi), and which has been suggested as part of the Vedic lineage system would probably be unacceptable to many who are familiar with the lineage system from other sources, but its possibility in this specific case seems plausible; and this particularly where its association with the lineage system eventually leads to the weakening of the latter and the emergence of a peasant economy. A certain degree of hopefully creative speculation has gone into this analysis.

The use of the term 'lineage society' is preferable to 'tribal society' which is what has been used in the past for Ṛg Vedic society. Tribal society in the Indian context is ambiguous and includes a range of cultures from stone-age hunters and gatherers to peasant cultivators. Lineage society as defined here narrows the connotation somewhat and is perhaps more precise. This term also emphasizes the centrality of lineage in all its aspects which is of the essence in such a society, particularly in relation to power and access to resources, whereas 'tribe' remains vague on this point.[42] Significantly there are fewer references to individual chiefs in the Vedic sources and more frequent ones to lineages, thus indicating that power was still based on legitimacy through lineage.

In the Indian situation lineage society gave shape and form to caste structure. Lineage elements such as kinship and marriage rules are important to caste. When differing forms of stratification begin to emerge an attempt is made through the *varṇa* framework to draw them together into a holistic theory of social functioning. In the later stage the occupational groups employed in production, the *śudras*, are added on as a fourth category but denied a lineage form, so that their exclusion is made explicit. At the same time their origin as a group is determined by occupation and locality and this marks a major difference in the *varṇa* system itself. When lineage-based societies gave way to state formation, the socio-economic changes reflected in the transition are also reflected in the structure of caste with the emergence of what is seemingly a duality between ritual status and actual status. The continuance of *varṇa* is in a sense the continuance of an aspect of lineage society and of

[42] A. Béteille, 'On the concept of tribe', *International Social Science Journal*, 1980, vol. XXXII, no. 4, pp. 825-8; M. Fried, *The Evolution of Political Society*, pp. 154-74.

ritual status. The latter becomes the survival of the lineage system and is most clearly articulated on ritual occasions. Economic status arises from new changes and has to be adjusted to ritual status. The latter is strengthened in those situations where the two statuses coincide.

The study of the early forms of the state is particularly relevant for Indian history since the process of state formation was a continuing one throughout the centuries with new areas being brought into state systems. It has been said that there was a pathological fear of anarchy defined as the absence of a king: it can be argued that it was not the fear of anarchy but the justification for the continual process of state formation which was being emphasized. The emergence of the state in any of the regions of the Indian subcontinent was not a uniform change affecting the entire region but very often was initially limited to small nucleii. A study of the earliest forms therefore may provide a pattern which was either repeated or modified or reorganized in later periods, but of which the constituents would remain substantially the same. Apart from the early form taken by the state it is equally relevant to analyse the pre-state form and examine the condition from which the state emerged, as these pre-state forms are also met with in later periods in areas adjoining the major states.

State formation has its own interest for the historian. But an attempt is being made in this study to relate the early Indian historical tradition to phases of historical change which correspond to the transition from lineage to state systems. The *itihāsa-purāṇa* tradition embedded fragmentarily in Vedic literature and the epics and more substantially in the *Purāṇa*s, such as the *Viṣṇu Purāṇa* and later texts, has often been dismissed as a fanciful rendering of the past, since it does not conform to the recognized models of historical writing. It is being argued here that the failure to recognize the format of this tradition, derives mainly from the inability of modern historians to perceive the essentials of this tradition in the context of the earlier society which can perhaps be better defined if viewed in terms of a lineage society and its mutation in time to a state system. In other words, the *itihāsa-purāṇa* tradition is seeking to record such a change but the record becomes legible, as it were, only when viewed in terms of its relations to particular social formations. The linking of the historical tradition with historical change will be attempted in the fourth chapter. By way of contrast the Buddhist handling of the historical tradition takes on its own distinctive form and although the constituent elements are present, their articulation relates even more closely to historical change and their form is more easily recognizable. A detailed discussion of these historical changes therefore becomes the preface to comprehending the meaning of the *itihāsa-purāṇa* tradition. The continuity of the form of the early historical tradition may also be explained by the continuing process of state-formation, particularly in those areas which are characterized by an earlier lineage society.

II LINEAGE SOCIETY

The archaeology of the Indo-Gangetic divide and the western Ganga valley indicates that the settlement of this area goes back to the second millennium B.C. The upper Doāb in particular receives the stragglers of the Late Harappan culture and is the hub of a possibly unrelated people of the Ochre-Colour Pottery culture. Ultimately the much more impressive sites of the Painted Grey Ware[1] culture come to dominate the region. This culture seems to have spread from northern Rajasthan and southern Punjab in the late second millennium B.C. into the western Ganga valley with a heavier settlement in the upper Doāb. Recent excavations in the Beas-Sutlej *doāb* indicate an overlap between the Late Harappan[2] and the Painted Grey Ware Cultures which, apart from other aspects would point to some continuity of Harappan traditions, albeit indirect and probably dilute, into the first millennium B.C.

The changing of river courses in southern Punjab and northern Rajasthan where the Painted Grey Ware is found in abundance, may have necessitated a movement south-eastwards to avoid the ensuing ecological uncertainties.[3] Sometimes the sites are located

[1] V. Tripathi, *The Painted Grey Ware,* Delhi, 1976.

[2] J.P. Joshi, 'Interlocking of Late Harappan Culture and Painted Grey Ware Culture in the Light of Recent Excavations', *Man and Environment,* 1978, vol. I pp. 100-3.

[3] R.C. Raikes, 'Kalibangan: death from natural causes', in *Antiquity,* 1968, 42, pp. 286-91; Suraj Bhan, 'The Sequence and spread of pre-historic cultures in the upper Sarasvati basin', in A. Ghosh and D.P. Agrawal, *Radio-Carbon and Indian Archaeology,* Bombay, 1972, p. 252 ff.; Suraj Bhan, 'Excavation at Mitathal 1968 (Hissar)', *Journal of Haryana Studies,* 1969, I, January no.1, pp. 1-15.; H.T. Lambrick, *Sind: A General Introduction,* Hyderabad 1964; H. Willhelmy, 'Das Urstromtal an Ostrand der Indusebens und dar Saraswati Problem', *Zeitschrift fur Geomorphologie,* Supplement Band, 1969, 8, pp. 76-93.; Gurdip Singh, *et al.*, 'Late Quarternary History of Vegetation and Climate of the Rajasthan Desert, India', *Philosphical Transactions of the Royal Society of London,* 1974, 267, no.889, pp. 467-501.; B. Ghose, Amalkar and Z. Husain, 'The Lost Courses of Sarasvati River in the Great Indian Desert: new evidence from Landstat Imagery', *The Geographical Journal,*1979, 145, pt 3, pp. 446-51.; *idem,* 'Comparative Role of the Aravalli and Himalayan River Systems in the Fluvial Sedimentation of the Rajasthan Desert', *Man and Environment,* 1980, IV, pp. 8-12.; Suraj Bhan, *Excavation at Mithathal (1980) and other Explorations in the Sutlej-Yamuna Divide,*

on dry river beds suggesting hydraulic changes. The Sutlej, described in post-Vedic sources as the river with a hundred channels has been known constantly to change its course. The Sarasvatī, the river of many pools, disappeared into the desert near Sirsa leaving only traces of its original bed. It has been argued that a change in the course of the Yamuna drew off the waters of the Sarasvatī and other rivers of the Indo-Gangetic divide. Added to this is the possibility of climatic changes with increasing aridity in northern Rajasthan.[4] Given the increase in the size of sites of the Painted Grey Ware, it is equally plausible that there was a demographic rise which led to a search, in a literal sense, for fresh fields and pastures new. The argument that a profusion of closely spaced settlements may point to shifting cultivation requiring new sites every few years would probably not apply in this case since the archaeological evidence suggests a more sophisticated agricultural activity. The Painted Grey Ware culture marks an assertive society, richer than its immediate predecessors. There is evidence of pastoralism and agriculture with the noticeable presence of a new animal, the horse, and with minimal use of iron (almost restricted to weapons) in the early part of the first millennium B.C. The finely made, wheel-thrown grey pottery with its floral and geometric designs provided a further distinction to the culture.

The *Ṛg Veda* refers to various tribes settled in the region between the Indus, the rivers of the Punjab and the now extinct Sarvasvatī, an area described in the text as the *sapta sindhavaḥ*.[5] The major concentration of settlements from archeological data points to the lower *doābs* of the Punjab and it is possible that the text may have been referring to the five rivers at their points of confluence rather than to their upper reaches. The Sarasvatī is described as eventually joining the ocean,[6] which it has since ceased to do. The possibility of hydraulic changes in this area would date to the latter half of the second millennium B.C., a date which would not conflict with the generally accepted chronology for much of the *Ṛg Veda*. Hydraulic

Kurukshetra, 1975.; Suraj Bhan and J.G. Shaffer, 'New Discoveries in Northern Haryana', *Man and Environment,* 1978, II, pp. 59-68.; K.N. Dikshit, 'Exploration along the Right Bank of River Sutlej in Punjab', *Journal of History,* 1967,45,pt II, pp. 561-68.; C. Ramaswamy, 'Monsoon over the Indus Valley during the Harappan Period', *Nature,* 1968, 217, pp. 628-9.

[4] Gurdip Singh, 'The Indus Valley Culture', *Archaeology and Physical Anthropology in Oceania,* 1971, vol.6, no.2., pp. 177-89.

[5] VIII. 24.27 ; III. 23.4.; X. 75; VII. 95; II. 41.16; VI. 61.

[6] *Vedic Index,* II, p. 434.

changes in northern Rajasthan and the watershed may well have required migrations of a large scale such as are suggested in the movement of the Bharatas and the Purus from southern Punjab and northern Rajasthan to Haryana and the upper Doāb or the wanderings of the Yadus to Mathura and Saurashtra. Desiccation and changes in river courses would have caused major population movements.

Ṛg Vedic society was essentially pastoral. This did not preclude agriculture although agrarian activities are more frequently described in the later section of the text. The pastoralists may well have controlled the agricultural niches without being economically dependent on them, particularly if the cultivated areas were worked by people other than those who belonged to the pastoral clans. The society of the Ganga-Yamuna Doāb as reflected in the Later Vedic texts was more dependent on agriculture although cattle-rearing remained a significant activity. Historically the west bank of the Yamuna has been associated with continuing pastoralism whereas the Doāb itself became prime agricultural land fairly early. Sedentary settlements become characteristic of the increasing emphasis on agriculture, although here again the change was evidently not rapid. Settlements in the Doāb would have had to adjust with the smaller settlements of earlier populations indicated by the Ochre Colour Pottery and the Copper Hoard cultures,[7] which may well have been assimilated by the more dominant culture. The existence of earlier agricultural communities in the region may have formed the nucleii of the larger communities as is suggested by the evidence from those sites where settlements of the Ochre Colour Pottery culture are succeeded by the Painted Grey Ware. It is not surprising then that both the Kurus and the Pañcālas are in origin confederations of earlier clans some of which were known to the *Ṛg Veda*. Neither the Kurus nor the Pañcālas as such are referred to in the *Ṛg Veda*. Whereas the Kurus emerged after the confederation of the Purus and the Bharatas in the main, the Pañcālas, as the name suggests, were an amalgam of five clans.[8] It would be reasonable to ex-

[7] B and R. Allchin, *The Birth of Indian Civilisation*, Harmondsworth, 1966, p. 200 ff. The Copper Hoard culture which seems to have had its provenance in the middle Ganga valley but the artefacts of which are found in large numbers in the Doāb, remains controversial since some archaeologists associate it with the Ochre Colour Pottery culture on the basis of its having been found with this pottery at a few sites, but others regard it as a distinct culture which cannot be precisely dated because the copper objects are found in caches and rarely in excavations.

[8] *Śat. Brāh.* XIII. 5.4.7 ; *-āla* as a termination is difficult to explain as an Indo-Aryan root. But it is worth noting that in Proto-Dravidian *āḷ* has a distinct meaning

pect that this confederation was the result of a re-alignment arising out of new settlements and some degree of conquest and subordination. In the case of the Kurus it is the Puru lineage which is listed as the dominant one.[9] The subordination was not necessarily of non-aryans by aryans (whoever the latter may have been!) but equally of various weak clans by the strong, all or whom could have called themselves aryans. The emergence of what came to be identified as the Kuru-Pañcāla region was clearly important as it is called *madhya-deśa* and *āryavarta,* the land of the *ārya*s in later tradition,[10] and is regarded as the epitome of *āryan* society. However, the assimilation of earlier populations would also have resulted in the inclusion (in later texts and rituals) of earlier traditions surviving among indigenous groups.

The pastoralism of Ṛg Vedic society made livestock breeding, and more specially, cattle herding the major activity. Pastoralism is dependent on assured grazing grounds and the ability to accumulate and increase the herd, this being the primary source of wealth. It required what the *Ṛg Veda* describes as 'meadows rich in grass'.[11] Its political implications demanded that grazing grounds be demarcated and a constant watch kept to exclude trespassers. The accumulation of cattle, *gāviṣṭhi*, comes through breeding as well as capturing other herds.[12] Cattle raids are therefore a form of acquiring fresh stock and the same word is used for such raids. The winner of cows, *gojit*, is an epithet for hero.[13] The Kuru-Pañcāla *rājā*s we are told, raided in the season when the dew falls.[14] Inevitably the worst enemies are the Paṇis, given to cattle lifting.[15] Cattle raiding is often accompanied by the capture of herders who are often enslaved. Leadership in this situation requires the ability to protect not only the herd, since cattle are the chief form of wealth, but also one's clan, and to defend the claim to ownership of cattle and control over the grazing ground or *vraja*. Hence the synonyms

which would suit the present context. *DED* 341 *āl* refers to one who rules or controls. *DED* 342 gives āḷ the connotation of a man or hero. Pañcāla could therefore mean the five chiefs, as a confederacy, provided one can accept a bilingual and therefore a mixed form of Indo-Aryan and Proto-Dravidian.

[9] F.E. Pargiter, *Ancient Indian Historical Tradition,* London, 1922.

[10] *Ait. Brāh.* VIII. 14; *Kauṣitiki Up.* VI. 1.; *Manu* II. 17-74.

[11] I. 42.8.

[12] *Ṛg V.* VIII. 86.2.

[13] *Ṛg V.* II. 21.1; I. 102.6; IX. 78.4.

[14] *Tait. Brāh.* I. 8.41.

[15] *Ṛg. V.* II. 24.6-7; IX. III.2; *Vedic Index,* I. 471

of *gopa, gopati* and *janasya gopati* for the *rājā*,[16] as against the later terms *nṛpati* and *nareśvara*,[17] the lord of the herd eventually giving way to the lord of men. Leadership in the context of cattle raids and protection also became the incentive for winning loyalties and establishing the rights of lineages.

Grazing lands are liable to change since the same pastures may not remain constant year after year and cattle herders have to be mobile. Since the economy is dependent on the increase of the herd, identification with land plays a peripheral role and the search for pastures remains crucial. Thus the Pūrus are earlier said to be settled along the grassy banks of the Sarasvatī,[18] but later become the core of the Kuru lineage in the Ganga-Yamuna *doāb*.

Wealth is frequently computed in heads of cattle and in this the cow has a special status. The *gomat* is the man of wealth.[19] The cow is a unit of value, a man's life being calculated to be worth a hundred cows (*śatadeya*). It gains religious sanctity and is sacrified on the more auspicious occasions.[20] It acquires the sanction of a totem animal in that its flesh is eaten on specified occasions in association with rituals,[21] or equally specially when welcoming a guest. The condemnation of the arbitrary killing of cows would point to their ritual importance.[22] Wealth is also computed in heads of horse, crucial to cattle raids and migrations. The horse too acquires religious sanction but less so than the cow. Its sacrifice is symbolic of fertility and power but its flesh is not eaten. The horse appears to have been more valuable than the cow.[23] In the enumeration of wealth the numbers of cattle are invariably much larger than those of horses. The latter is not ritually sacrificed in the same number as cattle. This may well have to do with the necessity of importing horses into India. Apart from the north-western borders the Indian ecology was not generally conducive to breeding horses of quality.

[16] *Ṛg. V.* III 43.5; IX. 35.5; 97.34; X. 67.8; *Ait. Brāh.* VIII. 12.17; *Śat Brāh.* II. 6.4.2. ff. R. S. Sharma, 'Forms of Property in the Early Portions of the *Ṛg Veda*', P of I.H.C., 1973, pp. 94-101; 'From Gopati to Bhupati', in *Studies in History,* July-Dec. 1980, II, no. 2,pp. 1-11.

[17] *Ṛg. V.* II. 1.1; IV. 20.1; VII. 69.1 ; X. 44.2-3; *Atharvaveda,* V. 18.1.

[18] *Ṛg V.* VII. 96.2.; IV. 38.

[19] *Ṛg V.* IX. 107.9.

[20] *Ṛg V.* II. 7.5; VI. 16.47 ; X. 91.14 ; X, 169.3 ; *Atharvaveda,* X. 10.

[21] *Vedic Index,* I. p. 10 ; *Ait. Brāh.* I. 15 ; *Tait. Brāh.* II. 17.11.1 ; *Śat. Brāh.* III. 4.1.2 ; *Apa. G.S.* VIII. 22.3-11

[22] *Atharvaveda,* XII. 4.38,53 ; 5. 36-9.

[23] *Ṛg. V.* I. 83.1 ; IV. 32.17 ; V. 4.11 ; IX. 63.

The *rājā* or chief was the successful leader of a raid and by extension, of a battle.[24] The booty thus acquired was distributed among the clan, but the distribution was already unequal. Some of it was retained by the *rājā,* but a substantial amount was also claimed by priestly families on the grounds that their rituals ensured success in battle and they were the bestowers of praise and therefore of immortality on the hero. The heroic ideal, apart from bravery, included generosity in gift-giving and thus, implicitly, access to wealth. The *dāna-stuti* hymns of the *Ṛg Veda*[25] refer to the established heroes as gift-givers in extravagant terms. Cattle, horses, gold, chariots and female slaves are said to have been bestowed in their hundreds and thousands on enthusiastic bards and priests. The wealth is as mobile as the chiefs from whom it comes and its recipients. The figures may be exaggerated but wealth was distributed at least among the families of the priests and the chiefs, a redistribution which increasingly neglected the rest of the clan. The ability to conduct a successful raid was in part motivated by the capacity to acquire wealth in order that it be distributed or even destroyed in a potlatch type ceremony; this is reflected in increasing references to the bestowal of wealth on ritual occasions, particularly to priests.[26]

The reciprocal relationship between chief and priest undergoes its first change in the period after that of the *Ṛg Veda* as is reflected in the other Vedic texts. Pastoralism, even in the earlier period did not exclude agriculture but the balance between the two gradually shifted in favour of agriculture. The more elaborate ceremonial sacrifices of the later period such as the *rājasūya* include offerings made of grain together with milk, *ghī* and animals.[27]. Plough agriculture is referred to in the *Ṛg Veda,*[28] generally in the later *maṇḍalas*, but curiously some of the major agricultural implements carry names which are linguistically non-Aryan, such as *lāṇgala.*[29] That there were sedentary agriculturalists in this region prior to the Ṛg Vedic period is evident from archaeology. The Asuras for exam-

[24] *Ṛg. V.* I. 116.21 ; VI. 32.3.

[25] *Vedic Index,* I. p. 336; II. p. 82.

[26] Romila Thapar, '*Dāna* and *Dakṣinā* as forms of Exchange', in *Ancient Indian Social History : some interpretations,* New Delhi, 1978, p. 105 ff.

[27] Ibid.

[28] I. 23.15; I. 176.2; I. 117.21; X. 34.13; X. 117.7 ; X. 101.3; a hymn addressed to the *kṣetrapati* in IV. 57 is believed to be late although included in the early section of the text. E.W. Hopkins, 'Pragathikani', *JAOS* 1896, 17, p. 84.

[29] Romila Thapar, 'The Study of Society in Ancient India', in *AISH*, p. 211.

ple are said to have had a correct knowledge of the seasons for agricultural activities.[30] The subordination of such groups to pastorally based power is not unknown and could be explained in terms of environmental circumscription, where, in favourable areas cultivators prefer not to migrate when encroached upon by pastoralists.[31] Alternatively, the close proximity of herders to agriculturalists may well have led to a symbiotic relationship of mutual dependence. Thus herders might graze their animals on the stubble of fields or be provided with fodder in return for protection. Such agriculturalists would then accept the authority of the herder chiefs without necessarily being conquered by them. At the individual level this would require a relationship simultaneously drawing on notions of alienness and friendship which is perhaps what is reflected in the complex meaning of the word *ari*. Such symbiotic relationships could encourage circuits of exchange of a simple and direct kind, should the herders practise transhumance. They would also presuppose a situation of bilingualism should the two groups be speaking different languages. It has been suggested that the presence of non-Aryan features, particularly Proto-Dravidian and Austro-Asiatic, in Vedic Sanskrit may have resulted from situations of bilingualism between speakers of Indo-Aryan and other languages.[32]

The migration into the Doāb carries few references to the conquest of or battles against local populations. Most of the celebrated battles were among the major clans and conflicts involved claims to territorial control and rights of succession to these territories. Apart from the famous *dāśarājña*[33] when the Bharatas fought against a confederacy of ten clans, the best known of which were the group of five, the Pūru, Druhyu, Anu, Turvaśa and Yakṣa/Yadu; the Bharatas were also involved in battles against the well-established *dāsa* chief Śambara and raids against the cattle-lifting Paṇis.[34] The Turvaśa and the Yadu fought against the Bharata Divodāsa and were defeated by his son Sudās,[35] the Sriñjayas were victorious against[36] the Turvaśa and Vṛṣivant as also

[30] *Śat. Brāh.* I. 6.1.2-4.

[31] R.L. Carneiro, 'A Theory of the Origin of the State', in *Science*, 1970, 169, pp. 733-8.

[32] M.M. Deshpande and P.E. Hook, *Aryan and Non-Aryan in India*, Michigan Papers on South and South-east Asia, no. 14, 1978, Ann Arbor, 1979.

[33] *Ṛg V.* VII. 83; VII. 18; *Atharvaveda*, XX. 128.12.

[34] *Ṛg V.* I. 51.6; II. 19.6; VII. 8.4. [35] *Ṛg V.* VII. 18. [36] *Ṛg V.* VI. 27.7.

against the Bharatas and the Satvant.[37] Such references come from the *Ṛg Veda* or refer to earlier events in the later texts and the location of such hostilities was in areas to the north-west of the Doāb and prior to the migration into the Doāb. There appears to have been systematic settlement on the new lands with the indigenous population either being absorbed, or being pushed to the margins of the settlement. Such settlements would have been clearings in the monsoon forests which covered the Ganga valley at the time. The proximity of the forests is always present in the consciousness of the settlers as is evident from the contrasting images of *grāma* and *āranya,* where the forest is the place of exile, of demons and *rākṣasas*, but also where the hermitages of *ṛṣis* were situated. The latter were in a sense the vanguard of the new society and the hermitages could act as the nucleii of new settlements. This might also explain why there was such hostility towards these hermitages from those who regarded the forests as their hunting grounds.[38]

The story of Pṛthu Vainya, the first righteous ruler according to tradition, is pertinent in that Niṣāda, the original chief created by the *ṛṣis*, whose name becomes synonymous with hunting and gathering tribes, is expelled to the forest to become a hunter and gatherer. Pṛthi Vainya who is created subsequently introduces cattle-rearing and the plough, an action for which the grateful earth goddess Pṛthvī bestowes her name on him.[39] The entire process would not have been too difficult for those acquainted with the superior technology of iron weapons, with the horse and chariot, and no longer pastoralists but familiar also with the advantages of agriculture That land was now recognized as an item of wealth is evident from its ownership being vested in the clan. The *rājā* Viśvakarma Bhauvana was rebuked by the earth, Pṛthvī, when he tried to make a grant of land and it is also stated that the *rājan* cannot settle people on land without the consent of the clans (*viś*).[40] There is no reference to the sale of land in the Vedic texts.

In the initial stages of settled agriculture pastoralism retained its importance. Apart from the milk provided by cattle, the grazing of cattle in fallow fields resulted in the manuring of these fields not to

[37] *Śat. Brāh.* XIII. 5.4 11; *Ait. Brāh.* II. 25; *Vedic Index*, I., p. 64 ff. R.S. Sharma, *Śūdras in Ancient India*, 2nd ed., Delhi, 1980. p. 17.

[38] Romila Thapar, *Exile and the Kingdom: some thoughts on the Rāmāyaṇa*, Bangalore, 1978. See also *Ṛg V.* X. 146. 1-3.

[39] *Atharvaveda*, VIII. 10.24; *Viṣṇu Purāṇa* I. 13. Romila Thapar, 'Origin Myths and the Early Indian Historical Tradition', in *AISH*, p. 294 ff.

[40] *Ait. Brāh.* VIII. 21.8; *Śat. Brāh.* XIII. 7.1.15.

mention the use of cattle in providing power for traction. This was known to the earlier people of the *Ṛg Veda*[41] and doubtless intensified as agriculture began to take precedence over pastoralism. Not only does agriculture become more important than cattle rearing in the Doāb but it may also have been the utopian land yielding two crops a year. Reference is made in later sources to harvests of barley in summer and rice in autumn and to the best fields yielding two crops.[42] It has recently been argued from archaeological evidence that double cropping in the Doāb appears to have been regular at this time.[43] Whether it was a system of double cropping or one of rotation remains uncertain, but of the increasing importance of agriculture there can be no doubt. The *Ṛg Veda* refers to the cultivation of *yava* (barley).[44] The later texts mention *vṛhi* (rice).[45] The cultivation of both was possible in the lower Doāb, as for example at Atranjikhera (Etah Distrct). The sites from which rice remains are available are located in the more elevated areas of the Doāb and its environs, and this was clearly not wet rice cultivation. Since it was grown in rotation with barley and wheat its cultivation was neither as labour intensive nor as demanding of irrigation as was the cultivation of rice in the middle Ganga valley. It is equally possible that some of the rice was not locally cultivated but brought from the area to the east of the upper Doāb where it was more widely grown and where wheat and barley played a lesser role. In the later texts there are references to heavy ploughs drawn by anywhere between six to twenty-four oxen,[46] which would be indicative of the heavier wetter soil east of the Doāb. The *Ṛg Veda* mentions wells and doubtless these were used for irrigation as well in the watershed area and the western Ganga valley.[47] Given the obsession with the theme of release of waters in the frequent references to the conflict between Indra and Vṛtra, it is tempting to think that agriculture was primarily dependent on rainfall.

The gradual transition to agriculture made an impact, perhaps indirectly, on other aspects of Vedic life. Among these was the

[41] *Ṛg V.* I. 161.10, *Atharvaveda*, II. 1.1.7; XII. 4.9.

[42] *Strabo* XV. 1.13 and 20, quoting Megasthenes of the late fourth century B.C.

[43] K.A. Chaudhuri, *Ancient Agriculture and Forestry in Northern India*, Bombay, 1977.

[44] *Vedic Index*, II., p. 187

[45] *Vājasaneyi Saṃhita* XVIII. 12.

[46] *Atharvaveda* VI. 91.1; *Śat. Brāh.* VII. 2.2.6; *Kaṭhaka Saṃhita* XV. 2.

[47] X. 101. 5-7; I. 105.17.

pattern of change in different sections of society. The vedic *jana* (tribe) incorporated a number of *viś* (clans). These may in origin have been more egalitarian but by the time of the Ṛg Veda were bifurcated into the *viś* and the *rājanya*, the latter constituting the ruling families. The description of the *rājanya* even in the Later Vedic literature depicts him as sporting a bow, shooting arrows with accuracy, running chariot races, drinking *śūra* and being in effect the epitome of the hero. It was from among these families that the *rājā* was chosen. In one place it is said that those who successfully complete the *aśvamedha* sacifice will share in *rāṣṭra* and become *rājā*s worthy of consecration whereas those who fail to do so will remain members of the *rājanya* and the *viś*.[48] The original relationship between the *viś* and the *rājanya* must have been close.

The bifurcation of Ṛg Vedic times suggests a division into the senior lineages of the *rājanya*s and the lesser, junior or cadet lineages which continued to be called *viś*. Clan lands were held in common by both lineages but worked by the lesser lineage, since the permission of the *viś* was necessary before the *rājā* could settle people on the land. The clans were the original settlers which is the literal meaning of the word *viś* and when land was converted to agricultural use or agricultural land was incorporated into the territory over which the *viś* claimed usage, it belonged jointly to the *viś*. In the past *viś* has been translated as peasantry.[49] This has led to some ambiguity in determining the beginnings of a peasant economy in the Ganga valley. ('Peasant economy' is here differentiated from 'peasant society' since the former entails specific obligations and dues which may be absent in the latter where the emphasis is on the presence of cultivators.) That *viś* means a clan is generally accepted and it is used as such for *dāsa*s and *ārya*s. The *viśpati* is in some contexts the chief of the clan and in others the head of the household.[50] Rights on land were probably of usage since ownership is not recorded. The demarcation and measurements of fields mentioned in the late books of the *Ṛg Veda*[51] may well have been lineage and family allotments rather than indications of ownership. Pastoral land raises no problems, remaining common to the village as *vraja* and most animal grazing took place on waste land and forest, of which there was plenty at

48 *Śat. Brāh.* XIII. 4.2.17.

49 E.g. R.S. Sharma, 'Class Formation and its Material Basis in the Upper Gangetic Basin, *c.* 1000-500 B.C.', *IHR*, July 1975, II, no. 1., p. 1 ff.

50 *Atharvaveda* IV. 1; IV. 5.6; IV. 22.3; *Tait. Sam.* II. 3.1.3.; *Ṛg V.* VII. 55.5.

51 I. 110.5.

that time. The allocation of holdings was probably made by lots; hence the symbolic significance of dicing and its association with wealth. Cultivation could also have been carried out by rotation with no claims to ownership.

The bifurcation of clans into those of higher status and others is not unusal. It often comes about through a claim to differentiation between elder sons and younger sons or the ability of some to lead in cattle-raids, to protect the clan, to establish new settlements as also through the control of alliances with other clans. In the Ṛg Vedic case there was a distinction between the chariot-riding warriors who were pre-eminently the guardians and protectors of the *viś* and the latter who were more sedentary and were the producers of both pastoral and agricultural items. The *viś* as the junior lineage provided prestations, informally extracted on special occasions, to the *rājanya*s who redistributed these among a limited group with *dāna* and *dakṣinā* given to *brāhmaṇ*s and bards and oblations offered at the *yajña* rituals. The link between the *rājanya* and the *viś*, suggesting an earlier, closer relationship, is referred to obliquely, for example in the statement that the *kṣatra* and the *viś* should eat from the same vessel,[52] which in a society placing a high value on commensality was a substantial statement of relatively equal status. It is also said that the *kṣatra* is created out of the *viś*, the analogy being to *soma* the ritual drink which when purified leaves the substance for the more common inebriant, *śūra*.[53] A comparison is also made then in terms of one being *soma* and the other various plants or of Varuna and the Maruts or Indra and the Maruts or Yama and the Pitṛs.[54] It is interesting that these comparisons are to superior and inferior statuses in the same species. Had the *viś* in origin been commoners with no lineage status or links with *rājanya*s it is unlikely that so much effort would have gone into stating the obvious, that the *viś* was inferior to the *rājanya* and the less powerful.[55] That some awareness of the earlier relationship of common origins persisted is indirectly suggested by the statement that those who seek to equate the two produce chaos.[56] The *rājanya*s as the senior lineages doubtless kept a larger share of the booty from raids but as long as the wealth came from pastoralism in the main it had a relatively more equitable distribution. The relationship between the *rājanya*

[52] *Śat. Brāh.* IV. 3.3.15

[53] *Śat. Brāh.* XII. 7.3.8.

[54] Ibid., III. 3.2.8.; II. 5.2.27.; VII. 1.1.4.

[55] Ibid., XIII. 2.2.15, 2.9.6.

[56] Ibid. V. 1.3.3.; XII. 7.3.15; V. 3.4.11.

and the *viś* in the *Ṛg Veda* is not as distant as it was to become in the Later Vedic period. The *viś* brought its prestations in the form of *bali* to the *rājā* or the chief[57] and the relationship is a subordinate one since the *rājā* is generally chosen by other *rājā*s and the *viś* is essentially the provider of tribute. It is this which sustains the families of the *rājanya*s, together of course with the booty from raids.

Within the broad framework of this dual division there is a further expansion of both those who utilized this wealth and those who produced it. The redistribution expanded from the *rājanya*s to include the priests who legitimized them through the performance of rituals. This in turn required a larger amount of wealth and when booty could not provide enough then the *viś* had to increase its agricultural output. Sacrificial rituals drew off a large proportion of extra wealth and in this process the status of the *rājanya* was not only ensured but gradually raised through priestly legitimation and eventual association with deities. The redistribution at the sacrificial ritual became a fee for the priest. The *viś* was involved as the provider of items to be used as oblations and as the gifts bestowed by the *rājanya* on the *brāhmaṇ*. The *rājanya* of the *Ṛg Veda* was gradually replaced by the *kṣatriya* of the later Vedic period, the term deriving from *kṣatra* meaning power. The power was based on a greater control over the *jana* and its territory which is partly expressed by the territory being named after the *kṣatriya* lineage; to this was added the increasing investment of the ruling chief with attributes of deities by the *brāhmaṇ*s as also the demands made by the *kṣatriya* on the *viś*. The latter is succinctly summarized in the sentiment that the *yajamāna* ensures cattle to the *vaiśya* which leads to the subordination of the *vaiśya*, and the *kṣatriya* then requires that the *vaiśya* bring out what he has stored away.[58] That the demands were met was because the *kṣatriya* led the settlement in new lands and protected those already in existence. The advantage of an increasing emphasis on agriculture was that wealth could be augmented without resorting to many cattle raids and this was encouraged by the *kṣatriya*s asserting their superiority. Cattle raids did not cease but began to play a more marginal role in the access to wealth.

The distance between the *kṣatriya* and the *viś* brought about a certain tension and ultimately took the form of the *kṣatriya* claim-

[57] *Ṛg V.* x. 173.6.

[58] *Śat. Brāh.* I. 3.3. 15.

ing more rights of appropriation and the *viś* being reduced to subordination.[59] The tension between the two is indicated in remarks such as, the *kṣatra* eats the *viś*,[60] the simile being that of the deer eating grain, or the repeated reference to the *rājā* as the *viśāmattā*,[61] 'the eater of the *viś*' and the *kṣatriya* being more powerful than the *viś*. The *viś* sets apart a share for the *kṣatriya*,[62] the latter having a share in whatever belongs to the former; suggestive of the germinal idea of what later became a tax and where terms for taxes in later periods such as *bhāga* (a share) and *bali* (a voluntary tribute) can be traced back to these times. In all accounts the *viś* is made obedient to the *kṣatriya*. Despite the distancing between the *kṣatriya* and the *viś* there is no ritual and social exclusion as there was with the *śūdra*s who were not even allowed to enter the sacrificial enclosure (*śālā)* to which only *brāhmaṇ*s, *rājanya*s and *vaiśya*s had access.[63] But the *vaiśya* was treading a tight rope for those with wealth could associate with senior lineages whereas those who were impoverished were doubtless treated on par with the *śūdra*s. The difference begins to be evident in occasional statements, for on the whole the *viś* was still included in with the *brāhmaṇs* and the *kṣatriya*s.

The necessity for the *viś* to increase their production to meet these new needs was met partly by new settlements and more land coming under cultivation and partly by incorporating the services of those who were outside the lineage system and could be employed. In this situation the *śūdra*s and *dāsa*s would be the ones available for such work. This ultimately brought about a householding economy in which the extended fámily constituted the household and employed labour in a series of service relationships. The overall lineage structure did not require a radical change since the flow of wealth still pertained essentially to the requirements of prestations which were consumed in sacrificial rituals and gift-giving. The word for wealth, *rayi* has its origin in the root **rā*, to give.[64] The prestations made by the *viś* to the *kṣatriya*s and the labour provided by the *śūdra*s was a sufficient basis for stratification although the maintenance of stratification

[59] *Tait. Sam.* v. 4.6.7.; VIII. 7.1.12.; x. 4.3.22.; XII. 7.3.15.

[60] *Ait. Brāh.* VIII. 12.17; *Śat. Brāh.* VIII. 7.1.2.; VIII. 7.2.2.; IX. 4.3.5.

[61] *Ait. Brāh.* VIII. 17.; *Śat. Brāh.* III. 3.2.8.

[62] *Śat. Brāh.* IX. 1.1.25.; IX. 1.1.18.

[63] *Śat. Brāh.* III. 1.1.9.

[64] *Ṛg V.* I. 96.7.; *Nirukta* IV. 17.; S. Varma, *The Etymologies of Yaska*, Hoshiarpur, 1953, p. 51.

did not require the machinery of a state, the importance of lineage still being central and adequate for asserting authority. It is perhaps in this context that the *viś* and the *prajā* are said to go down before the *kṣatriya*.[65] *Prajā* is a new concept and presumably includes the non-kin groups as well as the non-lineage groups such as the *śūdra*s. A further exclusion of the *viś* from their original status lies in the statement that the *viś* cannot eat the offerings at the sacrifice.[66]

A group of clans constituted a *jana* and the territory where they settled was referred to as the *janapada*, literally where the tribe places its feet. Since the economy of the *jana* included hunting and pastoralism, large forested areas adjoined the settlements and could even carry the name of the *jana*, as for example, the Kuru-vana. Actual control over territory was limited to smaller areas of cultivated land. As long as the settlements were comparatively small (as is suggested by archaeological evidence), lineage authority was sufficient as a mechanism of control. This is in part indicated by the fact of the *janapada*s being named after the *kṣatriya* lineages which had established their control in the area. Thus apart from the Kuru and Pañcāla, mention is made of Kekaya, Madra, Matsya, among others.

The *ksatriya* lineages claimed control over the territory of the *janapada* but the notion of a well-defined territory was uncertain at this time. The boundaries between *janapada*s tend to be topographical features such as forests, rivers and streams and hills. Territory was seen as the clearly indentifiable settlements and the more liminal areas of forests and waste land between settlements. The term which in the post-Vedic period is used for territory, *rāṣṭra*, is mentioned at this time, but its meaning does not seem to be that of a well-defined area over which absolute control is claimed. *Rāṣṭra* from the root **rāj*, to shine, is used more in the sense of realm, sphere or authority. Both in the *Ṛg Veda* and later Vedic texts it is the sustaining of the *rāṣṭra, rāṣṭrabhṛt*, which is crucial.[67] In the reference to the *rāṣṭrabhṛt* oblations the idea of nourishing is further endorsed by the oblations being of *ghi* (clarified butter).[68] This would hardly suggest territory in a literal sense. It is also stated that the *rājā*s are the *rāṣṭrabhṛt* and because of their association with the deities they are permitted by the gods to offer

[65] *Śat. Brāh.* III. 9.3.7. [66] Ibid., II. 5.2.24. [67] *Ṛg V.* X. 173
[68] Śat. Brāh. IX. 4.1.1.

the *rāṣṭrabhṛt* oblations. Even more important is the statement that only he becomes a *rājā* who is allowed by other *rājā*s to assume the title. This suggests a strengthening of the demarcation between lineages to which the *rājā*s belonged and the lower status lineages which played little or no role in the choice of the *rājā*.

There is some controversy as to whether the *rājā* was elected by the clans or was the choice of a more select group. In one hymn of the *Ṛg Veda* it is clear that those who chose the *rājā* are distinct from the *viś*.[69] The nature of the bifurcation between the senior and junior lineages would support the former selecting the *rājā* if only to further curb the power of the *viś*. The demand of *bali* would have been weakened if the *viś* had the right to elect a *rājā*. The *Śatapatha Brāhmaṇa* asserts that ruling power and social distinction are attached to a single person and multiplicity is the characteristic of the clan.[70] Yet in another hymn of the *Ṛg Veda*, again of a late section of the collection, there is a reference to the *viś* chosing a *rājā*.[71] Possibly this was the earlier custom which was later discontinued when the *rājanya*s became more powerful.

The title *rājā* has frequently been translated as king rather than chief. In many cases the later meaning of the term is applied to these early sources. Yet even in later periods the connotation of *rājā* has varied from landholder to king. The office of *rājā* in the Vedic sources was primarily that of a leader in battle and the protector of the settlements. This is evident both from the functions of the office and the association of *rājā* with Indra. Gradually the notion of the *rājā* as the nourisher and as the symbol of prosperity and fertility took precedence and the deities associated with the office were suitably enlarged. Reference to *rājā*s as in an assembly[72] would suggest members of the *rājanya* lineages or an assembly of chiefs. Later references even when the role of the *rājā* had changed still occur, often in the plural, and suggest persons belonging to a superior social group rather than individual kings, for example, the *rājā*s sharing the wealth among themselves and offering a sixteenth share at the *yajña* or the prayer for the prosperity of the *rājā*s.[73] It was at these assemblies that one among the *rājā*s was chosen to preside and to protect. The office was not hereditary to begin with and the choice and the consecration of the *rājā* would have occurred with every vacancy. It is curious that of the many

[69] *Ṛg V.* x. 173.1.
[70] *Śat. Brāh.* IX. 3.1.13-14.; IX. 4.3.10.
[71] *Ṛg V.* x. 124.8.
[72] Ibid, x. 97.
[73] *Atharvaveda* II. 6.4.; *Tait. Sam.* v. 7.6.4.; *Vāj. Sam.* 18.48.

close associates listed as the *ratnins*, there is no mention of any heir-apparent as would be expected in a system of kingship with hereditary succession. In the later Vedic period the consecration of the *rājā* became more elaborate with claims to *kṣatra* and consecration became an avenue to power. Claims to sovereignty and increasing demands of prestations were sought to be justified through consecration rituals. The absolute, secular authority associated with kingship appears to be absent in these sources and the income from prestations is poured into the rituals and given to those who perform the rituals. This also led to the greater inter-dependence of the *kṣatriya* and the *brāhmaṇ*, a relationship which is pointed to in the *Śatapatha Brāhmaṇa*. It is said that the *brāhmaṇ* was the god Mitra and therefore the conceiver and the *kṣatriya* was Varuna the doer. At first they were separate and thus undermined each other's power. Then Varuna called for unity with Mitra and conceded pre-eminence to him, after which both prospered.[74] Thus the *kṣatriya* must always have a *brāhmaṇ* (the reverse is too obvious and is left unsaid!). In the absence of both the hereditary principle and primogeniture the consecratory rituals had special significance to legitimation. In the search for power, consecration became the hall-mark of the *rājā* backed by senior lineages of the *kṣatriyas* and the cultivation of land was left to the householding families of the *viś*.

The inclusion of the householding system in the lineage structure was probably a marginal change to begin with. Gradually it became the thin end of the wedge which was partially responsible for erosion of the lineage system with the eventual arrival of the notion of private ownership of land and of the development of commerce as more than just exchange. The significance of non-kin labour in the householding economy can be seen at the point where in some areas lineage society underwent a change and the householding economy emerged but in a different framework incorporating a peasant economy and commerce.

Initially the householding system was probably common to both the *rājanyas* and the *viś*. Hence the *gṛhapati* or the head of the household could be from either and is mentioned with respect in the texts. In the late sections of the *Ṛg Veda* and in the *Atharva Veda* the *gṛhapati* appears to be of the higher lineage since the term is brought in when describing the nuptials of the daughter of *Sūrya* the sun-god.[75] Elsewhere in the *Ṛg Veda* Agni is called the *gṛhapati*

[74] *Śat. Brāh.* IV. 1.4.1 ff.

[75] *Ṛg V.* X. 85.; *Atharvaveda*, XIV. 1 and 2.; XIX. 31.12.

and the sacred household fire is the *gṛhapatya*.[76] That the *gṛhapati*s are associated with wealth is indicated by a hymn in which Pūṣan is urged to make them generous in their gifts.[77] In the later Vedic literature there are references to *gṛhapati*s and *yajamāna*s which suggest *kṣatriya*s but do not preclude *vaiśya*s. The principal ritual role of the *gṛhapati* was that of the *yajamāna* (he who orders the sacrifice) and it is possible to trace the growing importance of the *gṛhapati* through the rituals. The *vaiśya gṛhapati* occurs in the later Vedic literature but more often in the context of the *grāmaṇī*. It is said that all *vaiśya*s wish to become *grāmaṇī*s, probably because *grāmaṇī*s were thought to be wealthy.[78] That the *grāmaṇī* was from the *viś* is clear from the ceremony when the *rājā* visits the home of the *grāmaṇī* and offers oblations to the Maruts and it is said that the Maruts are the *viś*, a connection which is frequently mentioned, and that the *grāmaṇī* is also the *viś*.[79] The *grāmaṇī* was among the lineage heads and important families of the *viś* who had both power and wealth. Their wealth did not come from prestations but was produced by their own efforts, its abundance dependent on an economy which may be termed householding.

With the increasing shift to agriculture and the decreasing interest in pastoralism the role of the *rājanya*s as chariot-riding chiefs carrying out cattle raids and bringing in booty was not as conducive to producing wealth as it had been earlier. When the *rājanya*s were converted into *kṣatriya*s and they acquired power and became the hub of the redistributive system they came to depend more on the agricultural activities of the *viś* and the prestations which the *viś* could provide. Since numerically the *kṣatriya*s as chiefs would have been considerably smaller than the members of the *viś* such a dependence was not impossible. Gradually therefore the householding economy came to be associated with the lineages of the *viś* rather than with those of the *kṣatriya*s. In a more sedentary phase the household became the unit of agricultural production and doubtless began to claim permanent usage over the land which it worked and in which it invested its labour, a permanency which was acceded to by the community when it saw that it was necessary to agriculture and that it ensured a predictability in prestations. With the weakening of clan control over agriculture and probably more so in new areas of settlement the permanency of

[76] *Ṛg V.* I. 12.6.; I. 36.5.; I. 60.4.; VI. 48.8.
[77] Ibid., VI. 53.2
[78] *Tait. Sam.* II. 5.4.4.
[79] *Śat. Brāh.* V. 3.1.6.

usage was likely ultimately to be transmuted into family ownership. This was probably aided by a greater concern on the part of the *kṣatriya* lineages with demanding prestations than on asserting ownership over clan lands. Prestations were stored in the *kṣatriya* household for consumption in rituals, for using in gift-giving and to furnish the basis for the generous hospitality expected of the *kṣatriya* household. However the storage seems to have been short-lived as the references to such 'treasuries' are few and far between.[80] The households of the *viś* also began to maintain a minimal storage in cases where the *gṛhapati*s of the *viś* are described as *yajamāna*s. The eventual emergence of the *gṛhapati* as a social category was in relationship to the *viś*. When *viś* is replaced by *vaiśya* it suggests an altered status, the clan element decreasing and the individual status becoming more apparent. At this stage the *śūdra* is also mentioned more frequently and a distinction made between the *vaiśya* and the *śūdra,* as in the famous passage which states that the *vaiśya* can be oppressed but the *śūdra* can be beaten or slain.[81] This raises the question of whether the actual cultivation was done by the *vaiśya*s or the *śūdra*s.

The cultivator in the technical sense of the word was the *kīnāśa* of the *Ṛg Veda*[82] and is referred to as the *karṣaka/kassaka, kṣetraka* and *śūdra* in post-Vedic literature. *Vaiśya* is not used for the cultivator although the *vaiśya* may have derived his wealth from agriculture. The explanation for this may lie in the need to differentiate between three categories of cultivators: the primitive cultivator, the cultivator in a system which has been called the householding economy and the cultivator in a peasant economy. Primitive cultivation is almost limited to swidden and subsistance agriculture and is outside our context. In the second category the household is the unit of production and consumption based on agriculture and livestock breeding. In borrowing the term 'householding' from Polanyi[83] an attempt is made here to use it with reference to a pre-state society. Although in the Vedic period

[80] *Ṛg. V.* x. 97.6.; x. 191.; *Atharvaveda* III. 29.1.

[81] *Ait. Brāh.* VII. 29.4.

[82] IV. 57.8. *Kīnāśa* in later texts has an ambiguous meaning. The general sense is that of a cultivator who may not own the land he cultivates and is therefore better translated as a ploughman working for a wage and dependent on the owner. B.N.S. Yadav, 'The Kali Age and the Social Transition', *IHR*, 1978-9, v., nos. 1 and 2, pp. 37-8. Ṛg Vedic references to *kṣetra* suggest cultivated land rather than individual holdings (I. 100.18.; I. 33.15.; x. 85.4; x. 91.6).

[83] K. Polanyi, *Dahomey and the Slave Trade*, p. 70 ff.

householding does not emerge as an independent social formation in the terms in which Polanyi describes it, certain attributes of the form can however be usefully extracted from Polanyi's model and can perhaps elucidate Vedic data.

Polanyi describes the household as consisting of agnatically related men and their families claiming membership of a patrilineal lineage. The household as a unit is often made up of smaller houses functioning as an entity. Inheritance remains within the kin group and alienation of neither house nor land is permitted. The cult of the ancestor is the focus of the household and is maintained by hereditary priests. To this may be added other features: the household utilizes family labour as well as some specialists—herders and craftsmen for example—who are not kinsmen and are more in the nature of retainers except that they are not paid a wage but maintained by the household and paid in kind. Presumably such labour could be extended to cultivators helping in the fields. Slaves would be attached to the families of chiefs and they would be mainly domestic slaves. The household consumes much of what it produces but the excess is taken by those to whom it is politically subordinate in the form of prestations and gifts. This system is marked by the absence of two factors which distinguish it from a peasant economy. Firstly the family exercises rights over the land which it cultivates and there are no tenants since cultivation is carried out by family labour and by those who are attached to the household in various occupational capacities. Secondly there is no regular contractual payment of rent or tax to the political authority or to the state since it does not presuppose the existence of a state. The point at which taxes start to be paid by the household is also the point at which cultivation through membership of a landowning lineage weakens and individual ownership is asserted, even though lineage ties would still be respected and often seen to be effective.

The *viś* was by now characterized by the householding system, with the *gṛhapati* as the patriarchal head, commanding both family labour and that of *śūdra*s and *dāsa*s. Neither of the latter were helots and could well have been impoverished members of the *dāsa-varṇa*, their subordination arising as much from their being aliens outside the lineages as from their impoverishment. It is difficult to describe the *śūdra*s or the *dāsa*s as helots in the strict sense as there were clans of each which co-existed with the *ārya*s and some of the chiefs of these clans are described as wealthy or are spoken of with respect in the earlier texts. In time however the terms *śūdra* and *dāsa* came to be used for those performing labour services. The interchangeability of *ārya* and *dāsa* status in the post-Vedic period and the fact that an *ārya* could become a *dāsa* for a temporary period precludes a system of helotage.

The mention of *bali, bhāga* and *śūlka* has been interpreted as reference to taxes of various kinds. But none of these were collected at a specified time and regularly, nor were they of a precisely defined amount and there is no mention of specific occupational groups from whom they were collected or of designated persons who made the collection. All these conditions were fulfilled in the post-Vedic period when taxes were collected and these terms were used as terms for taxes. In Vedic literature their connotation would appear to differ. The *balihṛt* is clearly the tribute paid by a conquered tribe in one instance.[84] More frequently *bali* is a generalized offering made by the *viś* and may better be translated as tribute or a prestation rather than tax.[85] If there was any seasonality associated with the *bali* then it related to the performance of rituals or occasions of consecration. It may in origin have been the tribute of a defeated tribe but came to be extended to offerings brought by subordinate groups to those in authority. Terms such as *balihṛt* and *balikṛt*[86] can be rendered as the bearers and providers of tribute rather than as tax-paying groups, as in the case of the reference to the *vaiśya* as the *balikṛt*. This is further clarified by the request to the gods to distribute the wealth thus collected.[87] *Bali* therefore remained a prestation. *Bhāga* in the sense of share relates to the distribution of spoils after a raid or the division of prestations on ritual occasions. Its origins may be traced to the offering of the first fruits as a token to the sanctity of the chief, an idea which is known to other early societies.[88] It is connected with *bhāgadugha* which because of the word *dugha* (milking) can be interpreted as the collector of the share or in the association of *bhāgadugha* with Pūṣan, the distributor.[89] The share of the chief is not stipulated and this is in contrast to the later

[84] *Ṛg V.* VII. 6.5.

[85] E.g. *Ṛg V.* I. 70.5.; V. 1.10. See also J. Gonda, *Ancient Indian Kingship ...*, Leiden, 1969, pp. 12-13.

[86] *Ṛg V.* VII. 6.5.; X. 173.6.; *Ait. Brāh.* VII. 29.

[87] *Atharvaveda*, III. 4.2-3.

[88] Goldman, *Ancient Polynesian Society*, p. 509; cf. *Śat. Brāh.* V. 2.39.

[89] *Tait. Sam.* I. 8.9.2; *Kāṭhaka Sam.* XV. 4; *Tait. Brāh.* I. 7.3.5; III. 4.8.1. *Śat. Brāh.* I. 1.2.17; V. 3.1.9.

period when it is said that the king is to receive one-sixth of the share as a wage for protecting the people,[90] and still later when in the post-Mauryan period the designation *ṣaḍbhāgin* (the receiver of one-sixth share) comes to be used for the king.[91] The term *śulka* in the *Ṛg Veda* does not mean a tax but is used in the sense of a measure of value and in the *Atharvaveda* the context is generally that of the weak paying a price to the strong.[92] In the *dharma-śāstras* of the post-Vedic period and in Pāṇini there is the meaning of a tax but also the meaning of a nuptial gift or dower, suggesting that it might have been used for bride-price or dowry.[93] This meaning could well have gone back to the Vedic Period when such gifts were a part of marriage alliances. The words *bali, bhāga and śulka* do change their meaning from tribute, distribution and price (in the sense of value) in the *Ṛg Veda* to forms of taxes and dues in the later *dharma-śāstra* literature. Whether they meant the former or the latter in the intermediate period of the later Vedic texts would depend largely on the context of their occurence and the context suggests the greater likelihood of the former meaning. The change of meaning carried with it a major change in the relations between the chief and the clan. From voluntary giving with a pattern of mutual honouring it changed to compulsory giving with a pattern of unequal reciprocity. As long as status was based on genealogy the inequality was symbolic, when it was based on land it became substantial.[94].

The *vaiśya* as the *gṛhapati* was the source of wealth for the *kṣatriya* and the *brāhmaṇ* through prestations for the *kṣatriya* and through *dakṣinā* as well as the items consumed in the course of the sacrificial rituals for *brāhmaṇs*:[95] hence the statement that *vaiśyas* can be oppressed, presumably to extract further wealth.[96] The *vaiśya* was beholden to the *kṣatriya* for protection as well as the provision of lands to settle and cultivate. The prestations necessary for the sacrificial ritual precluded a completely self-sufficient village economy and established links across lineage segments and consequently a circuit of villages as well. With the disintegration of

[90] *Baudhāyana* D.S. I. 10.18.1.

[91] *Arthaśāstra* II. 15; *Viṣṇu D.Śā.* III. 22.

[92] *Ṛg V.* VII. 82.6; VIII. 1.5; *Atharvaveda,* III. 29.3; III. 4.3; *Śat. Brāh.* XI. 2.6.14 qv.; *Vedic Index*, II, p. 387.

[93] Pāṇini, IV. 3.75.

[94] Goldman, *Ancient Polynesian Society*, p. 509.

[95] *Śat. Brāh.* IV. 4.2.15; IV. 6.9.5; IV. 6.9.25; XI. 8.4.1 ff; XII. 1.1.1 ff.

[96] *Ait. Brāh.* VII. 29.4.

clan holdings, the *gṛhapati* who had earlier cultivated lands held jointly gradually came to exercise ownership, though perhaps still as the head of the family, over land cultivated by the family, since the *Dharma-sūtra*s in the subsequent period invest him with the right to bequeath property to his eldest son or divide it among his sons.[97] The transition from clan ownership to family holdings was probably accelerated when clan settlements became more scattered in new clearings together with the establishment of the economic viability of the household as a unit. In such a situation voluntary prestations were perhaps less forthcoming and the need for protection in new areas was paid for by a regular contribution which was to assume the character of a tax in the post-Vedic period. This became feasible when, with the intensification of plough agriculture, such an economic surplus was possible. Ultimately, in the post-Vedic period the decline of the householding economy would lead to the rise of peasant tenures in which the *śūdra*s were to emerge as the major peasant group. This change is reflected in the statement in a *Gṛhya-sūtra* that the *gṛhapati* should have his fields ploughed, suggesting thereby not only the working of the land by another[98] but possibly also the individual ownership of land since the *gṛhapati* is not described as a member of a lineage.

The changing relationships wrought by agriculture and the new settlements in the western Ganga valley would also have required some readjustments within the *viś*. Those who were able to establish a household and farm would have aspired to *gṛhapati* status and constituted a part of what came to be the *vaiśya varṇa*. Others reduced to the condition of labourers and artisans would have moved increasingly to the edges of society to finally become part of the larger population of *śūdra*s. At a still further remove, *dāsa* came more frequently to mean a slave. Most references suggest domestic slavery as in the case of the hundreds and thousands of slaves employed in the household of Yuddhiṣṭhira and who are listed as part of his wealth staked in the game of dice.[99] The figures are almost certainly exaggerated, for the functions which they performed would not have required such excessively large numbers.

These developments resulted in a series of contrasting status stratifications which were sought to be arranged into a system through the scheme of *varṇa*. The earlier texts speak of an *ārya-varṇa* and a *dāsa-varṇa,* suggesting a dual division.[100] The words

97 *Baudhāyana D.S.* II. 2.3.2 ff.

98 *Aśvalāyana G.S.* II. 10.3.

99 Sabhā Parvan, 46 ff

100 *Ṛg V.* I. 104.2; III. 34.9.

occur as *ārya* and *dāha* in Iranian sources and *ārya* connotes a man of wealth and possessions,[101] a frequent association in Vedic sources too. A contemporary lexicon explains it as an owner or master[102] and Pāṇini glosses it with the statement, *āryah swami vaiśyayoḥ*,[103] the wealth of the *vaiśya*s being an indication. The *dāha* of the early Iranian becomes *dasa* in Vedic texts and means 'a male, man, a hero', in much the same sense as *manuṣa*. This is often the meaning of the names taken by tribal groups.[104] Tacitus refers to the Arios and the Dahas settled along the Indus river.[105] (That *ārya* was a term of respect is clear from Buddhist sources where *bhikkhu*s are often addressed as *ārya* and where the *ārya* and the *dāsa* are juxtaposed to mean master and slave, especially with reference to lands beyond the Indus.[106]) The dichotomy is expressed in Vedic sources by regarding the *dāsa-varṇa* as alien and therefore of a different symbolic colour. In the *Ṛg Veda* they are associated with wealth, fortified settlements, and with darkness or blackness.[107] But they were apparently not a helot group or slaves since their wealthier members are mentioned by name. These were evidently people of some substance and *dāsa* chiefs such as Balbutha and Tarukṣa and Ambaṣṭhya are eulogized by *brāhmaṇ*s for their munificence or else, as Śambara, are feared for their strength.[108] Some *dāsa* chiefs are so powerful that Indra is said to have battled against them.[109] The *viś* of the *dāsa* are referred to in the *Ṛg Veda*,[110] indicating that they were distinct and separate. Possibly the *dāsa*s of the *Rg Veda* were agricultural communities

[101] H.W. Bailey, 'Iranian *Arya* and *Daha*', *Transactions of the Philological Society*, 1959, p. 71 ff.

[102] *Naighantaka* 2.6.

[103] III. 1.103.

[104] Curiously the area inhabited by the *daha/dāsa* being the Indus valley would suggest an earlier nomenclature which I have argued elsewhere applied to this region and that is Makan. This in Proto-Dravidian would convey the same meaning of a man, or hero or male. The name Suvira is also indicative of the same meaning, being used for this region in a still later period and occurs frequently as Sindhu-Suvīra. Romila Thapar, 'A Possible Identification of Meluhha, Dilmun and Makan', *JESHO*, 1975, XVIII, pt 1, p. 30 ff.

[105] *Annales* 10-11.

[106] *Maj. Nik.* II. 144; *Samantapāsādikā* II., p. 238.

[107] II. 12.4; 20.8; III. 12.6; IV., 16.13. 30.13; VIII. 40.6; X. 69.5-6; *Atharvaveda*, VII, 90.2. Blackness is also associated with the *asura*s and the *rākṣasa*s and was probably symbolic of all those who were not speakers of Indo-Aryan.

[108] *Ṛg V.* VI. 31.4; VII. 99.5; *Ṛg V.* VIII. 32, 40 and 46; *Ait. Brāh.* VIII. 12; *Chand. Up.* IV. 2.1-5; *Vedic Index*, II. p. 355.

[109] *Ṛg V.* I. 51.5-6, 103.8, 104.2; V. 30; VI. 20.7.

[110] II. 11.4; IV. 28.4; VI. 25.2.

of the Late Harappan or post-Harappan cultures of the area, perhaps even of the agricultural niches scattered in the region. That the word eventually came to mean 'slave' may initially have had more to do with the hostility towards them than with their actual subordination. The *Dasyu*[111] are noted for their variant religious beliefs and customs which the *ārya*s saw as the negation of their own and which appear to have been the chief distinguishing characteristic. The assimilation of these groups was facilitated by their being given subordinate status. Reference to *ārya-kṛita* in later texts indicate a status to which a person can be restored after having been a *dāsa*.[112] *Varṇa* was to become a system of putting together the structure of the society and the colour symbolism was retained. The four *varṇa*s were latter associated with the colours white, yellow, red and black.[113] In the dual division of *ārya* and *dāsa,* the *ārya* was distinguished by wealth and status. The *ārya*s would be those who either belonged to the senior or to the cadet lineages (*rājanya*s and the *viś*) as well as those who were included in the circuit of prestations and redistribution, that is, the *brāhmaṇ*s. The *dāsa*s were excluded from this circuit even when they were wealthy enough to bestow gifts on the *brāhmaṇ*s. With the sharpening of stratification and the beginnings of professional specialization, the constituents of the *ārya*s were more clearly demarcated into *brāhmaṇ, kṣatriya* and *vaiśya,* with the *śūdra*s incorporating an amorphous group of excluded clans and low status professions. The former described as *dvija* or twice born (the second birth being initiation) in later texts deepens the demarcation and underlines the connection between initiation and lineage customs.

Another contrast of a more broadly cultural kind but going back to Iranian sources was that between the *deva*s and the *asura*s. Among the Iranians the *deva*s were hostile and the *ahura/asura* god-like. In Vedic sources both are described as the progeny of Prajāpati[114] and the *asura*s in some cases are treated with respect but eventually come to represent evil, hostile forces. The *asura*s though feared are depicted as the more sophisticated of the two. They lived in permanent habitations whereas the *deva*s moved about in carts.[115] They were acquainted with the right seasons for

[111] *Vedic Index*, I. p. 347; *Ṛg V.* I. 33.4; I. 51.8; VII. 6.3.

[112] Pāṇini IV. 1.30; *Arthaśāstra* III. 13. In the *Ṛg V.* VI. 22.10 the *dāsas* and *āryas* are jointly invoked.

[113] *Aśvalāyana G.S.* II. 8.6-8; cf. *Ṛg. V.* X. 20.9. The Licchavi clans are distinguished by a difference in colour, *Mahāvagga* VI. 30.3-4.

[114] *Sat. Brāh.* I. 5.3.2; I.7.2.22; II. 2.2.8; VI. 6.2.11.

[115] Ibid. VI. 8.1. 1-2.

agricultural activities[116] and associated with wheel-thrown pottery.[117] The *asura* form of marriage involved a bride-price[118] and they performed regular burial rites.[119] The magical power of the *asuras*, perhaps a subtle concession to their superiority, which plays a role in the narrative of the *Mahābhārata*, is mentioned in the *Ṛg Veda* in association with the bringing of rain.[120] The ambiguity towards the *asuras* revolving around common origins, power and hostility, remains a constant feature in Vedic literature.[121]

To this list may be added a further social duality, recorded only in later Vedic literature.This essentially linguistic distinction to begin with, between the *ārya* and the *mleccha*, separating the speakers of Indo-Aryan from others, takes on a social connotation as well, with *mleccha* meaning a barbarian or one outside the pale and ritually impure.[122] The recognition of basic differences in these dualities of *deva-asura* and *ārya-mleccha* is an indication of the recognition of heterogeneity and the need to juxtapose the differences within a working system.

The integration of groups through particular forms of kinship was a parallel process and is more often referred to in the concept of the *gotra*, literally meaning a stockade for cows, which was used to identify descent groups among the high status *varṇas*. Initially it appears in more frequent association with the *brāhmaṇs* and was to remain essential to *brāhmaṇ* identity. Later sources mention certain *kṣatriyas* (such as the Andhaka-Vṛṣṇi, Śākyas and Licchavis) using *gotra* identities. But among them it was more a means of differentiating between families within the clan than for wider social identification. The *gotra* was an exogamous clan where exogamy was emphasized in the prohibition on marrying *sagotras*, and marrying those related upto seven generations on the father's side and five on the mother's. The latter would preclude cross-cousin marriage, so a special exception had to be made in case of *brāhmaṇs*

[116] Ibid. I. 6.1.2-4. [117] *Tait. Brāh.* II. 2.95; *Maitrāyani Saṃhitā* I. 8.3.

[118] *Yajñavalkya Smṛti* III. 61; Manu III. 3.

[119] *Śat. Brāh.* XIII. 8.1.1. *Chāndogya Upaniṣad* 8.8.5. [120] V. 63.3.

[121] A curious reference to the bull *asura*, Vṛṣṇa, in the *Ṛg Veda*, III. 38.4 calls to mind the bull as a clan name which occurs so frequently in early Indian tradition in the form of Vṛṣṇi, Vṛṣabha, Ṛṣabha, not to mention the frequeny of the bull on the Harappan seals.

[122] *Śat. Brāh.* III. 2.1.23. Romila Thapar, 'The Image of the Barbarian in Early India', in *AISH*, p. 152 ff.

[123] E. Senart, *Le Mahāvastu*, I, pp. 283-361, *Pāṇini* I. 2.65 ff.

from the south.[124] The exogamous basis of the *gotra* system doubtless facilitated the induction of outsiders of high or appropriate status; the insistance on marrying out meant the necessity of bestowing equal status on new groups and inducting such groups into the *varṇa*. This is reflected in the increase in the number of brahmanical *gotras* from seven to eighteen and forty-nine, and many more by the end of the first millennium A.D. Doubtless the increase was partly due to segmentation among the main *gotras*, although this generally took the form of a new *gaṇa* or *pravara*, a new sub-group. More likely this was also the result of co-option of new groups. This might account in part for *brāhmaṇs* of non-*brāhmaṇ* ancestry. The counterpart to exogamy was that inheritence of property was open only to members of the same *gotra*.

For the *kṣatriyas* to adopt the *gotra* system was something of an anomaly since they were identified by lineage or *vaṃśa*, preferred endogamy and are known to have made cross-cousin marriages as well as to have married into collateral lineages. There is a greater frequency of variation in the actual types of marriages among *kṣatriyas*. The classic example would be the implications of marriage alliances in the three generations of Pāṇḍavas from Pāṇḍu to his sons and grandsons who subscribe to endogamy, fraternal polyandry and cross-cousin marriage, but all among *kṣatriya* lineages. Within the *vaṃśa* there was a differentiation between the senior lineages and the rest as is interestingly demonstrated by the story of Yayāti and the interchange of status between his eldest and youngest sons, Yadu and Puru;[125] the inheritance having gone to the youngest, it became necessary to justify this action. Endogamy among the *kṣatriya vaṃśas* was doubtless encouraged because land rights were vested in kinship links and birth. In the initial transition to agriculture, genealogical links would have acted as a means of narrowing access to status and resources; genealogies of increasing depth in later sources would perhaps point to wider mobilization, particularly among the Candravaṃśa lineages which tend to follow a segmentary pattern. There is evidence of a fairly widespread movement of peoples not only from the watershed to the Ganga valley, but also into the Vindhyan region. The assimilation of local populations must certainly have been part of the reason for the frequency of breaking away or

124 *Baudhāyana* D.S., I. 1.2.1 ff.

125 *Mahābhārata*, Ādi Parvan, 71; cf. Udyoga Parvan 104.121 and 147.3-13.

a fissioning off from the main lineage, although migrations were also a form of easing tension and establishing new settlements.

The nuclear unit in such a society was the *kula,* the family, and a group of such families made up the *grāma* or village. *Grāma* by extension therefore also referred to a community. In some instances it conveyed the meaning of a body of men.[126] It was therefore a larger unit than the *kula* but smaller than the *viś*. The term *grāmaṇī* used for a village headman in many sources was also at this stage the chief of an aggregate of families or of a community settled in the same place. The larger unit *viś* or clan is recorded even among the *dāsa*. It counted in turn towards the identity of the tribe or *jana*. The word *jana* carries the notion of people as well as growth and fecundity.[127] A characteristic phrase of this literature is *pañca-janāḥ*, the precise meaning of which remains elusive.[128] It has been suggested that it may refer to five specific tribes whose eponymous ancestors are the founders of the clans, namely Yadu, Turvaśa, Druhyu, Anu and Puru, or that it may symbolize the totality of the people, the image deriving from the five fingers of the hand.[129] The notion of the *pañca-janāḥ* seems to have been basic to the pattern of one of the two major *ksatriya* lineages, that of the Aila or Candravaṃśa as given in the *Purāṇa*s and the *Mahābhārata*.[130] The main lineages are described as descended from the five sons of Yayāti of which the Paurava and the Yādava are the most important and the descent lines close with the victory of the five sons of Pandu at the Kurukṣetra battle. At crucial points of geographical diffusion, the genealogies list a pattern of five brothers such as the reference to the five sons of Uparicara establishing themselves along the southern bank of the Yamuna as far as Magadha[131] or the five sons of Bali establishing themselves in eastern India.[132] At one level the concept of the *Panca-janāḥ* could have referred to all the clans, but at another level it carried a

[126] *V.I.*, I., p. 245 ff.

[127] Minoro Hara, 'A Note on the Sanskrit Word Jana', *Pratidānam*, The Hague, 1968, p. 256 ff.

[128] *Vedic Index*, I, p. 269; II., pp. 466-7. D.D. Kosambi, 'The Vedic "Five Tribes"', *JAOS*, 1967, 87, pp. 33-9. Yāska's *Nirukta* III. 8.8.; IV. 23.1, explains it as the five categories of *pitṛ*, *gāndharva*, *deva*, *asura* and *rāksasa*.

[129] *Ṛg V.* I. 108.8; W.P. Lehman, 'Linguistic Structure as Diacritic Evidence on Proto-Culture', in G. Cardona *et al.*, *Indo-European and Indo-Europeans*, Pennsylvania, 1970.

[130] *Viṣṇu Purāṇa* IV. 18.

[131] *Mahābhārata*, Ādi Parvan 57.

[132] *Viṣṇu Purāṇa* IV. 18.

symbolism which remains obscure.[133] If it is to be interpreted as the symbol of the totality then its derivation would probably be from the notion of the four on all sides and the one in the centre, thus reflecting the idea of the four quarters as well.

The *kula, viś* and *jana* was a spatial distribution moving in widening circles from the nucleus to the rim. A vertical hierarchy was also evident in the *jana* with the distinction between the *rājanya* and the *viś*, where the *rājanya* was increasingly identified with the senior lineages aspiring to power and the *viś* represented the lesser lineages. Among the *rājanya* were those who had been consecrated as chiefs.[134] The *rājanyas* had access to power, *kṣatra,* and came to be called *kṣatriyas*, and the gradual displacement of the term *rājanya* by *kṣatriya* would indicate the emergence of a new focus of power among the ruling clans. The etymology of *rājā* remains uncertain and the later view that it derived from the verb 'to please' is unacceptable. The roots **raj, *rañj, *riñj*, suggest the connotation of the verb 'to glow' or 'to shine'. This could be extended to mean the one who shines and is resplendent and therefore the chief.[135] It has also been suggested that the Indo-European root **reğ* for *rex* in Latin indicates the one who leads, directs, follows what is right or proceeds in a line,[136] a meaning which would suit the idea of a head of a lineage. The increasing emphasis on the special status of the *rājanya/kṣatriya* had its counter-weight in the declining status of the lineages of the *viś*. The *viś* perhaps consoled themselves through a control of the householding economy in which they continued to have access to wealth as the *gṛhapatis*. Nevertheless the wealth of the *rājanya* was considerably greater since he was the recipient of prestations and

[133] Echoes of the idea seem to continue in the later concept of the *pañca-vīra* or five heroes of the Vṛṣṇis, a segment of the Yādavas. The five heroes were eventually worshipped as part of a cult in Saurashtra, southern Rajasthan and Mathura. The Tamil tradition of the Aimperumvelir, the five great *vel* chiefs is also curious, particularly as the Velir claim to be of Yādava descent. The notion of five constituting a unit is often found in the Indian subcontinent. The sacrificial ritual in the *Śat. Brāh.* involves five animals, listed as man, horse, bull, ram and he-goat, and the *gṛhastha* is required to perform five *yajñas* during the day, etc.

[134] This is evident from even later references to the *gaṇa–saṅgha* system as in Pāṇini VI. 2.34.

[135] Yāska, *Nirukta*, II. 3. This presents a parallel with the Proto-Dravidian *vel.* DED 4562 and 4524 would suggest a homophone meaning the chief and the resplendent one.

[136] E. Benveniste, *Indo-European Language and Society*, London, 1973, pp. 311-12.

doubtless also took a substantial share of the booty. Although much of this wealth went into the *yajña*s some of it would certainly have been temporarily stored since the *rājanya* was expected to use it to make gifts on frequent occasions.

The emergence of the *kṣatriya* was linked to clan rights over land as well as to the sanction given to the new status by the *brāhmaṇ*. In the definition of the *ārya,* three groups are mentioned, the *brāhmaṇ, kṣatriya* and *viś*. Whether or not one subscribes to the theory of the tripartite function in viewing the relationship between the three,[137] or to the definition of these three which such a function assumes, it is clear that an attempt is made to link them. But gradually, this link is broken when the *vaiśya* is more often included with the *śūdra* and the two are regarded as of lower status than the *brāhmaṇ* and the *kṣatriya*. Kinship links between the *brāhmaṇ* and the *kṣatriya* are occasionally conceded but the formal systems remain quite distinct. The ranking order between *brāhmaṇ* and *kṣatriya* is ambivalent to begin with where the former is dependent on the latter for *dāna* and *dakṣiṇā* and the latter requires that his power be legitimized by the former.[138] In any case the two are superior to the rest of the community, a superiority which is clearly expressed in the formula that the *vaiśya* and the *śūdra* should be enclosed by the *brāhmaṇ* and the *kṣatriya* at the sacrifice in order to make the former submissive.[139] Even in burning wealth, so characteristic of the *yajña* ritual, the decision to do so is controlled by those who had access to the maximum wealth—the *kṣatriya* and the *brāhmaṇ*. The redistribution of wealth was therefore curtailed by the requirement of reciprocity between the *ksatriya* and the *brāhman* where the reciprocal relationship enhanced the status of each. The *kṣatriya* provided the *brāhmaṇ* with what was essentially a sacrificial fee disguised as it may have been in ritual gift-giving. The *brāhmaṇ* not only bestowed legitimation on the *kṣatriya* but also gave him access to special skills and knowledge intermeshed with the ritual which inevitably augmented the power of the *kṣatriya*.

[137] G. Dumezil, *Mythe et Épopée*, I and II, Paris, 1968, 1971; *Flamen-Brahman*, Paris, 1935.

[138] Later sources mention *kṣatriya*s moving to brahmanhood such as the Kanvas who were of the Ajamīḍha lineage. *Viṣṇu Purāṇa* IV. 19; Garga who was a Bharata, ibid.; Mudgala of the Candravaṃśa lineage, *Bhāgavata Purāṇa* IX. 21; and Harita of the Sūryavaṃśa, *Viṣṇu Purāṇa* IV. 3.

[139] *Śat. Brāh.* VI. 4.4.13.

In addition to the first three the other distinctive unit included in the overall definition of a caste society was the *śūdra*, associated with servility in the earlier texts. The *śūdras* were described in the later *Dharma-sūtras* as including *sankīrna* or mixed *jātis*. Each *jāti* was born out of a hypergamous (*anuloma*) or a hypogamous (*pratiloma*) marriage from among the three *dvija* or upper castes, *brāhmaṇ*, *kṣatriya* and *vaiśya* or their progeny. The number of *jātis* could theoretically increase on each new intercaste marriage but in effect the increase occured whenever there were major changes in which new social groups and professions were established. The *śūdra* as a *varṇa* was clearly a category added onto the original structure at a time when artisans and cultivators had to be accommodated and when alien groups were assimilated into caste society and had to be assigned varying statuses. That the concept of the *sankīrna-jāti*, was a later attempt at explaining a *de facto* situation is evident from the divergence in the texts regarding the particular combinations of castes producing *śūdra* offspring.[140] The elimination of kin-body in the case of *śūdras*, by assigning them only the status of their parents, was a means of excluding them by denying them a lineage connection. In a strongly lineage-oriented society this would in itself place them outside the social pale. The occasional substitution of *śūdra* and *dāsa* would suggest that many of the groups included in the *śūdra* category may have earlier been *dāsas* prior to the technical meaning of the word as slave. Etymologically *śūdra* could have been derived from *kṣudra* meaning small. Both these are known to have been the names of particular peoples at some stage. Latin sources mention the Oxydrakoi and the Sudracae and Sodroi as tribes of north-west India.[141] The Kṣudraka are linked with the powerful Mālava (the Malli/Malloi of the Greeks) almost as a compound to mean the small and the big. Mention is also made of the *gaṇas* of the Śūdras and the Abhiras dwelling on the Sarasvatī [142] The sense of smallness was worked into that of lowliness, indicated in a statement that the *śūdra* is the servant of another, he can be made to work at the will of his master and even be beaten,[143] a sentiment endorsed in the later *dharma-śāstras* as well. The denial of a lineage and the insistence on mixed caste origins, if not the word *śūdra* itself, would

[140] Manu, x. 1-73 discusses the origins of various *samkīrna jātis* of *śūdras*.

[141] *Curtius Rufus* IX. 4; cf. *Mahābhārata*, Sabhā Parvan 48.14; Pāṇini v. 3.144.

[142] *Mahābhārata*, Sabhā Parvan 29.9.

[143] A. Sharma, 'An Analysis of the Epithets applied to the Sūdras in Aitareya Brāhmaṇa VII. 29.4', *JESHO*, Oct. 1975, XVIII, pt 3, pp. 300-18.

also point to the members of this group coming from a floating population of those who had fallen out of lineage ties and were available to serve whomever could provide them with a livelihood. As such the labour of the *śūdra* was to become an important factor in eventually augmenting the wealth of those whom they served.

Distance between the *dvija* and the *śūdra* was also maintained through the notion of pollution. This was to influence yet another category that, designated by the adjective *vrātya* or degraded, applied to degradation from the three upper castes, resulting from the non-observance of the required rituals. Thus *vrātya-kṣatriya*s was to become a useful category in which to place those who were politically powerful but were obviously not *kṣatriya*s in the true sense. The ultimate in distance and separation was of course the untouchable who is referred to in the later period. Purity and pollution, central to the question of ritual status was expressed in terms of bodily contact, through ceremonies relating to rites of passage; through touch, the one among the five senses which was crucial in this matter; through food taboos and through sex by the regulation of marriage relations.

The theoretical construct of caste society was not the simple unfolding of a class society, nor the mechanical measurement of ritual status. It was an attempt at inter-locking a series of social units based on diverse rules of functioning but all in the context of a lineage system. At least three formal structures were to evolve from this genesis: the exogamous *brāhmaṇ gotra*s, the preference for endogamy of the *kṣatriya*s and the *śūdra jāti*s identified by parental status in which lineage is negligible. The differentiation therefore includes the widest possible lineage system, the out-going *gotra*, as well as the narrowest social unit, the *śūdra jāti*. In its initial phase the notion of *varṇa* attempted to construct a complete social framework using differentiated lineage systems demarcated by distinctive kinship forms. Variations in marriage rules are sometimes indications of status where higher-status groups prefer exogamy and lower status groups endogamy. Descent however lies at the heart of status.[144] At the theoretical level this would be one condition for working out a hierarchy, although the emphasis lies in each unit constituting its own method of comprehending lineage. Added to this was the notion of ritual status which was made explicit in the idea of purity and pollution where the hierarchy goes

[144] Goldman, *Ancient Polynesian Society*, p. 418 ff

from the purest to the most polluting, and where, in an exchange of services, those not actively involved in production would claim higher status on the basis of intangible authority seeking justification from religious sanction through the performance of rituals. Yet implicit in this hierarchy is the attempt to define and limit the access of each group to economic resources by the gradually increasing insistence on occupational functions, accompanied by the channelizing and redistribution of wealth being limited to the castes claiming ownership of clan resources and higher ritual status. That the attempt was not entirely successful, would be suggested by economic stratification also taking place within each of these vertical *varṇa* groups. There are impoverised *brāhmaṇs*[145] and there are wealthy *śūdras*.[146] The inequality implicit in the process of an exchange of services was to the advantage of those who were dominant, who had access to resources and used these to claim higher status. In terms of economic status the wealthier *brāhmaṇ*, the *rājanyas* and the *gṛhapatis* among the *viś* would constitute the upper level, their wealth being comparable. The initial attempt therefore in the *varṇa* scheme was not to reflect a class system but a lineage system and seek to integrate and reflect the reality of a lineage system. When eventually the lineage system declined, the structure of caste society also underwent a change, even though it carried with it elements of the lineage system.

With ritual status as a criterion of hierarchy, it was relatively easier to induct groups into higher *varṇas*. *Brāhmaṇs* of *kṣatriya* origin are met with in the earlier sections of many genealogies and may even reflect common origins in some cases. What are equally evident are *brāhmaṇs* of non-Aryan origin. Agastya and Vasiṣṭha are said to have been born from jars.[147] Kavaṣa Ailūsa, the Ṛg Vedic seer was a *dāsiputraḥ* as was the well-known Dīrghatamas.[148] These may have been *dāsa* families of some standing who could have been profitably inducted into the *brāhmaṇ varṇa*. The associations of the early *brāhmaṇ gotras* are barely in conformity with orthodox āryan tradition considering that the Bhṛgus were priests to the *daitya* kings,[149] and Pulastya was the ancestor of the *rākṣasas*.[150] Induction would also have been easier through

[145] *Ṛg V.* I. 105.7 ff.
[146] *Śat. Brāh.* V. 3.2.2; *Pañcaviṃśa Brah.* VI. 1.11; *Maitrāyanī Saṃ.* IV. 2.7.10.
[147] *Ṛg V.* VII. 33.
[148] *Vedic Index*, I. p. 143, 366, II. 259.
[149] Pargiter, *Ancient Indian Historical Tradition*, pp. 197, 307.
[150] Ibid. p. 241.

exogamy. In later periods it was maintained that the *gotra* system was prevalent only among *brāhmaṇs*,[151] although it is conceded that *kṣatriyas* could take the *gotra* of their *purohitas*.[152] In the case of the *kṣatriyas*, recruitment to the *varṇa* meant latching onto one of the two major genealogies, Sūryavaṃśa or Candravaṃśa, which was done with considerable facility in the first millennium A.D., when low status chiefs acquired power and aspired to the best lineage links.[153] Within the *varṇa* however it often took economic reality to guarantee tangible status.

At the core of the *jana* the substantial division was the bifurcation of the *kṣatriya* and the *viś*. In the initial structure of the *varṇa* system, both the *brāhmaṇ* and the *śūdra* could have been, as it were, addenda. As priests attached to the clans, the ancestry of the *brāhmaṇs* went back to the shamans, mantics and seers of earlier times (the *vipras* and the *ṛṣis*), to which were added the reciters of hymns and the living manuals on rituals. The latter may have required co-option of priests from the indigenous cultures since the continuance of ancient rituals is strongly endorsed. The more priestly function of the *brāhmaṇ* comes into its own in the rituals of the Later Vedic texts. His special status is underlined by his privilege of being allowed to consume the remains of the sacrifice and this included the flesh of the sacrificed animal.[154] In the analysis of rituals, elements of earlier cultures may be seen to have survived.[155] It has been argued that the notion of purity and pollution may have been a survival of Harappan times. If Harappan society was ruled by an aristocracy claiming power through ritual and religion then it would be tempting to suggest that the *brāhmaṇ-śūdra* dichotomy went back to Harappan times, constituting the equivalent of an *ārya* and *dāsa varṇa* and into which the *jana* with its dual division of *kṣatriya* and *viś* intruded, and had to be accommodated. This is not to suggest that there was a continuity from Harappan times, but that some elements of an earlier culture can be recognized as part of the new lineage system.

[151] Medatithi commenting on Manu III. 5 maintains that the *gotra* and *pravara* system was prevalent among the *brahmaṇs* alone and quotes the *Aśvalāyana Śrauta Sūtra* I. 3 in support (P.V. Kane, *History of Dharmaśāstra*, II. 1, p. 493).

[152] *Āpastamba Śrauta Sūtra* 24.10.11-12

[153] Romila Thapar, 'Social Mobility in Ancient India with Special Reference to Elite groups', in *AISH*, p. 122 ff.

[154] *Vedic Index*, II, p. 83; *Ait. Brāh.* VII. 26; *Śat. Brāh.* III. 4.1.2; VII. 5.2.37-42.

[155] Romila Thapar, 'The Archaeological Background to the Agnicayana Ritual', in F. Staal(ed.), *Agni*, Vol.I., Berkeley, 1982.

The *varṇa* framework therefore was visualized as a structure for the integration of varying sub-systems rather than merely a reflection of the socio-economic hierarchy. This would account for the seeming changelessness of the rules of social functioning, although within each sub-system change was clearly registered. That the *varṇa* system was a consciously worked out structure by the mid-first millennium B.C. is apparent from the late hymn added onto the *Ṛg Veda*, the *puruṣasūkta*,[156] in which the origin of the four *varṇa*s from the body of Prajāpati is described: the symbolism being that of separate limbs performing different functions but co-ordinated in the unit of the body and listed in hierarchical order. The tying in of this description to a ritual event was perhaps an implicit emphasis on *varṇa* relating increasingly to ritual status.

Not only was the stratification rationalized in the concept of *varṇa,* but the function of each group was more clearly defined. The *brāhmaṇ* was now less of the seer and more of the expert on ritual. The more elaborate rituals such as the consecration sacrifices for the *rājā*s required an array of trained professional priests. The more simple *gṛhya* (domestic) rituals described in the *Gṛhya-sūtra*s, mainly concerned with rites of passage, required a single *brāhmaṇ* in most cases. The increasing importance of both categories of rituals emphasized not only the political role of the *brāhmaṇ* as a source of legitimization for chiefs but also as the authority and sanction of cultural identity in relation to the *gṛhapati*s, as also for the assimilation of new groups. The emphasis on *vāc* and *mantra*, the correct recitation of the right formula required meticulous training and memorizing with a comprehension of the language of the texts, which in turn became a criterion of aryahood together with the observance of *varṇa* rules. The Kuru-Pañcala region was noted for the excellence of the language and the relative purity of the rituals, suggesting that it was in this area and this period that the norms were decided upon—a time and a place which had already seen a considerable assimilation of varying groups of people and observances. Many of the people further away such as those in the *janapada*s of the Punjab and the middle Ganga valley are castigated for having discarded the rituals,[157] a rebuke which had more to do with other changes in these areas.

The importance of political authority is highlighted in the substitution of *rājanya* by *kṣatriya*. The context of the *rājanya* was

[156] *Ṛg V.* x. 97.
[157] *Atharvaveda* v. 22.14; *Baudhāyana* D.S., I. 1.32-3.

essentially status within the lineage. *Kṣatra* implied temporal authority and power which was based less on being a successful leader in battle and more on the tangible power of laying claim to sovereignty over territory, demanding prestations and also symbolizing ownership over clan lands. The status of the chief had been hedged around by his relationship to various clan-gatherings. Among these were the *gaṇa, vidatha, sabhā, samiti* and *pariṣad,* some of which, as nomenclatures at least, survived into later periods although their functions changed.

The *gaṇa* is identified by the name of a common ancestor and is also reflected in the *gotra* system in which sub-groups are referred to by *gaṇa*s. That it was at some stage a clan would seem evident from terms such as *gaṇapati, gaṇeśa* and *gaṇasya rājā,* which were synonyms for *rājā.*[158] It may have been a special body of selected members who held equal status and formed a peer group, as is suggested by the *kṣatriya gaṇa*s of later sources, and by the compound of *gaṇa-sangha*s for chiefdoms.[159] It may have been a cattle raiding peer group in origin since the leader is associated with cattle raids.[160]

The *vidatha* as its name suggests was probably a ritual occasion on which the distribution and sharing of wealth took place, among other things.[161] Booty being a major source of wealth, the *vidatha* would also be linked with cattle raids and heroic exploits.[162] The distribution doubtless had to carry the sanction of *brāhmaṇ*s as well as their inclusion as recipients, hence their presence at these gatherings.[163] Sāyana's gloss that the *vidatha* be equated with the *yajña*[16] would be expected in a system where redistribution or exchange of wealth was a ritual occasion. This in turn would explain the need for Indra-Mitra-Varuna being the presiding deities of the *vidatha.*[165] That the *vidatha* declines in the later Vedic period would reinforce its original function as the ritual occasion for the redistribution of wealth for, when other forms of economic redistribution became prevalent, the *vidatha* would have become

[158] *Ṛg V.* II. 23.1; *Ait. Brāh.* I. 21.

[159] *Vāyu Purāṇa* 88.4-5; 86.3; 94.51-2.

[160] *Ṛg V.* VI. 59.7; IX. 76.2.; III. 47.4.

[161] *Ṛg V.* II. 1.4; III. 38.5-6; VII. 40.1; *Atharvaveda* I. 13.4.; *Vedic Index*, II, p. 296. cf., ṚV. X. 11.8.

[162] *Ṛg V.* II. 1.16; I. 56.2.

[163] *Ṛg V.* X. 91.2-9

[164] Sharma, *Aspects of Political Ideas and Institutions in Ancient India*, p. 85 ff.

[165] J.P. Sharma, *Republics in Ancient India*, London, 1968, p. 72.

redundant. Although it has been argued that the *vidatha* was a folk assembly, a view which has been strongly opposed,[166] it was nevertheless of some consequence to Ṛg Vedic society judging by the frequency of reference to it. If it was an occasion for the distribution of wealth, then even its being a kin gathering rather than a folk assembly would be in keeping with such a function.

Indo-European cognates for *sabhā* mean the assembly of the kinsfolk which would make its membership exclusive.[167] In later periods the *sabhā* becomes an advisory body assisting the king. The association of the *sabhā* with gambling may have had antecedents in the division of grazing lands and arable lands by lot.[168] This would of course be a different function from sharing booty. This is indirectly supported at the symbolic level in the Sabhā Parvan of the *Mahābhārata*. The Pāṇḍavas lose their wealth and power in a game of dice which is held in the *sabhā* which was an assembly of kinsmen who not only witness the throw of dice but also discuss the question raised by Draupadi regarding the legal validity of Yudhiṣṭhira placing her as a stake when he himself had lost his freedom.

Dicing is not merely indicative of a weakness for gambling. The names used for the dice and the throws are heavily imbued with symbolic meaning. Dicing is not only associated with the *sabhā,* the most respected of the assemblies, but the one who throws the dice is on occasion referred to as the *sabhā-sthānu,*[169] literally, the pillar of the assembly hall. This gives dicing far greater importance than mere entertainment. Its significance may have derived from a time when the throw of dice determined the division of wealth. This can only be inferred from the frequent association of dicing with wealth and the notional significance of dicing with rituals conferring and legitimizing power. The inclusion of a simulated game of dice as part of the ritual of the Agnyādheya and Rājasūya sacrifices[170] would again point to its symbolic importance. Possibly lots were also transferred from one person to another by a throw of dice, an echo of which can be heard in the events of the Sabhā Parvan. Thus

[166] R.S. Sharma, 'Vidatha: The Earliest Folk Assembly of the Indo-Aryans', JBRS, 1952, xxxvii, pts 3-4, pp. 429-48; J.P. Sharma, *Republics in Ancient India*, p. 62 ff.

[167] *Atharvaveda*, XIX. 55.6; XII. 1.56; VIII. 10.5.

[168] *Ṛg. V.* X. 71.10; *Atharvaveda* VII. 12.3; *Āpastamba D.S.* II. 25.8.

[169] *Vedic Index*, II., p. 426.

[170] *Vedic Index*, I., p. 2; G. Held, *The Mahabharata: an ethnological study*, London, 1935.

the association of wealth and loss of wealth with gambling need not be taken in a literal sense but may refer to a more complex activity involving an exchange of wealth conditioned by a throw of dice. The stake was referred to as *dhana,*[171] generally meaning wealth and rarely, booty. The earlier texts refer to *vibhīdaka* nuts used as dice and since these cannot carry numbers, a computation must have been essential to gambling.[172] Later there are references to throws—Kṛta, Tretā, Dvāpara and Abhibhū or Kali—which suggest numbered surfaces of dice reading four, three, two and one. These terms are ultimately transferred to the division of the *mahā-yuga* into four *yuga*s or periods of cosmic time, thus linking the throw of dice with time and fate. The association of a share or distribution of wealth with the notion of fate is also evident in the use of terms such as *bhāga* and *bhāgya.*

The terms *sabhā* and *samiti* occur more frequently in the late books of the *Ṛg Veda* and in the later Vedic literature. In the *Atharvaveda* they often occur together.[173] There is also an association of the *rājā*s (in the plural) with these assemblies suggesting that they were the gathering points of the senior lineages, those of the *rājanya*s. The infrequency of the presence of the *viś* in these assemblies may reflect its declining status. The presence of the *rājā*s did not preclude the selection of one among them as the presiding *rājā.*[174] The *samiti* appears to have been a more open assembly than the *sabhā. The pariṣad* is mentioned even less frequently and appears to have had an even smaller membership.[175] If its later function is any clue to its origins then it may have been a body of specialized advisers, although such a body may not have been particularly relevant to the political needs of the time.

To the extent that some were plenary assemblies, and some limited to the *rājanya*s, they were essentially occasions for reiterating hierarchy and order; consultation was more a ritual function than an administrative necessity as it was to become in later periods. Over time, some of these gatherings declined in importance whilst others increased and even changed their function. To maintain that in the Vedic period different tribes used different forms of assembly is not indicated by the evidence as the gatherings are not

[171] *Vedic Index,* I., p. 388
[172] Ibid. p. 2 ff.
[173] *Atharvaveda* VII. 12.1; VIII. 10.5-11; XII. 1.8; XII. 1.56. *ṚV.* IX. 92.6; X. 97.6.
[174] *Ṛg V.* X. 124.8, 166.4, 173.1; *Atharvaveda* I. 9.3; III. 4; IV. 22
[175] *Rg V.* III. 33. 7; *Atharvaveda* XVIII. 3.22.

differentiated in accordance with tribes.[176] What is certainly feasible is that some types of assembly were more central to the functioning of certain tribes than others.

Sharing of wealth was an intrinsic part of raids providing booty. Cattle-herding and agriculture provided the items required for the performance of rituals. The redistribution and consumption of this wealth was channelled through separate acitivities. Booty from raids was shared by general consent in the assemblies where the larger shares presumably went to the chief who led the raid as well as to the priest who had invoked the deities and who would be doubly blessed if he was also to perform the role of the bard eulogizing the chief, as he often did in the *dāna-stuti* hymns of the *Ṛg-Veda*. This would serve to reinforce the status of the *kṣatriya* and the *brāhmaṇ* and further demarcate them from the lesser lineage of the *viś*. The wider distribution among other members of the *viś* who had participated in the raid was doubtless conducted in the assembly so that it would not be an arbitrary division. A decline in inter-tribal raids would lead to a corresponding decline in those assemblies where the wealth from such raids was allocated to the clan of those who were successful in the raid. The wealth listed in the *dāna-stuti* hymns, primarily cattle, horses, chariots, gold and slave girls were all items which could have been picked up in a raid. Wealth obtained from herding and agriculture consisted of objects offered as prestations at the ritual of sacrifice and therefore included the best animals of the herd, milk, *ghī*, grain, cakes and the like. The offering of these items had to be induced from the *viś* and the ritual occasion provided the incentive to part with wealth. The redistributive aspect lay not only in the gifts made to the priests but also in the sacrificing of the animals and the burning up of the other items as part of the prayer for the well-being of the *yajamāna* and the *viś*. The destruction of wealth in this fashion was a method of underlining the status of the *yajamāna* (either a chief or a *gṛhapati*) but at the same time, a subtle means of preventing the *yajamāna* from amassing excessive wealth.

The specific and precise functions of each of the assemblies remains unclear. With a changing social system the interlocking of functions and overlapping between them also changed and varied. The curb on the concentration of power in the hands of the *rājā* was not a legal formality, but was born out of a society in which power was not completely restricted to a few. With the narrowing

176 J.P. Sharma, *Republics in Ancient India*, p. 15. ff.

of kinship rights on land and an increase in prestation requirements, the more exclusive gatherings of kinsmen such as the *sabhā* became channels for the concentration of power and the more open assemblies were further diffused. The selection of the chief which was validated in the assemblies gradually gave way to succession being legitimized through ritual consecration by the priest.[177] The nature of these assemblies indicates that they relate to stratified societies and not to egalitarian clans.

The retinue of the *rājā* moves in inverse proportion to the concentration of power in his hands and includes widening circles of representation. This is reflected in his relationship with the *ratnins*,[178] a term frequently translated as 'treasure' but originally meaning 'a gift'. The list varies slightly from text to text but generally includes the *purohita, rājanya,* chief wife, favourite wife, discarded wife, *senāni, sūta, grāmaṇī, kṣattar, saṃgrahītar, bhāgadugha* and *akṣavāpa*. Some texts include the *go-nikartana* which has been taken to mean a slayer of cows or a butcher and by extension probably a huntsman. In the course of the *rājasūya* ritual the *rājā* goes to the home of each and there offers an oblation to a particular deity. The deity is generally one that is associated with the function of the *ratnin* and relates to either protection, fertility and the evil eye or wealth and its distribution. This procedure is referred to as the *ratna-havis* and symbolizes the *rājā* making a gift to the *ratnins*. In a society characterized by the system of gift-giving this would be seen not merely as a symbol of the status of the *ratnins* but also as a sign of the *rājā*'s dependence on them. It is for this reason that they are referred to as the makers of the *rājā*. (The post-Vedic concept of the *ratnāni* reflects a reaching back to the idea of the *ratnins* since it consists of the seven elements which are said to constitute the 'treasures' of the king : the wife, the minister, the general, the wheel, the elephant, the horse and the jewel. The inclusion of the latter four suggests a distancing of the king from his subjects, where each object provides an abstract concept associated with kingship.)

The *ratnins* are the support to the *rājā*'s office both at the symbolic and functional level. The *purohita* at this early stage rode in the *rājā*'s chariot and recited the appropriate *mantras* for his safety

[177] *Śat. Brāh.* v. 3.3.12; *Ait. Brāh.* viii. 5 ff; *Tait. Brāh.* i. 75; *Pañcaviṃśa Brāh.* xviii, 8 ff.

[178] *Vedic Index*, ii, pp. 199-201

and well-being.[179] His role as domestic priest to the royal household evolved with the coming of monarchy. The *rājanya* was clearly an important member of the clan. The inclusion of the wives points to fertility rituals, the avoidance of the evil eye from the discarded wife and marriage alliances. The latter would be particularly important in a ritual such as the *rājasūya* where even if the *rājā* had made fresh alliances through marriage, the earlier links had to be restated. The rest of the twelve would be members of the *rājā*'s entourage but with a wider concern with economic and political functions. The *sūta* (bard) remained close to the *rājā* and ensured his immortality in the land of the living. As *saṃgrahītar* the charioteer had responsibility for the well-being of the *rājā*. In one of the variant lists the significance of the chariot is further emphasized by the inclusion of the *takṣa-rathakārau* (carpenter and chariot-maker) amongst the twelve.[180] The *senāni* as a designation was used in later times for the commander of the army. In this context the latter probably refers more to the head of a troop since there is no reference to any regularly constituted army or to professional soldiers. Raids and battles seemed to have been the business of members of the *viś*.[181] The *kṣattar* is taken as the door-keeper or as one who distributes. The *bhāgadugha* and the *akṣavāpa* were both involved in distributive functions in the lineage system. The emphasis in this group is on the centrality of the *rājā* in his chariot, presumably symbolic of the cattle raid and of skirmishes highlighting his role as protector; of the dependence on fertility for prosperity; and of the persons involved in the procedure relating to the distribution of wealth. The twelve *ratnin*s represent the sanction of a wider circle but they remain essentially within the orbit of clan functioning. The extent to which they were regular office-bearers is limited since there is little reference to the periodic assesment and collection of taxes or to a separate armed force. It was however from the germinal functions of this group that the designations for some of the later offices were adopted. The *rājā* at this point remains the 'eater of the *viś*; the *viśāmattā*[182] and the *bhāgadugha*[183] assists him in this activity. Thus the *rājā* was surrounded by persons performing specific functions and some of them were even in a sense his retainers but there was no adminstrative machinery and no

[179] Gonda, *Ancient Indian Kingship ...*, London, 1969, p. 65 ff.

[180] *Maitrāyanī Sam.* II. 6.5; IV. 3.8; *Śat. Brāh.* V. 3.1.1 ff; V. 4.4.7; *Tait. Brāh.* I. 7.3.1 ff; *Tait. Sam.* I. 8.9.1 ff.

[181] *Śat. Brāh.* V. 4.3.8.

[182] *Śat. Brāh.* VIII. 7.1.2, 7.2.2.

[183] *Śat. Brāh.* I. 1.2.17, V. 3.1.9; *Tait Brāh.* I. 7.3.5; *Tait. Sam.* I. 8.9.2.

system of delegating powers. The existence of the *ratnin*s would point to two significant developments. One was the emergence of a group of non-kinsmen who ultimately took on the character of retainers to the *rājā* and who could contribute to the accumulation of power in the office of the *rājā*. It is also suggestive of a relationship between the *rājā* and others not based on kinship but on reciprocity.

Underlying the concept of *kṣatra* is that of *rājya*, temporal authority which is demarcated from sacred authority, and this is firmly stated at the time of the consecration when it is said that the *rājā* has authority over the people, *prajā,* but the *brāhmaṇ*s accept only the authority of the deity Soma.[184] Yet the actual relationship between sacred and temporal authority was one of interdependence. Various categories of *rājya* are listed of which the most eminent is *sāmrājya.*[185] This is often translated as 'empire', but a more realistic rendering would be to regard it as a high status among *rājā*s (chiefs) and with the increasing tendency for clans to confederate, the status of *samrāj* would become inevitable. As a corrective to the assumption that the *rājā* held excessive power it is well to keep in mind that the same chiefs who are associated with the performance of the consecration rituals as part of their claim to *sāmrājya* were also the ones who carried out their raids in the dewy season and received a share of the booty.

Exalted titles such as *samrāj, vairāj, parameṣṭha, ādipati* and so on are scattered throughout the texts and should not perhaps be taken too literally. The various ceremonies performed by the *rājā*s were in the nature of *saṃskāra*s, purification rituals and ceremonies for imbuing the *yajamāna* with power. These rituals were said to place the *rājā* in the proximity of the gods and gradually the *rājā* came to be accepted as divinely appointed. The gods were eligible to titles incorporating sovereignty, paramountcy and overlordship, and as a consequence of these ceremonies the *rājā* also felt himself eligible for such titles. Thus the attributes of Indra and of the chief of the clan tended to merge and the one was seen in light of the other. Divine appointment drew the chief towards kingship but this was still short of claims to divinity. The latter became more common in the period after the rise of the monarchical state. The analogy with the gods also underlined the role of the *rājā* as the nourisher and the protector and protection was so

[184] *Śat. Brāh.* v. 3.3.12.
[185] *Ṛg V.* III. 55.7, 56.5; IV. 7.1; IV. 21.1; VI. 19.2; VI. 27.8; VIII. 19.32.

important that it was equated with discipline and the avoidance of chaos.

It is stated that a people without a *rājā,* was a condition of anarchy.[186] The fear of anarchy is frequently alluded to which is not surprising in a society moving towards complex stratification. The *rājā* was in many ways the economic and political pivot of the lineage system. He integrated the control over territory with access to available resources as also production where productivity was a measure of the chief's efficiency. His position is symbolized in the linkage between the well-being of the clan and the physical well-being of the chief. This focus on the chief led to additional attributes associated with him. Not least among these was a connection with the gods and even if he was not himself regarded as divine, the insistence that the gods had intervened in his selection marked him out as a special person. This was not occasioned by a mere fancy for proximity to the gods, but the exigencies of an increasingly heterogeneous society demanded a category of persons who could be invested with authority. To concentrate power in one family could also have been the solution to tensions and hostility among the clans. In situations of migration to new areas, leadership plays an important part. Migration itself would help to stabilize political power by channelizing the potential for conflict into fission, provided settlements in new areas were attractive and did not involve constant battling against powerful indigenous inhabitants. A mechanism for assimilating indigenous populations would allow migration to act as a safety-valve which prevented a major change towards state formation. The continual proliferation of such a system could have been checked by an obstruction to fission which would possibly have forced the change.

With the gradual concentration of power in the families of chiefs, there followed other changes which were eventually to move in the direction of encouraging the emergence of kingship. It is not easy to locate the point of change but the tendencies were clear. Election and selection was superseded by attempts at hereditary claims[187] as is evident from the genealogies, admittedly shallow in the early stages, as for example that of Sudās.[188] Genealogies of greater depth occur in the *Mahābhārata, Rāmāyaṇa* and *Purāṇa*s, and were compiled in a later period. The gradual emphasis on primogeniture safeguarded succession within the lineage. The link

[186] *Ait. Brāh.* I. 14.6; *Tait. Brāh.* I. 5.9.1.

[187] *Ṛg V.* X. 33.4, 32.9.

[188] *Vedic Index*, II, p. 454

between the *brāhmaṇ* and the *kṣatriya* became stronger with the latter exchanging legitimization for gifts, *dāna*[189]. Implicit in this relationship was the idea that those who invest the *rājā* with divinity or legitimize him are alone permitted to remove him.[190] This was a far cry from the elected chief or legitimacy being based on kinship rights. The latter were still important but subject to brahmanical approval as is evident from the story of the wicked *rājā* Vena whom the *brāhmaṇs* had finally to strike down with stalks of the sacred *kuśa* grass.[191] Another important concession was the investment of the *rājā* with the right to punish (*daṇḍa*).[192] This was the necessary concomitant to his being made responsible for maintainance of law and order. However these aspects are not especially highlighted until the subsequent period.

Notions of divinity associated with the office of the *rājā* guaranteed the eventual transition to kingship. This restricted eligibility for the status of *rājā* to families already associated with the office. Earlier ideas of the well-being of the community being directly related to the health and well-being of the chief were reinforced at the rituals, particularly those focusing on rejuvenation, such as the *vājapeya*. Physical deformities of any kind invalidated claims to rulership and could create a crisis over succession. The blindness of Dhṛtrāṣṭra and the skin ailment of Pāṇḍu precluded both from uncontested succession and introduced the complication over the inheritance of the realm of the Kurus which had finally to be sorted out through a war. The sacerdotal status of the *rājā* also bestowed on him certain essential powers, necessary for the prosperity and fecundity of the kingdom, as for example, that of bringing rain. The king as 'rainmaker' is a widespread idea in many societies and its prevalence in the Indian tradition is recorded in a number of instances when drought accompanies the rule of an unrighteous *rājā* who has to be removed or goes voluntarily into exile before the rain falls again.[193]

The major sacrificial rituals such as the *rājasūya, aśvamedha, vājapeya,* became occasions for the consumption of wealth in lengthy ceremonies, some extending over many months. These were

[189] Romila Thapar, '*Dāna* and *Dakṣinā* as forms of Exchange', in *AISH*, p. 105 ff.

[190] *Śat.. Brah.* v.3.3.12.

[191] *Mahābhārata*, Śānti Parvan, 59; *Viṣṇu Purāṇa* I. 13.

[192] *Śat. Brāh.* v. 4.4.7.

[193] The story of Devāpi in some versions combines the disqualification of a physical ailment with legitimacy associated with drought and rain. *Ṛg V.* X. 98; *Nirukta* II. 10; *Rām.* I. 8.11 ff; *Bṛhaddevatā* VII. 148 ff; *Viṣṇu Purāṇa* IV. 20.

accompanied by lavish libations of milk and *ghī,* offerings of grain in various forms and the sacrifice of the choicest animals of the herd. The *yajña* took on some of the characteristics of the potlatch in literally burning up all this wealth. The redistribution of wealth through gift-giving on such occasions was primarily from the *kṣatriya yajamāna* to the *brāhmaṇ* priests. The change from animal herding to agriculture is reflected in the objects included as *dāna* and *dakṣinā* where heads of animals gradually gave way to preparations of grain and eventually to land. Only gold remains constant. The need for extensive consecration rituals would suggest that initially the position of the *rājā* as a superior among other *rājā*s was not so secure and required validation. If the *rājā* was selected to be the chief then he would not only have to prove himself but would also have to be invested with the requisite powers which would demarcate him from other *rājanya*s. This was prior to the assumption of such a status through the system of hereditary kingship. It is interesting that of the two families, it is the Pāṇḍavas establishing themselves at the new centre at Indraprastha who perform the *rājasūya* and not the well-entrenched Kauravas at Hastinapura.

Gift-giving served to reinforce social status and reciprocity between the dominant groups. The notion of obligation was seen as the priest performing services for the *rājā* and in return receiving gifts. Since in every case the gift was an object of considerable material value and therefore crucial to the livelihood of priests who had no other means of material support, it is ostensibly symbolic but in effect a fee.[194] Gift-giving was not restricted to an exchange between *kṣatriya*s and *brāhmaṇ*s. At the *rājasūya* sacrifice for example, initially gifts are brought by other chiefs as prestations to the *yajamāna,* the *rājasūya* of Yuddhiṣṭhira being such an occasion.[195] The chiefs vye with each other in making valuable gifts, partly because the value of the gift reinforces their status and partly because it is expected that when they in turn perform the *rājasūya* a still more valuable gift will be returned.

Spectacular sacrifices involving the resources of the *rājā* were not the only occasions for gifting or redistributing wealth. Periodic sacrifices relating to changing seasons or to phases of the moon were part of the regular calender of observances among those of high status.[196] Social obligations were also sources of economic

[194] Romila Thapar, '*Dāna* and *Dakṣinā*'.
[195] *Mahābhārata*, Sabhā Parvan, 30 ff.
[196] *Śat. Brāh.* I. 6.3.36; II. 5.2.48.; *Tait. Sam.* I. 6.10.3.

distribution. The *saṃskāra* rituals of the *Gṛhya-sūtra*s, and the domestic rituals enjoined upon every *gṛhapati,* were to be counted among such occasions both in expending wealth as part of the ritual and in prestations to the *brāhmaṇs*. In addition, expiatory *prāya-ścitta*[197] ceremonies became a regular requirement, particularly for those who travelled to areas beyond the pale, such as the *mleccha-deśa* of the Punjab and of the middle Ganga valley—areas which were looked upon as polluting, where the *yajña* rituals were not meticulously observed.

Food and feeding both for the living and the dead in the form of feasts and *śrāddha*s came to acquire central importance in the definition of prosperity. Hospitality and generosity even at the level of the *gṛhapati* was taken for granted. There are elaborate rules for the treatment of guests and the food fit to be served to guests.[198] These domestic rituals drew on the resources of the *gṛhapati*'s household and the wealth consumed was not booty from raids but the produce from cattle-rearing and cultivation carried out by the household. If a *gṛhapati* had obeyed the injunctions and observed each ritual as required by the *Gṛhya-sūtra*s it is likely that he would have been left with little to invest in other activities.

The *yajña* was a ritual occasion and one of major religious significance. But embedded in this and equally important was that a precondition to these rituals was the availability of an economic surplus which was consumed in the ceremony and in gift-giving. Wealth was destroyed rather than put to alternative use or invested. Even the gifts to the *brāhmaṇ*s had limited potential for creating a changed situation. The wealth was primarily provided by the *gṛhapati* in the form of tribute to the *rājā* and this was doubtless the reason for the statement that the *kṣatra* eats the *viś*. A successful raid or a victory in battle would also bring in booty which would contribute to the conspicuous consumption required in the *yajña*. Hence the heroic potentiality of the *rājā* was still of some consequence. The *dig-vijaya* or conquest of the four directions carried out by the Pāṇḍava brothers was an integral part of the *rājasūya* not only in terms of status and a declaration of political domination, but also to provide some of the necessities for the ritual. Tribute was the substitute for booty.

The burning of wealth through rituals was not just an irrational action, since the notion of long-term accumulation of wealth was

[197] *Śat. Brāh.* I. 1.4.9; XII. 4.1.6; *Atharvaveda*. XV. 2.
[198] *Atharvaveda* IX. 6.3; *Śat. Brāh.* VII. 3.2.1; *Tait. Upaniṣad* I. 11.2.

absent at this time. The burning of wealth was part of what might be called a prestige economy. Some degree of economic redistribution took place in an indirect, restricted and ritualistic manner but was nevertheless noticeable since we are told that the *rājā* consumes the wealthy in the same way as fire consumes the forest.[199] The consumption of wealth on ritual occasions was a statement of status and political power. There was a sense of reciprocity with the gods who were the ultimate recipients of the wealth and were believed to bestow wealth on those who offered lavish sacrifices. The change in the political meaning of the ritual is evident in the changing form of the *aśvamedha* sacrifice. Whereas in the *Ṛg Veda* it is a relatively small affair aimed at conquering foes and acquiring prosperity, in the later Vedic texts it becomes an activity of political supremacy where the claim to the subjugation of others is a sequence to the initial ritual and is also a means of legitimizing control over new territories.[200] Echoes of the earlier society are maintained in the *yajña*s in the simulated chariot-races, cattle-raids and games of dice, all of which are an essential part of the ritual. The sacrificial ritual enhanced the status of the *yajamāna* and the priest who performed it. The benefits of the latter were doubtless part of the reason why some *brāhmaṇ*s came to be called very wealthy (*mahāśāla*). Temporal and sacral power is also symbolized in the relationship between the *rājā* and the *purohita*. The latter, at most merely the domestic priest of the chief's family, eventually becomes a formal office with the advent of kingship.

The destruction of wealth in the ritual placed severe limitations on these chiefdoms, limitations which acted as an obstacle to the easy transition to a state system. The establishment of a state system would require among other things either the weakening of such ritual prestations and channelling wealth in other directions or the generation of additional wealth to finance alternative activities. The *yajña* rituals were questioned but only by those who were searching for a path to salvation. The discourses in the *Upaniṣad*s and *Āranyaka*s questioned the efficacy of *yajña*s but posited an opting out of society through renunciation rather than an alternative channelling of wealth. Renunciation in itself was of some, though limited, consequence to the stimulation of social change through possible changes in the *yajña* ritual. When renunciation was tied to

199 *Ṛg V.* I. 65.4.

200 *Ṛg V.* III. 53.11; *Śat. Brāh.* XIIIth *kāṇḍa*; *Tait. Sam.* VII. 4; *Vājasaneyi Sam.* XXIII.

a monastic community and this in turn was linked to lay support, then its role as a social catalyst began to take on serious dimensions.

The lineage system as it developed in the western Ganga valley resulted in a condition which might be called an arrested development of the state. The state was not by passed but the lineage system did not develop into a state in this area during this period. Certain trends inclined towards the emergence of a state but others remained impediments. There was a consciousness of territory and an identity with territory. The chief was required to integrate territory with resources and with economic production and distribution, a role which concentrated attention on him. Access to larger resources came about with intensified agriculture and a demographic rise leading to the extension of agriculture. But the increase in resources was not sufficient to finance a state system. The concentration of powers in the hands of the *rājā* raised his status and effective control, but at the same time, lesser chiefs were not his appointees and were chiefs in their own right. There was minimal delegation of authority.

The unity of society and internal harmony was sought through the *varṇa* structure. There were no formal procedures for legal action and redress of wrong was linked to social pressures and expiatory rituals. External protection was highlighted in the office of the *rājā* with some indirect attempt to sanction his control over physical force in the close association of the *senani* with his immediate retinue, as well as the tradition of leadership in battle being a prerequisite for the office. There were multiple prestations to support elaborate rituals maintaining the status of both the *rājā* and sacred authority but there was no systematic method of collecting an income to finance the institutions of a state, much of the wealth being consumed in the prestigious rituals.

The continuity of the lineage system was possible for various reasons. It was a successful mechanism for incorporating a diversity of ethnic and cultural groups where each group maintained its identity in a relationship of juxtaposition to each other. This probably accounts for the extensive segmenting off in the genealogy of the Candravaṃśi *kṣatriya*s the geographical reach of which included northern, western and central India. The working out of the *varṇa* structure at this stage was not the codification of a new social formation but an elaboration of the lineage system in a way enabling its use as a framework within which social change could be registered and up to a point confined. Where land was easily available the system could reproduce itself through fission rather than have to undergo a change of form to accommodate the need for further resources or meet the pressure of numbers. Again, where land was easily cultivable without major co-operative organization and agriculture was reinforced by a strong pastoral base, the lineage system would serve the function of cohering groups without their having to subordinate themselves to a state. The western Ganga valley being favourable to such conditions did not require the major changes which were necessary in the middle Ganga valley. If the suggestion that agricultural niches were left relatively undisturbed in the Ṛg Vedic period and that there were no major agrarian innovations from the second to the early first millennium B.C. is acceptable, then there would have been no substantial technological change in the agrarian system requiring new mechanisms of control. The use of iron does not seem to have influenced agricultural technology until the middle of the first millennium B.C. Its major impact in the earlier phase was to facilitate the clearing of land to a marginal extent, but much more significantly in its use in weaponry.[201] If the *kṛṣṇa ayas* of the Vedic texts is taken as iron, which is very possible, the use of iron would have been mainly in the making of arrow-heads, spear-heads, knives, etc. This would undoubtedly have been the monopoly of the *rājās* in their role as protectors. Clearing by burning was evidently possible in the Doāb as is described in the burning of the Khāṇḍava-Vaṇa in order to establish the settlement at Indraprastha.[202] Iron technology was to become more necessary in the clearing of the marshlands and monsoon forests of the middle Ganga valley.

In the western Ganga valley the resources were neither sufficient to finance the institutions required for the establishment of a state nor were they directed towards the creation of such institutions. Archaeological evidence from the Painted Grey Ware culture points to the size of these communities (although larger and more numerous than previous settlements), being smaller than those of the subsequent period, that of the Northern Black Polished Ware. Territory was not seen merely as an area over which a *jana* had political control, for the territorial dimensions of marriage alliances were far wider, particularly for the *kṣatriya* caste. Like

[201] R. Pleiner, 'The Problem of the Beginning Iron Age in India', *Acta Praehistorica et Archaeologica*, 1971, 2, pp. 5-36.

[202] *Mahābhārata*, Ādi Parvan, 199. 25 ff; 214-19.

lineage, *varṇa* was a mechanism for assimilation but reflected a stratified society. The experience in the Kuru-Pañcāla area, as evident from Vedic literature and archaeology, appears to have been one of developing methods of accommodating diverse groups into a workable system based on control by lineage. The importance of the lineage base is reflected in the description of the Kuru-Pañcāla as among the *rājaśabdopajīvinaḥ* ('taking the title of *rājā*s', a term generally applied to chiefdoms), a statement which occurs in a text as late as the *Arthaśāstra*.[203] What is even more interesting is that the reference to the Kuru-Pañcāla comes in the section of the text which deals with the policy of a monarchy towards the *gaṇa-saṅgha*s or chiefdoms. The Kuru and the Pañcālas are listed among the pre-eminent of the *gaṇa-sangha*s, those of the Licchavis and Vṛjjis, as one category of the variants within that system. This would tend to question the description of the Kuru and Pañcāla *janapada*s being full-fledged monarchies in the Vedic period. The relatively shallow lineage lists of Vedic literature and the continual segmenting off of the Candravaṃśi lineages would point to the feasibility of migration as a method of easing tension rather then the necessity of evolving a system of control through the state. The migration eastwards to the middle Ganga valley presented a different ecological scene and one in which the lineage system and the role of the *gṛhapati* both underwent a change, and particularly so with trade impinging as a new factor. In this new situation the *kṣatriya* claimed greater power and prestations were incarnated as taxes. The prising of the state therefore took place in the region adjoining the western Ganga valley and under changed circumstances.

[203] XI. 1.5.

III. THE TRANSITION TO STATE

The *Śatapatha Brāhmaṇa* describes the migration from the Sarasvatī to the middle Ganga valley in the story of Videgha Māthava who travels east but pauses at the river Sadānīra (? Gandak).[1] The land across the river is described as uncultivated and marshy because, 'it had not been tasted by Agni Vaiśvānara'. It became fit for settlement after Agni had crossed the river and this in turn became the boundary between the Kośalas and Videhas, both descendents of Māthava. The middle Ganga valley comes into historical focus with the migration and settlement of people along two routes. The northern route followed the foothills of the Himalaya and appears to be the one taken by Videgha Māthava; the second followed the south bank of the Yamuna and the Ganga at the base of the Vindhyan outcrops. Both routes ran along the elevated areas fringing the plain which were doubtless ecologically more familiar to those coming from the western Ganga valley, since the middle Ganga valley lies at a lower elevation and was probably even more densely forested and certainly given to large areas of marshland. The northern route turned south following the rivers, particularly the Gandak which joined the Ganga at a point not too far from Pāṭaliputra (Patna) where it also met the southern route.

Vedic literature has less to say about the middle Ganga valley which largely comprised lands beyond the pale, the *mleccha-deśa* of the Vedic sources. Much of the evidence for events in this area comes from Buddhist literature. Some comparative data, particularly on the functioning of the *gaṇa-saṅgha* chiefships, is available in the *Aṣṭādhyāyi* of Pāṇini, which often corroborates the statements from the Buddhist sources, even though Pāṇini was referring to *gaṇa-saṅgha*s in various parts of northern India and less specifically to the middle Ganga valley. There is a distinction between the types of *gaṇa-saṅgha*s described in the two sources. Those referred to by Pāṇini as spread over northern and western India such as the Madra, Andhaka-Vṛṣṇi, Kṣudraka and Mālava,[2] appear to be chiefships well before the emergence of the state

[1] I. 4.1. 14-17.

[2] Pāṇini, IV. 2.131; VI. 2.34; IV. 2.45 and the Kāśikā.

whereas those of the middle Ganga valley such as the Vṛjjis contain the rudiments of what were to become the essential characteristics of the state. Among the latter *gaṇa-saṅghas*, some were a single clan unit such as the Śākyas, Koliyas and Mallas located on the edge of the Himalayan *terai*. Others were confederacies of clans among which the pre-eminent was the Vṛjji of whom the Licchavis were the most important. The Vṛjji confederacy with its centre at Vaiśāli was a major political power, opposed to the expansion of Magadha. Monarchy with all its accoutrements is first established in Kośala and Magadha, although other areas such as Gandhāra, Kāśī (Varanasi district) and Kauśāmbi (Allahabad district) also provide indications of the evolution of monarchical systems.

The archaeological picture for the middle Ganga valley remains hazy for the second millennium B.C. and would require further excavation for clarification.[3] Neolithic-Chalcolithic sites occur in the Mirzapur and Varanasi districts as well as in the Saran and Gaya districts, suggesting that the earlier settlements lay between the northern edge of the plateau and the Ganga. This was geographically an area of attraction with a good drainage and therefore not given to marshland. It formed part of the southern route skirting the Ganga valley. The Neolithic settlements would point to an earlier population prior to the arrival of the Black-and-red Ware people who probably migrated along the southern route from western and central India. Painted Grey Ware occurs at Śrāvasti (Seth-Maheth in eastern U.P.) part of Kośala, indicating links with the western Ganga valley along the northern route as well as at Kauśāmbi and the Ganga-Yamuna confluence, indicating settlement along the Vindhyan outcrops. The main culture prior to urbanization is that of the Black-and-red Ware pottery, the sites of which seem to follow the migration along the southern route and then spread northwards into the middle Ganga valley. They are located along the rivers and more frequently near inter-fluvial confluences which were also the optimum catchment areas. The pottery ranges from crude to refined, and

[3] The data for this summary comes from *Indian Archaeology — a Review*, with particular reference to the section on the Explorations and Excavations in Uttar Pradesh and Bihar. In addition, A.S. Altekar and V. Misra, *Report on Kumrahar Excavations 1951-55*, Patna, 1959; A.K. Narain and T.N. Roy, *The Excavations at Prahladpur*, Benaras, 1968; A.K. Narain and T.N. Roy, *Excavations at Rajghat*, Benaras, 1976; B.P. Sinha and B.S. Verma, 'Preliminary Report of Chirand Excavations for the year 1969', *Patna University Journal*, July 1978, 23, no. 3, p. 97 ff; G.R. Sharma, *The Excavation at Kauśāmbi 1957-9*, Allahabad, 1960, p. 45 ff.

if it can be related to other Black-and-red Ware ceramics then its provenance would be western India with an extension eastwards south of the Yamuna and through central India. Its occurrence in the middle Ganga valley would be later in time and dates to the first half of the first millennium B.C.[4] That it is a precondition to urbanization, is suggested by the fact that it registers a demographic increase, shows in its late phases an acquaintance with iron technology and provides evidence of early cultivation of rice.

If ceramic industries can be taken as indications of cultural variation then the people of the Black-and-red Ware were culturally different although not entirely unrelated to those who dominated the western Ganga valley.[5] The Northern Black Polished Ware dating to about the sixth century B.C. marks a qualitative change. Its provenance is associated with the areas on both sides of the Ganga between Varanasi and Patna, which was also an area of concentration for the preceding Black-and-red Ware culture. The Northern Black Polished Ware is indicative of a more complex and sophisticated culture with some characteristics of urban living. The important sites are located at places which, from the literary sources, are known to have been urban centres. A confirmation of the archaeological processes towards urbanization in this area can only be ascertained after careful horizontal excavations which have still to be carried out.

The middle Ganga valley was a comparatively new ecological situation for the settlers, whether those of the Painted Grey Ware or of the Black-and-red Ware cultures, particularly with rice cultivation becoming the major agricultural activity. A domesticated variety of rice (*Oryza Sativa*) from neolithic settlements dating to the sixth millennium B.C. is claimed for sites in the Belan valley south of Allahabad.[6] Such cultivation would be essentially through scattering or at most in its more developed form, of the upland rice system, and organizationally different therefore from intensive wet rice cultivation which was to become characteristic of the middle Ganga plains. Nevertheless the presence of rice in the neolithic context permits the postulation of a gradual transition from one kind of cultivation to the other over a long period. Rice

[4] D.P. Agrawal and S. Kusumgar,' *Prehistoric Chronology and Radio-Carbon Dating in India*, New Delhi, 1974, p. 138.

[5] Romila Thapar, 'Purāṇic Lineages and Archaelogical Cultures', in *AISH*, p. 240 ff.

[6] G.R. Sharma, *The Beginnings of Agriculture*, Allahabad, 1980. pp. 22-3

grown by scattering or other less labour-intensive methods produces a low yield per unit of land. Where rice cultivation is being considered as one of the factors towards social change, the reference would be to wide-scale cultivation for purposes of more than subsistence harvests.

The clearing of land along the more elevated *terai* or at the base of the Vindhyan outcrops was still possible by burning. In the plains the land was more marshy and here iron technology would have been of greater use in cutting trees. The clearing of marshland was in any case more labour intensive and would have required a demographic increase.[7] River confluences, where many of the early settlements are located, would have sustained a larger population because they tend to be more fertile and these settlements may well have provided the labour. The yield of rice is higher per acre than of wheat; rice cultivation could therefore have supported a larger number of people. The demographic rise in the Northern Black Polished Ware period suggested by the increase in the size of settlements and their frequency would have required bigger yields to feed the growth in the population.

Kośala, in north-eastern Uttar Pradesh, was suitable for both barley and rice,but the wetness of adjoining north Bihar posed problems for the cultivation of barley. Its high temperatures and humidity made it ideal for rice cultivation. The wide flood plains of north Bihar, wider than those of the upper Doāb, provided good rice lands as also the banks of the *jhil*s (the semi-permanent lakes) and *chaur*s (the chain of temporary lakes formed during the rainy season), giving a marshland character to the landscape.[8] Buddhist texts[9] describe rice and its varieties with as much detail as the Ṛg Vedic hymns refer to cows.

The cultivation of rice[10] required a new orientation to agri-

[7] E. Boserup, *The Conditions of Agricultural Growth*, London, 1965; M.R. Haswell, *The Economics of Subsistance Agriculture*, London, 1967.

[8] O.H.K. Spate, *India and Pakistan*, London, 1964, p. 515. R.L. Singh argues that substantial areas of the *bhangar* (old alluvium) were also suitable for rice cultivation (*Regional Geography*, Varanasi, 1971, p. 204, 5a).

[9] Buddhist texts differentiate between the ordinary variety or *vrīhi* and the fine quality grain, *śāli*. Among the latter were the *raktaśāli*, *kalamāśāli*, *mahāśāli* and *gandhaśāli*. H.N. Jha, *The Licchavis*, Varanasi, 1970, p. 33, n. 6; cf. V.S. Agrawal, *India as Known to Panini*, Varanasi, 1963, pp. 204-6.

[10] R.L.M. Ghose, *et al.*, *Rice in India*, ICAR, New Delhi, 1960; *The IRRI Reporter*, 5/75, Nov. 1975. The discussion on rice in the middle Ganga valley relates not to the type of rice cultivation which was known to the western Ganga valley at places such as Hastināpur, Atranjikhera and Noh, but rather to the large-scale and

cultural activity. Where it was unaided by irrigation the cultivation of rice meant single crop agriculture using the summer monsoon rains. There being only one monsoon in this area, the crop was sown at the start of the monsoon and harvested before the onset of winter. A predominantly single crop system made it necessary to produce a substantial excess at each harvest, to be stored and used during the fallow season. There was a need therefore to considerably increase the yield of the single crop. This required more land to be brought under cultivation, more labour on the fields and in addition the construction of irrigation systems such as embankments, channels, tanks, to ensure a constant supply of water should there be drought — the water requirement of rice being larger than of any other crop of similar duration. Irrigation could be used both to supplement rainfall and to cultivate a second crop. The major form of irrigation remains the building of *bandha*s across small streams converting them into tanks. These are temporary and have to be carefully maintained. Canals are either taken off rivers or more frequently are inundation cuts. This appears to have been the general form of irrigation in earlier times as well. There is little evidence to show that construction of large reservoirs with sluices and water control in this area was undertaken as there is in some other rice growing areas.[11] The sources do however speak of tanks in the vicinity of Vaiśāli[12] and even though they seem to be small in size they may have been used for irrigation. Similarly, mention is made of tanks in Ayodhyā.[13] There is comparatively less reference to wells. Channels taken off rivers and *bandha*s are also mentioned as forms of irrigation and had to be maintained by constant clearing. This did not however require any large-scale state apparatus for maintenance of hydraulic machinery. It did require the use of slaves and labourers as is related in the story of the conflict between the Śākyas and the Koliyas[14] on the division of irrigation

widespread cultivation of rice as the single major crop and its impact on food-production and on the land-man ratio.

[11] The most impressive example being that of ancient Sri Lanka (R.L. Brohier, *Ancient Irrigation Works in Ceylon*, Colombo, 1934).

[12] Krishna Deva and V. Misra, *Vaiśāli Excavations 1950*, Vaiśāli, 1961; D.P.P.N. II., p. 943.

[13] *Rāmāyaṇa* II. 94.37. In verse 39, Rāma specifically inquires from Bharata whether there are sources of water for irrigation other than rainfall.

[14] *Kunāla Jataka*, London, 1970, p. 1 ff; *Dhammapada* III. 254. These texts are of course not contemporary with the Buddha but they do reflect the continuity of some ideas and the preservation of a perspective on the recent past.

water taken off the Rohinī river which separated their fields. Even in later periods, although irrigation works were encouraged by the state they were effectively constructed and maintained by local bodies of a private nature. The preparation of the field in the 'puddling process' is facilitated by the use of an iron plough-share in the continual reploughing of the land under water.[15] The use of iron plough-shares for this period and region has not as yet been attested to from archaeological sources but there is the mention of the term *ayovikāra kuśi*[16] which has been taken to mean an iron plough-share and there are descriptions of deep ploughing. Wet rice cultivation, the highest yielding form of rice cultivation in the lowlands of the middle Ganga valley does not permit of rotation with any other dry land crop and legume is the main crop after the rice harvest. Apart from irrigation aids providing a further harvest, yields could be increased by extending the area under cultivation, and this method appears to have been used judging by the references to cultivated land in large units of measurement. Irrigation is not so frequently or emphatically described as is the size of the areas under cultivation. Areas with access to upland rice such as the Himalayan foothills,[17] (*terai*), where a number of *gaṇa-saṅgha* chiefships were located, would have had the advantage of more than one crop per year, but a yield per unit of land which was lower than that of a comparable area of lowland wet rice.

That irrigation was a significant variable in social change does not necessarily imply a link between irrigation and despotism but rather suggests a relation between water control and the sources of power among ruling élites.[18] As has been pointed out, irrigation is in any case not an independent factor and is dependent on ecology, crops, land size, climate, water-balance, soil and the actual mechanisms of obtaining, transporting and storing water in addition to calendric activities. Rights over water are not monolithic but they tend to go together with those who have access to other resources as well. There is also a difference between irrigation systems which function more efficiently under a centralized authority and those which are better in a decentralized system.

[15] *The IRRI Reporter*, 5/75, Nov. 1975.

[16] Pāṇini IV. 1.42; V. 4.58-9 *Sutta-Nipāta*, 81.

[17] This was referred to as *nivāra*, generally translated as wild rice. Pāṇini III. 3.48; R. Mehta, *Pre-Buddhist India*, Bombay, 1939, p. 190.

[18] E. Hurt and R.C. Hunt, 'Irrigation, Conflict and Politics: A Mexican Case', in R. Cohen and E.R. Service (eds.), *Origin of the State*, pp. 69-124.

Where land, labour and irrigation was made available the production of a surplus was feasible and this could support a larger population or intensify the social base of stratification. There are references to the *dāsa-karmakaras* (slaves and labourers) in the fields of the *rāja-kulas* (the land-owning *kṣatriya* clans)[19] and there is evidence of economic disparities among social strata. The dual stratification of *dāsa-karmakaras* employed by the *rāja-kulas*, with an absence of *gṛhapatis* (or *gahapatis* as they are called in Pāli texts), in the *gaṇa-saṅghas* is prior to private ownership. *Gahapatis* are occasionally mentioned in the sources relating to the *gaṇa-saṅghas* but rarely as agriculturalists. (*Gahapatis* are more evident in the monarchies of the middle Ganga valley). There is therefore a sharper stratification between the *kṣatriyas* and the *non-kṣatriyas*. In the middle Ganga valley, in contrast to the western Ganga valley, the use of land and irrigation in itself required not only intensive labour but the organization of labour on lines of co-operative interaction. In areas other than those of the *gaṇa-saṅghas*, although the major part of the produce was still household production, nevertheless the household unit was in competition with the larger clan holdings. Initially the latter seem to have been the richer and had the greater potential. With the increase in the size of effective holdings, a hierarchy of control over the resources and their working became necessary since there was more than a single resource-base and the interlinking of these required a co-ordinating group invested with authority. It would seem that the rich *gṛhapatis* were noticeably richer and this would have made for greater stratification. The survival of the *gaṇa-saṅgha* system in the heart of the rice-lands as evident from the Vṛjji confederacy, would point to the efficiency of the larger clan holdings being able to provide the wealth required for the continuation of the system. However, in competition with the peasant and commercial economies as they emerged in the middle Ganga valley the clan holdings could not survive and finally went under.

The association of livelihood (*vṛitti*) was essentially with agriculture although other activites began to assume importance. The unit of settlement remained the *grāma*/village[20] and villages were classified according to size and predominant activity (*gonisādinivittho gāma, nalakāra gāma, lonakāra gāma*).[21] Land

[19] *Kunāla Jātaka; Aṅg. Nik.* I. 128, 206; II. 205; *Dig. Nik.* III. 189.

[20] Pāṇini VII. 3.14.

[21] *PED*, p. 84; *Maj. Nik.* II. 206; *Aṅg. Nik.* II. 182; *Mahāvagga* VI. 33.4.

was classified as *ūṣara* (waste land, especially that which was saline), *gocara/vraja/ghoṣṭha* (pasture land) and *karṣa* (cultivated land).[22] The last-named is also described as *sītya* (furrowed) and *halya* (ploughed).[23] Separate holdings in the form of fields are mentioned as also the measurement and enclosure of these.[24] Terms such as *khetta* and *vatthu* are used to mean a field and a farm.

To argue that the technical feasibility of a surplus was sufficient to start a chain reaction which automatically led to state formation would be too mechanical an interpretation of the change. Surplus is in any case not an event but a process, as it has been rightly suggested.[25] The form of control is as important as the existence of the surplus, as is also the direction towards which it is channelled. In this not only is the contrast with the western Ganga valley an indication but there is also the variation between the *gaṇa-saṅgha* chiefdoms and the kingdoms in the middle Ganga valley. The preconditions were similar and yet the state system evolved more clearly under the aegis of a monarchical form. A comparison between the *gaṇa-saṅgha*s and the monarchies may serve to indicate the features which were crucial to the establishment of the state and which seem to relate to the control of economic resources and the form of political authority.

Migration into the middle Ganga valley was motivated not merely by a search for new land. Other possible causes could be a demographic growth which, if the land could not support the increased numbers or if there was no technological change to sustain the population, would be reason enough for tension and hostility within the initial group and would encourage migration to new areas. The movement eastwards may have been the result of a process of fission, so common in lineage systems. This is suggested, in the frequent theme of the segmenting off or fissioning among the *kṣatriya* clans as described in Buddhist sources.[26] Members of a *rāja-kula* family migrate to new areas, often from Varanasi northwards towards the Himalaya, and establish a new *janapada*. Such is the origin of the Śākyas, the Koliyas and the Licchavis.

Kṣatriya lineages with their ruling clans claimed the ownership of cultivated land. Territory was named after the *kṣatriya* lineage

[22] Pāṇini v. 2.107; v. 2.18; iii. 3.119. *Kauśika-sūtra* 24.2; *Gobhila G.S.* ii. 1.4.

[23] Pāṇini iv. 4.91 and 97.

[24] *Dīg.Nik.* i. 5; *Baudhāyana D.S.* iii. 2.2.2.

[25] R. McC. Adams, *The Evolution of Urban Society,* Chicago, 1966.

[26] Romila Thapar, 'Origin Myths and the Early Indian Historical Tradition', *AISH, p. 294 ff.; Dīg. Nik.* i. 92 ff; *Sumangalavilāsinī* i. 260 ff; Papañca Sūdanī, i. 258.

although it included categories of labour not related through kinship with the lineage. Possibly at the earliest stage the land had been cultivated by the clan, who claimed ownership over it but later began to employ labour when the size of the holdings was too large for a single family to manage. Since the land was held jointly by the clan and the right to ownership was based on birth, the produce as wealth was probably distributed among its members following certain rules of procedure. (The *Vinaya* texts not only refer to the distribution of food in the monastery but also discuss the ethics of how and what is to be distributed.[27] This may have been an adaptation from *gaṇa-saṅgha* procedures, given that food collected as alms would be the equivalent of wealth for a monk, quite apart from the symbolic role of food *vis-à-vis varṇa* regulations.)[28]

The *gaṇa-saṅgha* (or assemblies of a *kṣatriya gaṇa*) as a lineage system registers two important changes as compared to the Vedic lineage system. Possibly because in the middle Ganga valley they seem to have been chronologically later and the founders of the *gaṇa-saṅgha*s are often described as younger members of the established *kṣatriya* lineages, the fact of the *kṣatriya* lineages owning the land is clearly indicated. They have little use for prestations and the rituals are marginal, but the claim to land-ownership on the basis of birth into the lineage is established. Secondly, there is a noticeable absence of junior lineages. There is a demarcation between *kṣatriya* lineages as owners and the various non-kin groups who worked on the land as their employees and slaves. Production therefore was directly controlled by the *kṣatriya* families. Individual ownership is known to the Buddhist theory of the state, but the evidence on the *gaṇa-sanghas* suggests a joint ownership of land since it is referred to in the name of the *kṣatriya* lineage.

The middle Ganga valley had no uniform political system, since some *janapada*s supported kings and others retained the *gaṇa-sangha* system. That in some cases kingship is said to have been replaced by the *gaṇa-saṅgha* system points to the tenuousness of the idea of kingship or alternatively and more likely the misinterpretation of the term *rājā*, literally a chief, but assumed to be a king by modern commentators. The *gaṇa-saṅgha* system, variously rendered by modern historians as republics and oligarchies, can perhaps be more precisely described by the terms chiefships or

[27] *Cullavagga* IV. 4.1.

[28] Romila Thapar, 'Renunciation: the Making of a Counter-Culture?', *AISH*, p. 63 ff.

chiefdoms, where the ruling clans were differentiated from non-*kṣatriyas*. The members of the ruling clans are also referred to as the *rājās*, *rāja-kulas* or consecrated *kṣatriyas* (*abhiśikta vaṃśya kṣatriya*).[29] Thus the Mallas had five hundred *rājās*[30], the Vṛjji confederacy boasted of seven thousand seven hundred and seven,[31] and the Cedis had sixty thousand.[32] Every household had its head or *rājā* and the *saṅgha* is characterized by the use of the title of *rājās* or what is described as *rājāśabdopajīvinaḥ*.[33] Within the *rāja-kulas* status was equal[34] although a distinction was made between the older (*vṛddha*) and the younger (*yuvan*) generation.[35] Decisions were taken by voting.[36] The *gaṇas* had their own symbols[37] which doubtless were used on punch-marked coins. Categories of *gaṇa-saṅghas* are listed as *pūga,*[38] *vrāta,*[39] and *śreni.*[40]

Chiefdoms are characterized by a central leadership legitimized on the basis of birth. Genealogies, whether actual or fictionalized, are therefore of considerable importance and ancestry becomes crucial. The difference between the rulers and the ruled is initially that between certain descent groups having access to power and others who are excluded and among whom are the non-kin groups, generally providers of labour.[41] This last category could consist of indigenous people conquered by the lineages who settle on their land or else could be captives or labouring groups brought from elsewhere. The *jana* name was to apply only to those who were descendents of the ruling *kṣatriya* lineage and not to the *dāsa-bhṛitaka* (the slaves and hired labourers).[42] That the social demarcation is sharp is reflected in the story of how the king of Kośala, Pasenadi's son by a Śākya *dāsi* was not recognized as being of equal status by the Śakya *kṣatriyas* even though he became the king and the Śākyas accepted the suzerainty of Kośala.[43] In the conflict

[29] Kāśikā on Pāṇini VI. 2. 34; IV. 1.137.
[30] *Maj. Nik.* I. 231; *Dīg. Nik.* III. 207.
[31] *Mahāvagga* VIII. 1.1.; the same figure is repeated in late texts such as the Tibetan *Dulva*, W.W. Rockhill, *Life of Buddha,* London, 1907, p. 62.
[32] *Cetiya Jātaka* no. 422.
[33] *Mahābhārata*, Sabhā Parvan 14.2 refers to, *grihe grihe hi rājānaḥ*; *Arthaśāstra* XI. 1.
[34] *Mahābhāṛata*, Śānti Parvan, 108.30.
[35] Pāṇini I. 2.65; IV. 1. 162-3; *Dīg. Nik.* III. 74 emphasizes veneration of elders.
[36] Pāṇini IV. 4.93.
[37] Ibid., IV. 3.127
[38] Ibid., V. 3.112.
[39] Ibid., V. 3.113.
[40] *Mahābhārata*, Karṇa Parvan, 5.40.
[41] Patañjali II. 269 on Pāṇini IV. 1.168.
[42] *Kātyāyaṇa* IV. 1.168. 2-3.
[43] *Bhadda-sāla Jātaka* no. 465; *Dhammapadaṭṭhakathā* I. 339 ff.

between the Śākyas and the Koliyas over the distribution of the irrigation water of the Rohinī river, the quarrel breaks out among the *dāsa-karmakara*s on both sides, but the actual fighting takes place among the members of the *rāja-kula*[44] since it becomes a matter of prestige and the *khattiya*s alone could defend their honour.

Since power was retained through birth, marriages tended to be made among those of equal status, sometimes within the lineage in the form of cross-cousin marriages. It has been argued that such references derive from the fact that these texts were collated and edited and revised in Ceylon and south India where cross-cousin marriages prevail and were not part of the original social system of the middle Ganga valley.[45] However, the cross-cousin marriage connections of the Śākyas occur even in the texts from the northern tradition of Buddhism.[46] Furthermore, cross-cousin marriage often prevails in areas where it is necessary to keep property inheritance intact within a small group and this would be suitable to a system of chiefdoms where the link between property and lineage rights was very close. Inequality is, as it were, hereditary, since lineages are given a rank which is determined by the best property going to the higher lineages.

The maintenance of high status sometimes requires marriage with a close kin as a mark of differentiation and references to sibling marriages are common as symbolic forms in the origin myths of the Śākyas, Koliyas and Licchavis.[47] This could also symbolize the purity of lineage, the ultimate source of descent being a single set of parents. The mutually supportive role of the mother's brother and the sister's son is referred to in the context of familial responsibility and inheritance and the mother's brother is the most important kinsman outside the household.[48] Even in the *Dharma-sūtra*s, the kinsmen to whom the *madhuparka* (the oblation of honour, as it were), can be given, apart from the bridegroom, are the mother's brother and the father-in-law.[49] (Was this to ensure equal respect for agnatic and affinal relations or was the inclusion of the latter two an indication of their being identical in a cross-cousin marriage?)

44 *Kunāla Jātaka*

45 T.R. Trautmann, 'Cross Cousin Marriage in Ancient North India', in T.R. Trautmann (ed.), *Kinship and History in South Asia*, Michigan, 1974, p. 61 ff.

46 S. Beal, *Romantic History of Buddha*, London, 1907, p. 18 ff.

47 Romila Thapar, 'Origin Myths and the Early Indian Historical Tradition', *AISH*, p. 294 ff.

48 N. Wagle, *Society at the time of the Buddha*, p. 92 ff.

49 *Baudhāyana D.S.* II. 3.6.36.

The chief had a retinue of followers, often the younger members of the family, who performed the functions of a rudimentary administration. The administration of the Licchavis was looked upon with admiration by the Buddha,[50] and was more than rudimentary. There were said to be 7707 *raja*s resident at Vaiśāli, the capital of the Vṛjji confederacy.[51] These were the heads of the *rāja-kula* families who were eligible to sit in the Vṛjji assembly which met in the assembly hall (*santhagāra*). The figure is nominal and exaggerated but the Vṛjji assembly would in any case have been large since it was a confederacy of eight clans. The assembly elected one person among them to preside. The *gaṇa-rājā* or *pramukha* was assisted by an *upa-rājā*. Regularly assigned seats suggest a ranking within the *gaṇa*.[52] A quorum was necessary[53] and voting by proxy was permitted. The resolution before the *gaṇa* was moved, discussed, had three readings and was finally put to vote.[54] Later commentaries refer to an elaborate judicial procedure which sounds more ideal than actual, in which a case could move through six levels of appeal before coming to the president of the assembly as the final appeal.[55] Mention is also made of officers such as the *senāpati* and the *bhāṇḍagārika*,[56] responsible to the *gaṇa*, reflecting a specialization in function arising out of military and fiscal needs. However there is no mention of a standing army (although the Vṛjjians are described as powerful)[57] nor of any periodic assessment and collection of revenue. These sources further refer to a toll on visitors coming to Vaiśāli which was paid at the gates and there is a reference to taxes paid by traders including *kṣatriya* members of the *gaṇa-saṅgha*.[58] Presumably if the land was held in common by the lineage there would be no occasion for the payment of land or agricultural taxes. There are references to *bhojaka*s and *amacca*s (*amātya*s) suggesting some delegation of administrative control.[59] Doubtless such offices were in the hands of the *kṣatriya rāja-kula*s. This did not preclude them from inviting non-kin persons of high status from outside the *janapada* who were also appointed to some

[50] *Dīg. Nik.* II. 73 ff.

[51] *Mahāvagga* VIII. 1.1.1.; *Ekapaṇṇa Jātaka* no. 149.

[52] *Cullavagga* XII. 2.7.

[53] *Mahāvagga* IX. 4.1; V. 13.12; I. 31.2; VIII. 24.6.

[54] Ibid., IX. 3.1-2.

[55] *Sumaṅgalavilāsinī* II. 59.

[56] *Sumaṅgalavilāsinī* II. 673.3.

[57] *Dīgha Nikāya* II. 72

[58] *Sumaṅgalavilāsinī* I. 338.

[59] *Kunāla Jātaka*, no. 536; *Dīgha Nikāya* I. 7; 136; III. 64; *Aṅg Nikāya*, II. 154; II. 279.

office.[60] However, these references come either from texts of a later period, or, are more frequently mentioned in the context of kingdoms superseding chiefships.

In the *gaṇa-sanghas* of the Ganga valley power still lay with the lineage as also the ownership of essential wealth and there is an absence of the collection of taxes by a superordinate agency. Such a system may be regarded as being a point in the process of state formation, an incipient state, or what Fried has called a stratified society.[61] Where the distinction between the non-state and the state is presented not in absolute terms but along a continuum, there the *gaṇa-saṅgha* system of the Vṛjjis would be a point along such a continuum, closer to state formation than, for example, the *gaṇa-saṅgha* system of the Vṛṣṇis of western India.

There is an oft-quoted passage from the *Mahāparinibbāna-sutta* where the Buddha maintains that the unity of the Buddhist *saṅgha* will survive as long as, among other things, it has frequent and formal assemblies, maintains concord, acts in accordance with the *Vinaya* (the discipline ordained for monk and monastery), and honours the elders.[62] This has been taken as an oblique reference to the functioning of the Vṛjjian *gaṇa-saṅgha* which is similarly advised in the preceding section.[63] The dependence on unanimity of decisions and distribution of wealth made harmonious relations an essential factor. Discord was a constant possibility in the *gaṇa-saṅgha* system and the resultant fission would be outside the control of the system. In such cases the dissenting group would branch off and found new settlements in fresh areas, provided virgin land was available. Origin myths of the major chiefdoms refer to the exiling of younger members of a *rāja-kula* family as the starting point of a new settlement. The cause for discord is not stated, but as it is the younger generation which migrates and the new *janapada* does not register any major change as compared to the original, it can be surmised that a change in the system was not what was being demanded. Segmenting off provides the possibility of repeating the pattern elsewhere and thus relieving the pressure on the original group. Possibly some members of the *rāja-kula* were exiled when the original *janapada* was on the verge of becoming a monarchy and power was being captured by a single segment of the lineage. The frequency of groups branching off meant a continually expanding frontier and encroachments into forests and waste land. This

[60] *Sumaṅgalavilāsinī* II. 522-4; Rockhill, *The Life of Buddha*, p. 63 ff.
[61] *The Evolution of Political Society*, p. 185 ff.
[62] *Dīg. Nik.* II. 76.
[63] *Dīg. Nik.* II. 74.

in one sense stabilized the political situation and at the same time eased the tension arising from demographic and other pressures, but did not encourage major internal changes in the original *janapada*.

It was probably in the process of fission and segmenting off, and the settling of new lands that slavery became important. The rapid clearing of forest or waste land would be facilitated by the use of hired labourers to which the *rāja-kula* were already accustomed. If the indigenous populations of the new areas were enslaved, they would tend to take on the characteristics of helots where the slaves formed a distinct class and were born into it. There is however no direct reference to helotage. That the *dāsa-bhṛtaka* or *dāsa-karmakara* working on the land are often referred to as a compound term suggests that helotage was not what was meant. The *dāsa* are not identified as a particular ethnic or tribal group or even constituting a separate community by this time. The *karmakara/bhṛtaka* was in any case a labourer working for a wage and therefore theoretically free. It seems more likely that indigenous populations were put to work on the land but not in a condition of helotage. There is also a more frequent mention of domestic slaves in larger numbers.

It can be argued that unlike the Greek peninsula where, because of its topography, agriculture had perforce to be intensified with multi-cropping in which the use of slave labour became a necessity, in the middle Ganga valley because of rice cultivation, the opening up of new land in the extension of agriculture was a more effective form of obtaining larger yields. The relative expense of buying a slave was certainly high later in the first millennium B.C. when the cost of a slave was a hundred *kahapana*s/*kārṣāpaṇa*s and that of a pair of oxen was twenty-four.[64] The same sources refer to a labourer earning anywhere between 1.5 and 4 *māṣaka*s per day where one *masaka* was the equivalent of one-sixteenth of a *kahapana*.[65] It may therefore have been cheaper to have hired a labourer to work in the fields than to buy a slave, given that the extra labour required on a farm was seasonal and that in many cases wages could be paid in kind.[66] The high expense of slaves may have been because, unlike the Greek system, not all prisoners of war could be enslaved. The distinction between *ārya* and *dāsa* would

[64] *Nanda Jātaka* no. 39; *Gāmaṇi-caṇḍa Jātaka* no. 257.

[65] *Sutano Jātaka* no. 398; Patañjali *Mahābhāṣyam*, I.3.72.

[66] *Sunakha Jātaka* no. 242; *Amba Jātaka* no. 474; *Taṇḍulanāli Jātaka* no. 5.

have to be maintained. If there was an availability of labourers, slaves would not be necessary to production and would remain an item of luxury. This may explain the high incidence of domestic slavery. Slaves are said to be acquired through predatory raids,[67] judicial punishment[68] or are born as such to slave women employed by a family. The lack of growth of a slave base had to do with the ascription of *śūdra* status to the peasant and artisan and the fact that caste rules kept the *śūdra* subordinated to the point where his labour could be exploited and justification found for this. Another source of slavery, debt-bondage, being technically limited to a specific period discouraged permanent enslavement. Household slaves ranged from hewers of wood and carriers of water to the more accomplished cooks, nurses, dancing girls and concubines.[69] Slaves were often a part of the dowry of wealthy young women.[70] The total number of slaves both in production and domestic work does not seem to exceed the non-slave population as happened in Athens during the same period. The figures mentioned for domestic slaves are far larger than those of slaves employed in agriculture and craft production.[71] The use of the compound *dāsa-bhṛtaka* or *dāsa-karmakara* makes it difficult to compute a percentage, unless the compound is interpreted as *dāsa* being an epithet describing the condition of the labourers — a reading which is not generally accepted. The relatively high price of slaves would also have tended to reduce their purchase in large numbers for production and there is no evidence of slave markets suggesting the conversion of slaves into a commodity. It would seem that slavery was not the crucial variable as was the functioning of the *śūdra*. Although the preconditions for slavery were to emerge in the private ownership of land with a sufficient concentration in some hands to need extra familial labour as a permanent work force and in the development of production for markets requiring a similar labour force,[72] there was nevertheless an availability of labour through the *śūdra* category which made the acquisition of labour force from elsewhere marginal. The *bhṛtaka/karmakara* in the compound *dāsa-bhṛtaka* would be of *śūdra* status. The *bhṛtaka* and *karmakara* were those employed on wages (*bhṛti*) but as unskilled

[67] *Cullanārada Jātaka* no. 477. [68] *Kulāvaka Jātaka* no. 31.

[69] D.R. Chanana, *Slavery in Ancient India,* New Delhi, 1960 p. 45.

[70] *Nimi Jātaka* no. 541; *Nānacchanda Jātaka* no. 289; *Uraga Jātaka* no. 354.

[71] D.R. Chanana, *Slavery in Ancient India,* p. 110 ff.

[72] M.I. Finley, *Ancient Slavery and Modern Ideology,* London, 1980, p. 73 ff.

labour.[73] The wages of skilled workmen — *śilpin*s — are referred to as *vetana*.[74] The term for hired labourers was either derived from the period for which a labourer was employed as for example, *māsika* or monthly, or from the amount of wages which a labourer happened to be paid as for example, *pañcaka* or five.[75] The description from a somewhat later period of the rich *gahapati* Meṇḍaka's household provides a range of categories employed and the *dāsa*, whether working in the house or in the fields, is one among a number of others.[76] Whereas the others receive salaries in cash or in kind, the *dāsa* is the recipient only of food.

Members of the *rāja-kula*s are sometimes identified by their *gotta/gotra*. Thus the Śākyas are of the Gautama *gotra* and the Mallas and Licchavis of Vasiṣṭha.[77] Some are described as high, *ukkaṭṭha gotta* and some as low, *hīna*.[78] This may reflect an earlier period when both *brāhmaṇ*s and *kṣatriya*s claimed descent from the same stock, reminiscent of the *brahma-kṣatra* group from the genealogical sources. Alternatively *kṣatriya* lineages may have associated themselves with the higher ranking *brāhmaṇ gotra*s for acquisition of status. That the *brāhmaṇ*s do not object to this would point to its being an acceptable custom.

Varṇa in Buddhist sources is listed differently with the *khattiyas/kṣatriya* as the highest followed by the *brāhmaṇa*, *vessa/vaiśya* and *sudda/śūdra* and the *caṇḍāla* as a frequent synonym for untouchable.[79] Equally often the list runs *khattiya, brahmaṇa* and *gahapati*[80] which seems to be a more realistic ordering of the socio-economic groups rather than that of ritual rank. The pre-eminence given to the *kṣatriya* would in itself suggest that the ritual ordering was absent in the Buddhist system, which is not surprising considering that brāhmanical ritual was unacceptable to Buddhists and other followers of what have come to be called 'heterodox sects' — Nirgranthas (Jainas), Ājīvikas and varieties of Cārvāka and Lokāyata sects. All the three high status *varṇa*s, —

[73] Pāṇini, III. 2.22.; I. 3.36. [74] Ibid., IV. 4.12. [75] Ibid., V. 1.80; V. 1.56.

[76] N. Wagle, *Society at the Time of the Buddha*, p. 153, *Mahāvagga* VI. 34.

[77] *Dīg. Nik.* II. 51 and 158. It has been argued that Gotama with reference to the Buddha is a personal name and not a *gotra*. D.D. Kosambi, 'Brahman Clans', *JAOS*, 1953, 73, pp. 202-8.

[78] In a division of high and low *Gotra*s, the Gautama, Maudgalyāyana, Kātyāyaṇa and Vaṣiṣṭha are considered high, whereas the Bharadvāja are low. *Suttavibhanga*, II. 1.2.2.

[79] *Dīg. Nik.* I. 97–107. [80] Ibid., II. 85. 109.

khattiya, brāhmaṇa and *gahapati* — are said to have as their aim the acquisition of wealth and wisdom.[81] The first does this through power to dominate territory; the second acquires it through Vedic learning and the fruit of the sacrifice which he conducts and the third through a craft and the result of his labour.

Varṇa as a system of social status and organization seems to be absent in the *gaṇa-saṅgha* areas. The lineage system in such areas is different from that in the western Ganga valley. Sacrificial rituals on a large scale played no role, whether religious or economic, and this made the *brāhmaṇ varṇa* redundant and altered the nature of the economy and the pattern of control. The emphasis was more on the availability and organization of labour and these societies were characterized by a demarcation into two broad groups, those who owned the land and those who worked on the land. The recognition of this demarcation made the *śūdra varṇa* unnecessary since the *dāsa-karmakara* were in effect performing the functions of the *śūdra*. In the absence of a householding system labour was provided by non-kin groups so that the changing status of the clan or *viś* is not recorded. Only the landowning families carry the label of *kṣatriya* and this differs from the definition of *kṣatriya* as it emerges in the western Ganga valley. Since the ritual status or *varṇa* is not given priority in these societies (the references to it in Buddhist sources relating generally to monarchical states), it is inevitably the *jāti* status which comes to be treated as the social reality.

Jāti is characterized by a dual distinction, that of the high and the low.[82] These are sometimes symbolized in the colours white and black with a range of shades in between.[83] The *khattiya* and the *brahmañña* invariably belong to the *ukkuttha, ucca* or high *jāti* and and the *sudda* and *caṇḍāla* to the *hīna, nicca* or low *jāti*. The *vessa* is not invariably among the high as was the case with the brahmanical *dvija* unless the *gahapati* is seen to replace the *vaiśya*. It would seem that the notion of *jāti* or endogamous groups was being extended to other *varṇa*s, and to this extent *jāti* appears to have a different meaning in Buddhist sources from that in the *Dharmasūtra*s. Endogamy would have conflicted with the exogamous *gotra* systems unless both *gotra* and *jāti* were being more flexibly and less rigidly interpreted to mean an adherence to marriage rules relevant to family and kinship. Significantly, it is said that these are impor-

[81] *Aṅg. Nik.* III. 363.
[82] Ibid., I. 162; *Suttavibhaṅga* II.1.2.2.
[83] *Aṅg. Nik.* III. 383.

tant at marriage.[84] The emphasis on *gotra* and *jāti* would also point to the numerical increase of groups included within each *varṇa*; a growth of some complexity and size which could only be identified by indicating the boundaries of endogamous and exogamous alliances.

The unit which appears to be even more central to the lineage system at this time was *ñāti*, which has been rendered as the extended kin group.[85] Thus whereas the Licchavis, Bullis, Mallas, Koliyas and Śākyas all claimed relics of the Buddha on his death in view of their being fellow *khattiyya*s, the Śākyas alone were the *ñāti* of the Buddha.[86] Both *gahapati*s and monks make claims on their respective *ñāti*s for support. In a kin-oriented society, the *ñāti* would be the crucial unit, lineages being ranked on the basis of *ñāti* connections. The *ñāti* was an agnatic group and the *ñātaka* was the affinal group. Decisions of the *ñāti* had a strong social sanction, for a Malla states that he finds the Buddha's teaching unacceptable but since his *ñāti* has decided to honour the Buddha he is also joining in.[87] The social nucleus in this society is therefore much more closely integrated with the kin group and the lineage and less so with ranking based on *varṇa*. It was doubtless this together with the rejection of Vedic rituals which made the area into a *mleccha-deśa* in brahmanical eyes. The dual stratification of high and low was more evident than other differentiations. The three upper groups are often demarcated by economic wealth. The *khattiya* as a term is said to derive from *khatta* and signifies having possessions, or alternatively from *kheta*, as the lord of the fields.[88] The economic status of the *brāhmaṇ* is emphasized in the references to the *brāhmaṇ*s having been given grants of land. These are primarily in the kingdoms of Kāśi, Kośala and Magadha and *brāhmaṇ gahapatis* living in *brāhmaṇ grama*s are referred to.[89] The grants of land are so large that the epithet *mahāśāla*,[90] wealthy, is applied to these *brāhmaṇ*s. In one case a Bharadvāj *brāhmaṇ* has so much land that he requires five hundred ploughs to cultivate it.[91] Some *brāhmaṇ*s are described as rich, and living in fortified palaces manned by armed guards.[92] The granting of cultivable land to

[84] *Dīg. Nik.* I. 99.

[85] Wagle, *Society at the time of the Buddha*, p. 127 ff; Agrawala, *India as Known to Panini*, p. 95.

[86] *Dīg. Nik.* II. 165 ff

[87] *Mahāvagga* VI. 36.2.

[88] *Dīg. Nik.* III. 93.

[89] *Maj. Nik.* II. 141-2; *Dīg. Nik.* I. 111-12.

[90] *Saṁ. Nik.* I. 175.

[91] Ibid. I. 172.

[92] *Dīg. Nik.* I. 104-5.

brāhmaṇs reflects not only the primacy of land as an item of wealth in contrast to the earlier grants of cattle and gold, but also a further weakening of the idea of land being held jointly by the clan and indicates that the householding economy was seen as the more normal condition in these areas, encouraging in turn the private ownership of land. Since the epigraphic evidence on the granting of land to *brāhmaṇs*, *brahmadēya*, is absent until the early centuries A.D., these descriptions could perhaps be interpolations of a later period. Yet the association of land with *brāhmaṇs* becomes more common at this time, and it is probable that in the process of establishing kingdoms those who performed the legitimizing rituals for the new kings may well have been given grants of land, seeing that land was now the most valuable form of wealth in the middle Ganga valley. References to *brāhmaṇs* in the Buddhist sources occur more frequently in the context of kingdoms (and particularly of Kośala and Magadha) than in the *gaṇa-saṅghas*, perhaps because Vedic ritual was generally absent in the latter areas. That some of the *Dharma-sūtras* disapproved of *brāhmaṇs* living by cattle rearing, agriculture and serving the king[93] does not seem to have bothered the *mahāśāla brāhmaṇs* who did just that. When the Buddha addresses such *brāhmaṇ* landowners he refers to them as *gahapatis*.[94] The same sources which speak of the very wealthy *brāhmaṇs* also refer to some impoverished *brāhmaṇs* in professions which would normally have been prohibited to them by the *Dharma-sūtras*.[95] The wealth of the *brāhmaṇ* according to the *Dharma-śāstras* was said to come from *dāna* and this was theoretically the only source of income permitted to him as he was not expected to practise a profession. The logical consequence of this was that the *brāhmaṇ* should not be taxed, a view which is strongly reiterated in the *Dharma-śāstras*.[96] If all *brāhmaṇs* were exempt from tax then presumably even those who worked for a living at some profession would try and claim the exemption.

The substitution of *gahapati* for *vaiśya* points to the final disintegration of the original *viś*. The *gahapati* is not only the head of the household but is often also the landowner[97] deriving his land through the breaking up of the lineage held lands into family

[93] *Baudhāyana D.S.* I. 5.10.24, 28. [94] *Maj. Nik.* I. 400 ff

[95] *Sam. Nik.* I. 170-71; *Gagga Jātaka* no. 155; *Somadatta Jātaka* no. 211, cf. *Āpastamba* II. 5.10.4 ff; *Gautama* VII. 8-21.

[96] *Manu* VII. 133-6.

[97] Wagle, *Society at the time of the Buddha*, pp. 151-2.

ownership. The *gahapati*'s household extended over three or four generations and included kinsfolk as well as a range of servants and slaves. In the *Dharma-sūtras* the occupation of the *gṛhapati* consisting of cattle herding, cultivation and trade is associated with the *vaiśya* of the later *Dharma-śāstras* who constitutes the economic backbone of society together with the *śūdra*. Buddhist sources define the *kulapati* as having access to the same three occupations.[98] The household also seems to have produced some of its basic requirements. There are references to the production of cloth in each household.[99] Doubtless most of this was for self-consumption but some may have gone towards the building up of exchange in the *nigama* or market. Gradually the householding economy may have sought links with groups of craftsmen (*grāmaśilpin*)[100] and thus built up an exchange nexus.

References to *gahapatis* include men of wealth who may be associated with professions such as carpentry, medicine, etc., but have links with land and property,[101] or else have changed from agriculture to a diversity of professions characterized by a lucrative income. That the term had an intrinsic link with the *gṛhapati* of Vedic times is evident from the interpretation given by the Buddha to the concept of the sacred domestic fire, *gahapati-aggi*,[102] which is not used for *saṃskāra* rituals but symbolizes the supervision of household well-being. This was the parallel to the Vedic *gārhapatya-agni* which the householder received from his father and transmitted to his descendents.

Associated with the status of the *gahapati* were the *kuṭumbika* and the *gāminī*. *The kuṭumbika* was again the head of a family and a man of property who, in the *Jātaka* literature, is associated either with a rich landowner who is often said to be collecting his dues, or with commerce and usuary.[103] An element of moneylending in rural areas is also associated with *kuṭumbika* but probably this again refers to a later period.[104] *Gāmiṇī* derived from the *grāmaṇī* of the earlier period refers to the head of a band or professional group or the head of a village, presumably in the capacity of the chief of a

[98] *Aṅg. Nik.* III. 281.

[99] *Āpastamba G.S.* IV. 10.10.

[100] Pāṇini VI. 2.62; V. 4.95. Pāṇini differentiates between those who work for daily wages at the homes of their employers and those who were paid at piece-rate.

[101] *Aṅg. Nik.* I. 229; III. 391.

[102] *Aṅg. Nik.* IV. 45; *Dīg Nik.* III. 217. cf. Pāṇini IV. 4.90.

[103] *Succaja Jātaka* no. 320; *Satapatta Jātaka* no. 279; *Kakkaṭa Jātaka* no. 266.

[104] *Sālaka Jātaka* no. 249; *Takkala Jātaka* no. 446.

group settled in a village.[105] The section of the Buddhist texts addressed to the *gāmiṇīs* includes professions such as soldiers, elephant and horse-trainers, and stage managers. Authority in the village was sometimes vested in the *gāminī* who was also on occasion associated with the *nigama*,[106] a larger settlement with some degree of exchange and market functions.

The *gahapati* is also met with in the *nigama*.[107] In one case, the name of the town, Āpaṇa meaning a place of exchange or a shop, indicates the origin of the town.[108] It is possible that the origin of some of the *nigamas* may also be traced to villages specializing in particular craftsmen such as potters, carpenters and salt makers,[109] which may have become small specialized markets and later more general market centres. A corroboration of the *nigama* as a market town is available from numismatic evidence where a series of early coins carry the legend *'negama'*[110] suggesting that they were issued by a *nigama*. In the context of very large cities the word has also been interpreted as the ward or section of a city[111] where professionals working in a particular craft would live and work, again indicating some commercial connections. The market was the gathering point for rural produce and could also be tapped by merchants locating resources. As such it would have impinged on village economy, particularly where production was specialized. The phrase, *gāme va nigame*[112] is frequently used suggesting a distinction between the village and the *nigama* and also linking the latter to a rural nexus.

The existence of the *nigama* may also have been the base to the rise of some towns. A distinction has to be made between the city as a political centre and one which combined both political and commercial functions. There is a difference in the ethos of towns which were primarily political centres such as Hastināpur, Indraprastha,

105 *Saṁ. Nik.* IV. 305 ff.

106 *Saṁ. Nik.* IV. 309 ff.

107 A Ghosh, *The City in Early Historical India*, Simla, 1973, p. 46.

108 Pāṇini III. 3.119; *Maj. Nik.* I. 359.

109 R. Mehta, *Pre-Buddhist India*, p. 213.

110 J. Allan, *A Catalogue of the Coins of Ancient India*, London, 1967, pp. CXXVI-VIII, CXXX: The word *negamā* in Pali or *naigāmah* in Sanskrit most likely refers to the market or mercantile area of the city. A. Cunningham, *A.S.R.* XIV, p. 20. Epigraphically the coins date to a later period, Mauryan and post-Mauryan, but the sense of the word remains the same.

111 Wagle, *Society at the time of the Buddha*, p. 22.

112 *PED*, p. 249.

Ahicchatra and Ayodhyā and those which combine political with commercial functions, such as Śrāvasti, Kauśāmbi, Vaiśāli and Rājagṛha. The former are the locations of palaces and courts, the hub of political activity, to which was added in later periods when taxes were collected, the redistributive mechanism of a collecting agency and a distributing agency which provided a modicum of public services — not forgetting the all-important *dāna* to religious groups. Palaces are however yet to be found in the excavations of the early political capitals and this is perhaps due to the transition to monarchy being weak at this time. Admittedly the absence of horizontal excavations may be a partial explanation. Kauśāmbi has revealed a palace complex although its date remains somewhat controversial.[113] There is a striking absence of monumental public buildings in the early towns of the Ganga valley. Even in the Mauryan period, Pāṭaliputra alone was associated with impressive buildings. It is not until the wealth from external trade pours in during the post-Mauryan period that the cities of northern India are embellished with monuments. Towns which combined the functions of commercial centres with political capitals are distinguished by a more evident activity on the part of merchants and traders and sometimes included a sector which was regarded as the *nigama*. In the early progression towards urbanization there is little indication of towns growing around religious monuments or ceremonial centres. Neither the Vedic religion nor the early phases of Buddhism and Jainism had monuments of any size or places of pilgrimage other than cult spots. The growth of urban centres may also have been quicker in the middle Ganga valley since the nucleii of the *gaṇa-saṅgha*s were the settlements occupied by members of the *rāja-kula*. Since they did not live on their lands but rather in a nucleated group there was a greater potential for the transition of such settlements into towns.

The term *pura*[114] was often employed for towns and originally meant a fortified settlement or a locality. Fortifications were associated with political centres which were either the residence of the *rājā* and his entourage or of the families of the *rāja-kula*s in the *gaṇa-sangha* system. The fortification enclosed the urban settlement and separated it from the surrounding areas or its umland, thus demarcating the urban from the rural. But this separation was by no means absolute since the links between the two remained

113 G.R. Sharma, *The Excavations at Kauśāmbi*, 1957-59, Allahabad, 1960.
114 Pāṇini IV. 2.122.

strong. Fortifications also served to segregate excluded social groups such as the *caṇḍāla*s who lived in villages in the vicinity. Early fortifications may have been in the nature of mud ramparts, with more elaborate structures belonging to the Mauryan and post-Mauryan period.[115] *Nagara* was the common term for a town and *mahānagara* used more frequently in the middle Ganga valley was the city.[116] Buddhist origin myths describing the emergence of the *janapada*s associate the earliest phase not only with the settlement of a lineage segment but also an urban centre.[117] Whereas in brahmanical sources, names of cities are often said to derive from names of kings, in Buddhist literature the names are associated with *ṛṣi*s, plants and animals, as in Kapilavastu and Koliyanagara.

The rise of the city as a commercial centre in addition to being a political centre is linked closely to the emergence of trading groups and professions connected with trade. It is from the ranks of the *gahapati*s that the traders evolve.[118] In the *Dharma-sūtra*s the association of trade is with the *vaiśya*s whose source of wealth is listed as the triple occupation of cattle-rearing, agriculture and trade, listed it would seem almost in order of historical change from *viś* to *vaiśya*. Clearly not all *vaiśya*s would have the surplus wealth to invest in trade and many would have continued to be cattle breeders and agriculturalists. The *grāmiṇī* is described as a *vaiśya* and the *grāmiṇī* would certainly be a *gahapati*. The *Gṛhyā-sūtra*s prescribe the rites to be performed for success in trade, the *pāṇyasiddhi*.[119] Occasionally there is mention of members of *kṣatriya* families taking to trade and generally it is the younger sons.[120] In Buddhist sources the *gahapati* often computes his wealth in terms of grain as well as of coined money as in the case of the *gahapati* Meṇḍaka.[121] The image of the *kāma-dhenu* (wish-fulfilling cow) gives way to that of the self-replenishing grain measure. The *gahapati* is both the symbol of wealth and of the tax-payer.

In the middle Ganga valley in areas other than Magadha, Kośala and Kāśi the major sacrificial rituals played a marginal role judging by the infrequency with which they are mentioned. The weakening of the brahmanical orthodoxy would doubtless have released the

115 A. Ghosh, *The City in Early Historical India*, p. 62 ff.

116 Pāṇini IV. 2.142 and the Kāśikā, VI. 2.89.

117 Romila Thapar, 'Origin Myths and the Early Indian Historical Tradition', *AISH*, p. 294 ff.

118 *Ang Nik.* I. 116-17; IV. 282-3.

119 *Hiranyakeśi G.S.* I. 1.4.8.

120 As for example the *Ghaṭa Jātaka* no. 454.

121 *Mahāvagga* VI. 34.

gahapati from ritual prestations and enabled him to use his wealth in a more generalized exchange. The economic fetters of the *yajña* in which wealth was consumed were now reduced and in some areas, were absent. With access to greater wealth in the middle Ganga valley through changes in agricultural production of various kinds, the *gahapati* would have used only a part of his wealth for ritual prestations. The other equally important aspect of the *yajña* which was the bestowal of status on the *yajamāna* and the reciprocity between the *yajamāna* and the *brāhmaṇ* could be acquired in some areas at least by a different mechanism, that of amassing wealth and making donations to the Buddhist *saṅgha* This had as much legitimacy in many parts of the middle Ganga valley as did the *yajña* in the western Ganga valley. Although the *gahapatis* are more frequently associated with the kingdoms, nevertheless the proximity and inter-links between the kingdoms and the *gaṇa-saṅghas* in this area would have weakened the influence of orthodoxy. Many of them appear to have been lay-followers of the Buddhist and Jaina sects which made it possible for them to use their wealth in forms other than the *yajña*. It is not unexpected that brahmanical sources are generally not very sympathetic to those who live in cities.[122] The *gahapati*, liberated from ritual prestations and lineage limitations, could be said to have emerged with a more clearly defined economic function.

That the trader was a person claiming considerable respect from society, in spite of the disapproval of trade as an occupation for the upper two *varṇas* in much of brahmanical literature, is evident from the word used for the trader, *śreṣṭhin* and its Pāli form, *seṭṭhi*, meaning, 'a person having the best'. *Śreṣṭhin* is used in a general sense in the later Vedic texts,[123] but it acquires a specific meaning in the Pāli texts. *Śreṣṭhin* is curiously, absent from Pāṇini who uses terms such as *vāṇija*[124] and *āḍya* and the word may therefore have been more current in Buddhist usage and in the middle Ganga valley. The use of *śreṣṭhin* probably originated from the link with the *gahapati* rather than with commerce *per se* or with the *varṇa* ranking of the *vaiśya* and was substantiated by the esteem given to merchants and traders in Buddhist sources. Trade is described as a

[122] *Baudhāyana D.S.* II. 3.6. 33.
[123] *Atharvaveda* I. 9.3; *Ait. Brah.* III. 30.3; *Tait. Brah.* III. 1.4.10.
[124] III. 3.52; VI. 2.13. In the *Rg. V.*, *vāṇij* suggests 'wanderers', I. 112.11; V. 45.6.

high status occupation, *ukkaṭṭha-kammam.*[125] The term *seṭṭhi-gahapati* is used for those whose wealth is measured in large sums of money. Banking was to become a separate and important profession. The *seṭṭhi-gahapati*s had close ties with existing groups of high status and the trader was not therefore an alien in society.

Among other factors associated with wider social changes some of which led towards urbanization, the gradual utilization of iron can be cited as one of the increasingly noticeable technological changes. As a technology[126] it is recorded for the early half of the first millennium B.C. (with sporadic occurrences earlier) but the quantity of artefacts found and their function in non-military activities initially remains small. If *kṛṣṇa-aya*s in the *Ṛg Veda* refers to iron then doubtless its use was known and the skill of the technology was familiar, but the location of iron was distant. This might account for the paucity of iron finds and the fact that they are mainly weapons at this time. The location of ores was limited in the Ganga valley to south Bihar, and haematite-bearing soil although more widespread, was nevertheless still confined to the middle reaches of the Ganga. The extensive use of iron would have had to wait until the metal workers could tap these resources. The occurrence of iron in central India may point less to local deposits and more to contact with the Ganga valley sources. This uneven distribution encourages a circuit of exchange and in this process the metal can even be used as a medium of exchange. The greater efficiency of the weapons — iron arrow-heads, spear-heads, knives and blades would doubtless have appealed to the *kṣatriya rājā*s. The social status of the blacksmiths is kept low partially because they were an itinerant group and therefore suspect in the eyes of sedentary peoples and partially to prevent them from using their skill in the new technology for acquiring power. The more specialized skill required for iron working also required a dependence on smiths and the uneven location of iron required smiths to be peripatetic. Iron technology therefore helped in preventing the emergence of self-sufficient villages.

The importance of iron technology is not merely that it introduces a change in the use of metals but that when the use of iron

[125] *Suttavibhanga* II. 1.2.1.

[126] R. Pleiner, 'The Problem of the Beginning Iron Age in India,' *Acta Praehistorica et Archaeologica*, 1971, pp. 5-36; D.K. Chakrabarty, 'The beginning of iron in India', *Antiquity*, 1976, 50, pp. 114-24; 'Distribution of Iron Ores and Archaeological Evidence of Early Iron in India', *JESHO*, 1977, XX. pt 2, pp. 166-85. G.R. Sharma, *Excavations at Kauśāmbi 1957-59*, Allahabad, p. 45 ff.

artefacts becomes more widespread the pace of change as compared to other metal technologies is accelerated. Its major significance at this time lies in its impact in the middle Ganga valley. Even if the direct evidence for the extensive use of iron at an early date is not very substantial, the indirect evidence would suggest that it had some impact. The Northern Black Polished Ware may have resulted from a high firing temperature which was made possible by the higher temperatures required for smelting iron as compared to copper. Further, the particular polished and shining quality of the pottery may derive from the presence of iron in the soil. The provenance of this particular pottery in the area between Patna and Varanasi, is in the vicinity of the iron mines of south Bihar and local haematite bearing soils. There is sporadic evidence of iron working in south Bihar and it is likely that initially the technology was in the hands of itinerant smiths (as it is largely even to this day in the servicing of many rural areas and more widely prior to the arrival of manufactured steel and iron goods). The routes of the itinerant smiths may have built up a circuit of trade connecting local levels of production.[127] An itinerant trade in salt may have played a similar role, the major salt mines being in the Punjab. Local circuits of trade linked the villages, *grāma*s, with the local market centres, *nigama*s, and these in turn with the towns, *nagara*s, the commodities in circulation being largely items of basic consumption. Some, such as metals and salt, would then enter into the larger circuits of trade which linked the *nagara*s with each other, a qualitatively different trade from the local circuits and where commerce was handled by the *gahapati*s and later the *seṭṭhi*s. This trade required investments of large amounts and close contact among the traders. Some of these contacts went back to earlier links between political centres and, with the growth of commerce, took on the character of commercial links.

The major routes (outside the local circuit) also linked the political centres. These links may originally have been forged through marriage alliances such as in the marriages between Gandhāri and Dhṛtrāṣṭra, Kaikeyi and Daśaratha. The *janapada*s to which they belonged — Gandhāra, Kuru, Kekeya and Kośala — were linked along the northern route, the *uttarapatha*. With the

[127] D.D. Kosambi, *An Introduction to the Study of Indian History*, Bombay 1956, pp. 11, 91.

growth of trade some of these political centres acquired commercial importance as well and in some cases the latter was to become the chief focus of activity. Thus Taxila in Gandhāra retained its commercial importance since it had access to west Asia, particularly after the sixth century B.C. when it lay on the eastern edge of the Achaemenid empire. Hastināpura met with disaster when the Ganga flooded the town and its inhabitants are said to have migrated to Kauśāmbi (near Allahabad). It was reoccupied in the mid-first millennium but never attained the status of other towns in the middle Ganga valley. Among these were the *mahānagaras* mentioned in Buddhist sources[128] — Śrāvastī (the capital of Kośala in the Buddhist period) seems to have replaced the Ayodhyā of the *Rāmāyaṇa*, possibly because the latter was too far south and therefore not on the main route running closer to the foothills, although Sāketa remains a major city on the route from Kośala to Kauśāmbi, thereby giving Kośala the advantage of two major cities; Rājagṛha the capital of Magadha commanding the fertile tract between the Ganga and the eastern outcrops of the plateau; Campā the capital of Aṅga (the Bhagalpur region of Bihar) and an active river port on the Ganga controlling trade going east; Kāśī, the centre of the kingdom of the same name and close to the confluence of the Ganga and the Gomati; Kauśāmbi near the confluence of the Ganga and the Yamunā with access to the route southwards through the Vindhyas. All these cities are characterized by their location on major routes or on rivers which were used as routes.[129] Most of these towns were also situated at the meeting point of two ecological zones. The early importance of the route from northern India along the foothills and then southwards following the Gandak, the *uttarapatha*, is indicated by its having been used by Bhīma, Arjuna and Kṛṣṇa when they travelled from Hastināpur to Rājagṛha in order to challenge Jarāsandha of Magadha.[130] The significance of the control over river traffic which grew in importance over time and superseded the *uttarapatha* is demonstrated in the rise of Pāṭaligrāma, as it was called in this period, to Pāṭaliputra, the capital of the Mauryan empire, located

[128] *Dīg. Nik.* II. 146; The term *mahānagara* especially in relation to the Ganga Valley is also used by Pāṇini in VI. 2.89.

[129] It is perhaps worth remembering at this point that until the railway network was established river traffic was of great importance in the Ganga valley and the siting of places was often in relation to river traffic. O.H.K. Spate, *India and Pakistan*, p. 558.

[130] *Mahābhārata*, Sabhā Parvan, 18. 26-30.

as it is, near the confluence of the major rivers of the Ganga valley. In a sense the rivers provided a wider circuit of exchange. The capitals of the *gaṇa-saṅgha*s such as Kapilavastu, Koliyanagara, Kuśinagara, Pāvā, are described as important towns but do not have the status of *mahānagara*s. Even Vaiśāli which controlled an important segment of the *uttarapatha* is not consistently listed as a *mahānagara*. In at least two cases, capitals which were political centres were shifted to locations on important commercial routes, the Kośala capital being moved from Ayodhyā to Śrāvastī and the Magadhan capital from Rājagṛha to Pāṭaliputra. Either the enhanced status of the *nagara* when it became a *mahānagara* grew with the maturing of the state and the description therefore relates to a somewhat later period, or else it would seem that the emergence of the state was a factor in encouraging commercial enterprise and thus indirectly contributing to the transformation of a *nagara* into a *mahānagara*. Ties between these cities are also indicated by references to wealthy *gahapati*s from the middle Ganga valley cities going to Taxila for professional training, as in the case of Jīvaka the physician from Rājagṛha.[131]

Trade within northern India extended over a wide geographical reach as is evident from the distribution of the Northern Black Polished Ware and related artefacts in the earlier phases of this culture. The degree to which commercial interests outside the Indian subcontinent acted as an incentive remains uncertain and would require further and more extensive excavations. In the north-west and particularly Gandhāra the demands of the Achaemenid empire may have laid the foundations for external trade, the fuller development of which dates to the Mauryan period. Another potential area would be Gujarat with its maritime connections extending into the Gulf area. The Assyrian empire in its twilight period may have had some trade connections with western India which are merely hinted at in the sources but require investigation. The revival of prosperity of Rangpur III (early first millennium B.C.) and the spread of the Lustrous Red Ware from Rangpur to Ahar, Navdatoli and Prakash may point to a possible linkage of coastal areas with a hinterland known for the availability of timber and semi-precious stones. Both these were commodities much in demand in west Asia.[132] The *Bāveru Jātaka* suggests a con-

[131] *Mahāvagga* I. 39; VIII. 1.4 ff., *Manorathapūrāṇi*, I. 216.

[132] Romila Thapar, 'A Possible Identification of Meluhha, Dilmun and Magan', *JESHO*, 1975, XVIII., pt., 1, p. 1ff.

nection with Baveru/Babylon which, in memory at least, probably dates to the pre-Alexandrine period when Babylon was still a major commercial centre. The importance of Bhṛgukaccha and Sopāra as ports on the west coast can only be explained in terms of a maritime trade with west Asia and with the emergence of the west coast from Sind to Sri Lanka as a circuit of trade with its own coastal network. The *dakṣiṇāpatha* or the southern route going through Ujjain southwards was, whether it branched off at the Narmada or continued to Pratiṣṭhāna, aimed at linking the Ganga valley with the west coast, a link which probably began in this period although it developed to major importance later.

The city was demarcated in contemporary sources by its size. An average of thirty to fifty square kilometres was considered quite normal for a city[133] even though the size of the mounds today is often as small as five kilometres in circuit. Allowing for the fact that much of the original city may have spread well beyond the inner core,[134] which is probably all that is contained in present-day mounds, the tendency to exaggerate the size is evident. A rough approximation of settlements of the Northern Black Polished Ware period indicating the start of urbanization does suggest a noticeable rise in population and a larger size for the settlement.[135] Even if the measurement of the city is exaggerated the consciousness of differentiation in size is important.

Archaeology also points to the early phase of urbanization having a certain similarity in material culture. There is evidence of an improvement in living conditions, concentrations of people of a higher density than before and therefore the need for drains and refuse disposal.[136] Mud-brick was the main building material and probably this was augmented with timber buildings.[137] Kiln-fired bricks and stone occur more frequently in the subsequent period.

[133] E.g. The Ayodhyā of the *Rāmāyaṇa* I. 5. 6-7; A. Ghosh, *The City in Early Historical India,* p. 52. The city of Vaiśāli is described by Hsüan Tsang as extremely large although in ruins (Watters, *On Yuan Chwang's Travels in India,* II. p. 63). Nevertheless it is not clearly defined as a *mahānagara* either in Buddhist or Jaina sources (J.C. Jain, *Life in Ancient India as Depicted in the Jaina Canon*, p. 257).

[134] *Mahāvastu* I. 271 refers to the suburbs as *bahira*.

[135] This was the case at sites in the Western Ganga valley such as Atranjikhera (A. Ghosh, *The City in Early Historical India*), and Hastinapur. B.B. Lal, 'Excavations at Hastinapur', *Ancient India*, nos. 10 and 11, 1954-5.

[136] A. Ghosh, *The City in Early Historical India,* p. 70.

[137] *Arthaśāstra* II. 36. Early Buddhist rock cut cave shrines carry traces of timber construction even where it was not necessary.

The extensively used black pottery might well have been luxury-ware and consequently an important item of trade.

The absence of a central market comparable to the Greek *agora,* highlights certain aspects of the lay-out of the middle Ganga town. It grew around the intersection of two main highways thus emphasizing the aspect of the four quarters, or along a river bank. The main roads became the spine of the urban centre linking it to rural areas and also providing the processional paths on ceremonial occasions, with the balconies of houses providing stalls for the audience, a scene so frequently depicted in Buddhist sculpture. Market areas or *nigama*s in the larger cities were located at the main gateways. Alternatively, transactions were carried out in areas where the commodity was produced. The *nigama* in large cities such as Rājagṛha and Śrāvasti may indicate an area which was once a market town before it was engulfed by the growth of the *mahānagara*. Monumental buildings, often listed as a characteristic feature of early cities, tend to be few and far between. This may have been in part due to the extensive use of wood for building,[138] or that neither political nor religious authority were powerful enough for prestige buildings during this period. There is little indication of a citadel or acropolis distinct from the residential area, a feature so characteristic of the towns of the Indus civilization. The cities built in the vicinity of Taxila have been horizontally excavated and a comparison of the early pre-Mauryan to Mauryan town of Bhir Mound with the later post-Mauryan town of Sirkap demonstrates the difference in the very lay-out of the cities.[139] It is difficult to differentiate the various areas of settlement at Bhir Mound whereas Sirkap is extremely well-planned. Admittedly Bhir Mound being the earlier settlement reveals the gradual evolution of the town whereas Sirkap represents a deliberately planned city. The absence of a citadel or acropolis at Bhir Mound or for that matter of any strikingly monumental building is very noticeable. The absence of large-scale warehouses or granaries in these towns again suggests that political authority was still relatively decentralized. The *gahapati*s have their own granaries, but state granaries are referred to only in the Mauryan period.

Commodities involved in the early trade included metals (iron, copper, tin, lead and silver) salt, pottery and textiles of a large

[138] A. Ghosh, *The City in Early Historical India*, p. 68.
[139] J. Marshall, *Taxila*, vol. I., Cambridge, 1951.

range among the more common items.[140] The elaboration of exchange on local circuits may have led to the marketing of the first two items. The distribution of luxury wares such as the Northern Black Polished Ware is doubtless what is later described as the wealthy potter owning five-hundred potteries and an equal number of boats for transporting the pottery to various river ports in the Ganga valley.[141] The quantity and volume of production and trade probably belongs to the subsequent period but the start of this pattern would date to the earlier period. Cotton-textiles and iron swords are especially remarked upon in Greek sources and remained associated with Indian trade for many centuries. More specialized items were woollen blankets from the north-west, particularly Gandhāra, ivory which was then abundant in the forests of the Ganga valley and the Himalayan foothills, and horses which came from Sind and Kamboja, and of which the chief market seems to have been at Kāśī.

The production of commodities for trade would involve the villages producing the raw material or even commodities (where villages had specialized craftsmen) and the sale of these at the market towns as well as to the merchants obtaining material and goods directly from the village either through exchange or through purchase. Certain commodities however, such as the finer textiles and more delicate ivory work among others are associated with skilled craftsmen in urban centres. Such artisans initially worked on their own, but gradually with the expansion of trade came to be organized into corporate bodies, the most commonly referred to being the *śreni* and the *pūga*, both names taken from the corporate assemblies associated with the *gaṇa-sangha* system. Included in the *śreni* were the artisans, and if the guild prospered then not only were assistants (*antevasika*) employed but also *dāsa-bhṛtaka*. In this period however there are few references to *dāsa*s employed by artisans or to advanced guilds. The *śreni* was gradually to evolve into a professional group bound by contractual ties. Its professional identity encouraged its evolution into a *jāti* and these were among the large number of occupational *jāti*s which were to be allotted a *śūdra* status in the *varṇa* system.

A distinction is made between the shopkeeper (*pāpanika)*, the retailer (*kraya-vikrayika*), the *vasnika* investing money, the small-

140 Agrawala, *India as Known to Pānini*, p. 245 ff.

141 *Uvāsagadāsao* (ed. R. Hoernle), Calcutta 1890, p. 184.

scale trader (*vāṇija*), and the *seṭṭhi-gahapati*.[142] The latter was essentially the banker or the investor interested in investing money and not involved in the actual production or transportation of commodities. The latter grew with the use of coined money, the evidence for which is available from the punch-marked coins found at various sites, most of which are associated with urban centres of this period.[143] The use of coined money although it had a wide horizontal spread is more frequently associated with urban centres; the excavation of rural settlements produce fewer coins at this level. Labourers in farms working for a wage would more likely have been paid in kind. Barter and the exchange of items prevailed on perhaps a larger scale elsewhere, as is suggested by the use of terms such as *nimāna* (value), *vasana* (that which is exchanged) and *go-pucha* (the value of one cow).[144] The coin of highest value in circulation was the silver *śatamāna* but the more standard coin was the silver *kārṣāpaṇa* and the copper *māṣa* and *kākaṇī*.[145] The *kārṣāpaṇa* is said to equal sixteen *māṣas* and was divided into a half (*ardha/addha*) and a quarter (*pada*). The *kākaṇī* was half a *māṣa* and the smallest denomination was the *ardha-kākaṇī*. The *kārṣāpana* or *kahapana* of the Pāli texts is also called the *paṇa*. The root *paṇ* provides a number of words connected with trade, as for example, *paṇya*, small-scale trade, *paṇāyitri*, a trader, etc. Punch-marked coins carry symbols which were the identification of the issuing authority, the combination and variety of symbols differing according to provenance and issuing authority. The issuing authority could either have been trading groups backed by the *rājā*s of their lineage and identified by particular symbols, or professional groups affluent enough to issue their own coins. The question of whether punch-marked coins were issued by royalty remains controversial. Punch-marked coins were therefore a transitional

[142] Pāṇini III. 3.52; VI. 2.13; IV. 4.13.; *Ang. Nik.* I. 115; *Sam Nik.* I. 92.

[143] S.K. Chakravorty, *Ancient Indian Numismatics*, p. 56 ff.; J. Allan, *A Catalogue of the Coins of Ancient India*, Oxford, 1967; A.K. Narain (ed.), *Local Coins of Northern India*, Varanasi, 1966; A.K. Narain and L. Gopal (eds.), *Seminar Papers on the Chronology of the Punch-Marked Coins*, Varanasi, 1966. D.D. Kosambi's papers on punch-marked coins have recently been edited by B.D. Chattopadhyaya and published in a volume entitled D.D. Kosambi, *Indian Numismatics*, New Delhi, 1981.

[144] Pāṇini V. 2.47; V. 1.27; V. 1.19.

[145] Ibid. V. 19-37. The value of the *Kārṣāpaṇa* varied according to the metal in which it was issued. In this period silver and copper *kārṣāpaṇa*s are more frequently referred to. *Samanatapāsādikā* II. 698; cf. *Manu* VIII. 1.

form between traders' tokens as units of value and legal tender issued by royalty. The backing of coins by the state is not referred to until the Kauṭilya *Arthaśāstra*.[146] Punch-marked coins from stratified levels of excavations and the comparative study of their symbols provides an indication of the trading links of that time. The introduction of coined metallic money, even if only in the urban markets, extended the geographical reach of trade as also the range of items traded and led increasingly to the computation of wealth in the form of coined money. Those who were wealthy were accorded a high status in urban life, which weakened the role of ritual status and, to a lesser extent, the monopoly of landownership as criteria of social rank.

Among the economic innovations associated with coined money which were to have far-reaching effects in the social life of the times were the introduction of the profession of money-lending and banking and as a further extension of this, activities associated with forward speculation. The new profession of financing trade and production was based on usury (*kuśīda, vṛddhi*) and attitudes to usury vary in the sources. The *Dharma-sūtra*s refer to a large variety of interest rates depending on the period for which the loan is taken and the purpose. The average rate is fifteen per cent per annum.[147] At the same time usury is regarded as a sin, *apātrīkarana* and the *brāhmaṇ* is prohibited from taking up this profession.[148] *Brāhmaṇ* usurers are to be treated like *śūdra*s. It is only permitted to *dvija*s if they derive an interest from those who are socially degraded. This was doubtless in part to discourage the *gahapati*s, particularly the *brāhmaṇ*s among them, from investing in trade at the cost of ritual prestations. Pāṇini describes usury as 'giving for a mean motive'.[149] This would be logical from the point of view of Vedic tradition since the accumulation of wealth was inimical to the furtherance of sacrifices and enabled the rich *gahapati* to invest his wealth in non-ritual activities. The encroachment of money into the lives of the *gahapati*s would of course have been restricted only to those who were wealthy, the same who in the brahmanical tradition should have been bestowing their wealth as *dāna* on *brāhmaṇ*s or as *yajamāna*s in sacrificial rituals. Certain *janapada*s are referred to as having fallen in status because they have ceased to perform the *yajña*s and not surprisingly those of the north-west along the *ut-*

146. II. 12. 24-5; D.D. Kosambi, *Indian Numismatics*, New Delhi, 1981.

147 *Baudhāyana D.S.* I. 5.10.22; *Gautama D.S.* XII. 29-42.

148 *Baudhāyana D.S.* I. 5.10. 23-5; *Vaṣiṣṭha D.S.* II. 40-2.

149 IV. 4. 30-2.(S.C. Vasu, tr.)

tarapatha are conspicuous in this regard.[150] As a counterpart to this the status of the *purohita* is sought to be enhanced by emphasizing the need for a permanent domestic priest.[151] Furthermore, the introduction of money would also tend to create a new set of impersonal professional ties not necessarily based on kinship nor subservient to the requirements of the ritual status of the *varṇa* hierarchy. Buddhist sources on the other hand endorse the status of the financier and carry no hint of disapproval of usuary. The *seṭṭhi-gahapatis* are highly respected and are frequently the more important patrons of the Buddhist *saṅgha*. The Buddhist sources depict the *gahapatis* in trade as an economic asset treated with respect by those in political authority.

The increasing complexity of trade may have led to the introduction of a script during this period. The earliest evidence of a script is that of the Aśokan *brāhmi* and *kharoṣṭhi* inscriptions. These assume literacy among at least the officers of the state. Regional variations in the language and the use of diverse scripts would suggest a literate tradition, no matter how limited, of at least a few generations. The compilation of a grammer, Pāṇini's, would also be indicative of the beginnings of literacy. Literate *gahapatis* would not have been viewed sympathetically by those who controlled the oral tradition and for whom literacy would be regarded as the preserve of the privileged.

It was from the families of the *gahapatis* that there emerged the *seṭṭhis* who had the surplus from agricultural activities to invest in trade. The interchangeability of the *gahapati* and the *seṭṭhi* as members of the same family is supported from references to *gahapatis* who are also described as *seṭṭhis*.[152] This inter-relation as a process is evident from later epigraphic sources as well.[153] It can also be observed in Buddhist texts, thus permitting extrapolation back to the preceding period. It is however necessary to emphasize that this link was common in the wealthier *gahapati* families and should not be seen as commerce replacing the income from agriculture or leading to a decrease in cultivation. The income from commerce would have been in the early stages a form of

[150] See ch. II. p. 52.

[151] *Baudhāyana D.S.* I. 10.18. 7-8.

[152] *Cullavagga* VI. 4.1; *Aṅg. Nik.* IV. 282; VIII. 1.16.

[153] *Epigraphia Indica* X. 1909-10, cf. *Dīg. Nik.* II. 176; Luders List nos. 1056, 1062, 1073, 1075, 1121, 1127, 1209, 1281; G. Bühler, Bhattiprolu inscription, *Epigraphia Indica*, II. 1894, p. 323.

augmenting the income from agriculture, and the transition to commerce as a profession was a gradual process.

The inclusion of trade as one of the activities of the *gahapati* contributed to the growth of towns but also brought about a change in the rural economy. The diversification of interest and investment in trade meant a diversification in the methods of cultivating the land owned by the richer *gahapati*s. Where the rich *gahapati*s began to invest in commerce, the direct control of cultivation through the employment of labourers and slaves would tend to be reduced gradually [154] and the land would be given out on a tenancy basis, either to erstwhile labourers or to other independent persons wishing to become tenant cultivators. Such changes are reflected in one of the rules in the *Dharma-sūtra*s that if a man has leased land from another and it fails to bear a crop that does not exempt him from payment to the owner, for he is still considered responsible for the crop and has to compensate the owner.[155]

The size of holdings seems extraordinarily large and in many cases would have required managers and tenants to make it worthwhile. A Licchavi *gahapati* renounced his wealth, retaining a small amount for his needs which in itself constituted five hundred ploughs, a hundred acres of land and forty thousand head of cattle.[156] Being a later reference this would date to the period after the breaking down of some clan holdings among the Licchavis and the emergence of the holdings of the *gahapati*s. Once land had been converted into private property, unless the rule of primogeniture was strictly applied, there would have been a continual subdivision of holdings through the generations with some sections of the family becoming impoverished.[157] Most sources refer to a fairly detailed partitioning of the estate, not necessarily in equal shares, among all the sons.[158] Drought and other calamities resulting in a poor harvest or none at all are also mentioned as leading to the impoverishment of landowners,[159] as also oppressive taxation. One source associates this with the Pañcāla *janapada*;[160] but may well relate to the subsequent period.

[154] The statement that the *gṛhapati* ploughs the land for a while and then gives the plough to the ploughman may reflect the employment of a cultivator or a tenant (*Kauśika-sūtra* 20. 1-24; *Baudhāyana D.S.* III. 2.2).

[155] *Āpastamba D.S.* II. 11.28.1.

[156] *Uvāsagadāsao*, II. pp. 52-4.

[157] *Vasiṣṭha D.S.*, XVII. 40 ff.

[158] *Baudhāyana D.S.* I. 5.11.11.ff; II. 2.3 2 ff.

[159] *Saṁ. Nik.* I.170-71; *Kāma Jātaka* no. 467; *Bilārikosiya Jātaka* No. 450.

[160] *Gaṇḍatiṇḍu Jātaka* no. 520.

The cultivation of land at this time can be classified into various categories. In some areas there was a continuation of clan holdings. In other areas, noticeably so in Kośala and Magadha, the pattern varied. Land could be cultivated by those who owned it either personally or with some help as was the case with the *gahapatis*. Land could be rented out to tenants who cultivated it and gave a share of the harvest to the owner, the latter most likely being a *gahapati*. Land could be brought under cultivation through the initiative of the state. The extension of land under cultivation as a source of wealth doubtless suggested the idea that the king should settle agriculturalists on waste land, converting it into arable land. Settlements established through the initiative of the state are mentioned in the *Jātakas*[161] and in Mauryan sources as one of the normal methods of extending agriculture but may have had their beginnings in the earlier period. The conquest of territory occupied by hunters, gatherers or primitive cultivators would, if brought under plough cultivation, have resulted in the conversion of such groups into castes and the agriculturalists would take on a peasant status. The sale of land is referred to very indirectly and that too in the context of a wealthy *gahapati* buying land to gift to the Buddhist *saṅgha*, as in the case of Anāthapiṇḍaka.[162] There is no clear testament of the sale of land in a generalized form, as for example in the *Arthaśāstra*.[163] The expansion of agriculture created a peasantry which worked the land neither as members of the kin-group owning the land nor as employees of the owners but on a contractual basis. The variation in landownership and tenures brought about a more complex stratification than had been known earlier. However, the relationship between the owner and the tenant was not necessarily entirely contractual, particularly where the tenants had earlier connections with the household. Both customary law and caste considerations tended to blur the sharpness of the change.

The emergence of the peasant is suggested in the use of terms such as *kassaka/karṣaka* which, together with *kṣetrika, kṛṣaka, kṛṣivāla*, became recognized terms for peasants even in later sources.[164] The peasant either owns the land he cultivates or rents it from the owner; he may cultivate it himself or with some assistance. He pays a tax to the state in the former case and a rent to the owner in the latter, for he is not an employee of either. The

[161] *Jayaddissa Jātaka* no. 513; *Arthaśāstra* II. 1.

[162] *Cullavagga* VI. 4.1.

[163] III. 10.9.

[164] *Dig. Nik.* I. 61: Pāṇini V. 2.112; *Manu* VIII. 241 ff.: IX. 53; X. 90.

tax is a stipulated amount, generally an agreed upon share of the produce or the equivalent which has to be paid at regular intervals and is treated as contract; obligations and dues may also be required in addition to the taxes. In one of the *Dharma-sūtras* it is stated that the cultivator should pay a tax of one-sixth of his produce to the king in return for the protection given by the king.[165] In another similar text the cultivator is required to pay the king a tax of one-tenth, one-eighth or one-sixth of the produce.[166] That this was not a rent is indicated by the subsequent statement that there should be a tax of one-fiftieth on cattle and gold and one-twentieth on the sale of merchandise. False evidence regarding land carries the threat of loss of caste.[167] It is also stated that the king has a preferential share in booty which otherwise should be equally divided.[168]

It would seem that the lineage system had not been completely converted into a peasant economy. It is significant that the payment is to be made not because the king claims to own the land but because the relationship between the king and the peasant symbolizes mutual rights and obligations. The question of land-ownership was to become a vexed one and contradictions in the sources of this early period suggest the probable co-existence of a variety of tenures varying from region to region. The emphasis here is less on the significance of the state claiming ownership and more on its entrepreneurial activity, an emphasis which is made more apparent in the major text on political economy, the *Arthaśāstra* of Kauṭilya. In this context there is much relevance in the statement, *kassaka gahapatiko kara karako rāsi vaddhako,*[169] the peasant who cultivates his land and the *gahapati* (both) paying taxes (i.e. performing their duties) increase the wealth. It is at this point that the peasant begins to crystallize as a social category quite distinct from the *gahapati*.

The epithet of *śūdra* in relation to cultivators would seem to mean the peasants. *Śūdras* employed in agricultural work were evidently small in number, judging from later Vedic literature, but by the Mauryan period *śūdra* agriculturalists come to mean peasants[170] and Megasthenes states that the cultivators are

[165] *Baudhāyana D.S.* I. 10.18.11. [166] *Gautama D.S.* X. 24.
[167] Ibid. X. 22-3.
[168] *Baudhāyana D.S.* II. 1.2.1.ff.
[169] *Dīg. Nik.* I. 61; *PED.* p. 209; cf. *Aṅg Nik.* I. 229, 239, 241.
[170] *Arthaśāstra* II. 1.

numerically the largest of the seven 'castes' which he describes.[171] The more general references to *śūdras* included artisans and craftsmen as well, working both in the villages and the towns. The economic importance of the *śūdra* made it necessary to define the *śūdra varṇa,* a definition which took the form of an elaboration of the *sankīrna jātis* in the *Dharma-sūtras*. The *varṇa* status of these *jātis* was kept low by arguing that it resulted from the polluting intermarriage between persons of the higer *varṇas* and combinations thereof: this was the counterpart in ritual status to the economic and social depression of both the peasant and the craftsman who had the most to lose with the erosion of kinship ties and the encroachment of contractual relations. The peasant was a new phenomenon tied to paying taxes instead of giving tribute and permitted little participation in the ritual. The peasant neither had the extra wealth nor did his status at the time allow him to participate more fully in ritual prestations.

Among the categories of *śūdras* reference is made to the *dāsasudda*. The term *dāsa* now carried the technical meaning of a slave characterized by an absence of legal status and rights.[172] The condition of a *dāsa* was to become a form of legal punishment, when an *ārya* had to serve as a *dāsa* for a stipulated period, particularly those unable to pay their debts.[173] Apart from prisoners-of-war and those born as slaves, another source of slaves would be debt-bondsmen although for a temporary period.

The hierarchical social stratification with a sharper consciousness of differentiated status in the middle Ganga valley, as compared to the earlier society of the western Ganga valley, derived from the more complex agrarian system and the commercial activities of the urban centres. The close control over land meant a clear distinction between indigenous populations and more recent settlers. Urbanization not only demarcated the umland from the city but also introduced a number of necessary although marginal occupations which were believed to be polluting and could only be carried out by uprooted groups. It is from these occupations and such groups that the untouchables in the main were drawn.

It has been suggested that untouchability arose from an urban

[171] *Strabo*. XV. 1.40.

[172] *Dīg. Nik.* I. 104; *Mahābhārata*, Udyog Parvan, III. 272; IV. 33. *Papañcasudani* III. 409.

[173] Chanana, *Slavery in Ancient India,* p. 68; Pāṇini I. 4.35. *Mahāvagga* I. 47.

setting[174] which might explain why there is a noticeable increase in references to and the presence of excluded groups in the literature of the post-Vedic period. The *caṇḍāla*s are described as *bahinagare,*[175] literally living outside the town in separate villages as excluded groups. Their association with pollution is explicit in this literature. The daughter of a *seṭṭhi* washes her eyes on seeing a *caṇḍāla*[176] and a *brāhmaṇ* is worried that a breeze which blows past a *caṇḍāla* will blow on him as well.[177] These sources predate the reference to *caṇḍāla*s as *aspriśya*/untouchable, yet the sentiment is present. The *caṇḍāla* in these stories is said to have been the Buddha or a *bodhisatta*[178] in an earlier birth, an attempt perhaps to suggest that the Buddha did not differentiate as did other members of society between the excluded and caste groups. The same source refers to a king marrying a *caṇḍāla* woman and making her son his successor.[179] In the *Dharma-sūtra*s however they are included among the *sankīrna jāti*s[180] and there was evidently a hierarchy of impurity from the *śūdra* downwards. There seems to be a co-relation between greater stratification and the existence of un-touchability, possibly because purity and pollution act as counterweights to each other, untouchability being the logical ex-tension of a hierarchy which uses pollution as one criterion. Yet the more frequent references to the *caṇḍāla*s as untouchables, recognizably different by their dress, accessories and speech, comes from *Jātaka* sources where the recognition of the purity of the *brāhmaṇ*s was minimal. The notion of pollution is often found in non-urban societies, particularly those described technically as primitive, in which there are periods of time, situations and objects which are regarded as polluting. This may well have been the source of the idea. The strategy of using pollution as a method of segrega-

[174] C. von Führer Haimendorf, in the Foreword to S. Fuch's, *The Children of Hari*, Vienna, 1949.

[175] *Mātanga Jātaka* no. 497; *Amba Jātaka* no. 474.

[176] *Matanga Jātaka* no. 497; [177] *Setaketu Jātaka* no. 377.

[178] *Chavaka Jātaka* no. 309; *Uddālaka Jātaka* no. 487; *Citta-sambhūta Jātaka* no. 498.

[179] *Mahā-ummaga Jātaka* no. 546. This story is interesting as it refers to the *rājā* of Dvāravatī, Vāsudeva of the Kaṇhagana who married the Caṇḍāli Jambavatī and was succeeded by her son, Śivi who ruled at Dvāravatī. These links with Vāsudeva, Kṛṣna and the Vṛṣṇis is curious.

[180] *Baudhāyana D.S.* I. 8.18.8; *Vasiṣṭha D.S.* XVIII. 1–6; *Āpastamba D.S.* II. 4.9.5; *Gautama D.S.*, IV. 16 ff.

tion would have reinforced the existing distinctions based on other criteria and intensified with increasing stratification.

The middle Ganga valley witnessed a sequential but variant social formation from that predominant earlier in the western Ganga valley. The difference is also reflected in the range of religious ideas which were prevalent at this time. The links between historical changes and the rise of religious sects such as the Buddhists, the Jainas and the Ājīvikas have been suggested elsewhere.[181] Before the rise of these sects the two main strands of religious ideas in this area were either those of earlier Vedic texts or in the *gaṇa-sangha* territories the worship of *caitya*s and *stupa*s. These as funerary monuments emphasized ancestral identity and lineage links, crucial to claims of rights over land but at a wider level providing a form for cosmic symbolism.

The leaders of the new sects preached to urban audiences in the main[182] and the tenets of their teaching held an appeal for such audiences although this did not exclude the village dwellers. Buddhism, for example, supports the investment of economic surplus in commercial enterprises rather than its consumption in rituals. The Buddha explains that a man should allot his income in the following manner : a quarter for daily expenses, a quarter to be put by as savings and the remaining half to be judiciously invested.[183] The patronage extended by the *gahapati*s to the Buddhist *saṅgha* and vice versa helped indirectly in forging new links which were not based on kinship. The Buddhist *saṅgha* with the monastery as its major institution supported by a lay following is, in itself, indicative of a changed socio-economic system in which, as the Buddha says, the village and the *nigama* were the mainstay of the monk.[184] The expenditure of wealth in this support was in exchange for a religious sanction which gave legitimacy to the pursuits of the *gahapati*s. Ritual prestations were replaced by *dāna* to the *saṅgha* which were said to be of enormous proportions as with the gifts of Jīvaka and Anāthapiṇḍaka.[185] Although *dāna* was ostensibly directed to non-economic channels, it went into the building of the *saṅgha* which, apart from bestowing status on its donors (as did

[181] Romila Thapar, 'Ethics, Religion and Social Protest in the first Millennium B.C. in Northern India', in *AISH*, p. 40 ff.

[182] In referring to places associated with the Buddha and his mission, the greatest number of references are to Rājagṛha, Śrāvasti and Kāśī.

[183] *Dīg. Nik.* III. 188. [184] *Maj. Nik.* I. 369.

[185] *Dīg. Nik.* I. 47; *Maj. Nik.* II. 112.

dāna through *yajña* in the earlier system), helped as an institution to provide a base and a network of contacts in new areas brought under the state system and across territorial boundaries. Such contacts were doubtless useful in places where clan and kinship ties were being slowly eroded and the ties built up on the basis of the *saṅgha-upāsaka* (lay follower) relations may have been seen as one among the possible replacements. With the increasing prosperity of the *saṅgha* as an institution, its social and political significance was also enhanced. Even more important was the implicit function of *dāna* : in order to obtain the surplus to give to the *saṅgha* it was necessary to lead a relatively austere life and invest one's wealth with care and caution. The Buddhist emphasis on investment was a boon to the commercial economy. Some of the new religious sects therefore provided an ethic in support of simple living and the investment of wealth. In an indirect manner royal patronage to Buddhist monasteries became a channel through which royalty could support the same ideology which the commercial groups supported, thus lending status to both the commercial groups (who otherwise had a low ritual status) and their religious ideology. Commerce as a new source of revenue[186], augmenting the taxes collected from agriculture, was doubtless one at least of the reasons for the encouragement of trade by royalty.

With the emergence of the monarchical state in Kośala there are distinctly fewer references to ritual prestations at the time of the *yajña* and more to the gifting of land to *brāhmaṇs*. The changes in the agrarian economy released a larger surplus and this was in turn matched by gradual changes in the concept of *dāna* and the content of ritual prestations. Gifting of land, particularly where it was waste land, would have had the added benefit of such gifts leading to the settlement and development of what was primarily the *āranya*. Gifts of land at this time did not carry any specific administrative rights.

The universalistic ethics of Buddhism, Jainism and similar religious movements extended to the entire range of castes in an effort to equate people not socially but at least at the level of ethical action. That the middle Ganga valley was generally outside the social pale by brahmanical norms and that these new religious sects had a susbstantial following, makes it a moot point whether they can be called the 'heterodoxy' in this area, although in terms of the

186 *Suttavibhaṅga* LXVI. 1, 2.1.

Vedic religion they certainly took a heterodox stand. The emphasis on renunciation for example was in part a continuing tradition of those wishing to seek salvation by opting out of society, but in narrower social terms it also functioned as the containment of dissent. In the brahmanical system of *āśrama*s, renunciation came as a termination in the life cycle after the completion of all social obligations so that the risk of the social effectiveness of dissent was reduced. That there was a strong group of dissidents is evident not only from the attitudes towards social conservatism on the part of the heterodox sects, but more so from the view of the many radical groups referred to as Cārvākas and Lokāyatas. The monastery became the institution which brought together diverse persons in a new relationship. Within the monastic network there existed a potential of power in that well-endowed monasteries could become sufficiently independent of the state as to assume an almost parallel form. Of this potentiality Buddhist thinking was aware, but it chose to work in conformity with the state rather than in opposition to it. This is reflected in the relationship which it envisages between the Buddhist *saṅgha* and the government. In the historiography of Buddhism, written by Buddhist monks, there is a constant attempt to link the major events in the history of the religion with political authority. as for example linking the Councils of Rājagṛha and Pāṭaliputra with Ajātaśatru and Aśoka.[187] Not only this but in describing the establishment of the religion in an area an attempt is made to involve royalty with the event.[188] The association with the state doubtless derived from the fact that some, even rudimentary, state system was a prerequisite to the establishment of a *saṅgha* or monastery in an area. The attack on heretical groups by the staunchly brahmanical authors of the *Arthaśāstra* and the *Manu Dharmaśāstra*[189] were, apart from sectarian diatribes, also motivated by the fear that monastic networks could become extremely powerful and could divert royal patronage.

The *janapada* was no longer merely the territory identified by *kṣatriya* clans; it is now defined as including villages, market towns and cities, and involving administration and revenue,[190] which in a sense symbolize the complexity of the change. The kingdoms of

[187] *Mahāvaṃsa*, V. 234-42; *Dipavaṃsa*, VII. 36-49.

[188] This is evident from the description of the coming of the first Buddhist mission to Sri Lanka brought by Mahinda, the son of Aśoka Maurya, and welcomed by Tissa, the ruler at Anurādhapura.

[189] *Artha* II. 1.40; Manu V. 90; IX. 225.

[190] *Dīg. Nik.* I. 136; II. 349.

Kośala and Magadha were qualitatively different from those of the Kurus and the Pañcālas, even if the latter can be called kingdoms. The establishment of the state had many implications. Power was concentrated in the family of the rulers who were not necessarily of the highest status. The ruling family of Kośala was regarded as somewhat inferior in status by the *rāja-kula* of the Śākyas who refused their daughter in marriage to the king of Kośala.[191] Yet the Śākyas accepted the suzerainty of Kośala.[192] Pasenadi, the king of Kośala is also said to have performed all the required *yajña*s, such as the *aśvamedha, vājapeya,* etc., involving the slaughter of many hundreds of animals, [193] so that he was assured brahmanical sanction in claiming legitimacy as a king. These ceremonies were by now a formality as there was considerable wealth from agriculture and trade which remained untouched by sacrificial ritual. The comment in the text is that the slaves, servants and craftsmen involved in preparing the animals for the sacrifice were emotionally upset by the killing of so many animals; evidently they were not overawed by the destruction of animal wealth.

It is also said that when a rich *gahapati* of Kośala died intestate his wealth was attached by the king's treasury.[194] This would point to the collection of taxes being so well-established that the king's treasury had the power to appropriate wealth in such circumstances as well. It was doubtless the efficiency of tax collection which enabled Kośala to carry out a prolonged struggle with the kingdom of Kāśi which it finally annexed and which in turn brought it into conflict with Magadha. The earlier terms for prestations are now more often used as technical terms for taxes. *Bali* came to mean a tax but could also refer to an offering at a sacrifice.[194] *Bhāga* and *ardha* are clearly used as a share of the total which constitutes a tax.[196] *Śulka* is a customs duty levied on a consignment and presumably relates to the value of the consignment rather than its size or its contents; the notion of value linking it to its earlier meaning.[197] Pāṇini makes a special mention of the taxes paid in the eastern region, *kāra nāmni ca prācām halādau,*[198] which is glossed as a series of taxes on households as well as a tax on land. The significance of the latter to the prosperity of the *kośa* is evident.

A treasury built on regular tax collection and able to finance a

[191] *Maj. Nik.* II. 110, and 127; *Dhammapadaṭṭhakatha* I. 339 ff.

[192] *Aṅg. Nik.* I. 276; *Maj. Nik.* II. 124.

[193] *Saṁ. Nik.* I. 75.

[194] *Saṁ. Nik.* I. 89.

[195] Pāṇini II. 1.36; V. 1.13.

[196] Ibid., V. 1.48; V. 1.49.

[197] Ibid., V. 1.47; IV. 3.75.

[198] Ibid., VI. 3.10.

standing army was among the requisites of a state system. A standing army implied campaigns in which territory was annexed and these were qualitatively different from the raids of earlier times. A professional army was dependent on the recruitment and training of full time soldiers, the manufacture of armour which was often a state monopoly and a well-defined military administration. These aspects were to receive particular attention from the rulers of Magadha. An indication of the sea-change in relation to military activities is provided by certain technical innovations in weaponry at this time. In the Magadhan campaign against the Vṛjjis two new 'war machines' were apparently brought into use. One was the *rathamūṣala*, a chariot with knives pointing outwards fixed to its body, which when driven rapidly through enemy ranks would mow them down. The other was the *mahāśīlakaṇṭika,* a giant-sized catapult for hurling heavy stones and rocks against the fortifications of a town under seige. The function of such weapons is a pointer to the change from raids to well-planned sieges and campaigns over long periods.

References in brahmanical sources to the Māgadha people describe them as of low caste, a *pratiloma jāti,*[199] although there is some difference of opinion among the *Dharma-sūtras* as to the combination which gave rise to the Māgadha.[200] The profession of the Māgadha is listed as that of the bard who composes eulogies on his patrons.[201] A later text describes it as that of trade, conducted on land routes.[202] Of the territory of Magadha, the early political centre called Girivraja, i.e. hilly pasture, gives way to a new capital adjoining the old and significantly called Rājagṛha, the dwelling of the *rājā*. Bṛhadratha is believed to have established a powerful kingdom at Magadha, such that his son Jarāsandha had to be vanquished before Yuddhiṣṭhira could perform his *rājasūya*, and clearly Jarāsandha is regarded as the most powerful ruler. Of a later period, Bimbisāra was also called Māgadha, suggesting his link with the people of that name and *seniya/śrenika* which would indicate the head of a *śreni* or corporate body, perhaps of the Māgadhas, which he might have used to establish his personal authority. His kingdom is said to have included eighty-thousand villages, the *grāminī* of which met in an assembly.[203] Its economic

[199] *Gautama D.S.* IV. 16 ff; *Arthaśāstra* III.; *Manu* X. 11, 17.
[200] *Baudhāyana D.S.* I. 9.7; *Gautama D.S.* IV. 17.
[201] *Mahābhārata*, Anuśāsana Parvan, X. 48.
[202] *Manu* X. 47.
[203] *Mahāvagga* V. 1.1 ff.

potential is clearly referred to in the *Mahābhārata* where it is described as heavily populated, rich in cattle, flowing with water, because it was a land never avoided by the clouds, inhabited by the four *varnas*, boasting of opulent shops and its people holding in veneration a vast *caitya.*[204]

Magadha was in many ways ideally suited for the founding of a state. The land was fertile and naturally irrigated. The gentle gradient towards the Ganga prevented the formation of marshes and yet had the advantage of the Son valley catchment. The plain between the Ganga and the Vindhyan outcrops was subject to temporary inundation which could by a series of *bandhas* be converted into short-term reserves of water, making it possible to get a dry weather crop of rice in addition to the normal crop. The forests of the Rajmahal hills would have provided supplies of timber and elephants and to the south were located the major iron ore deposits of the region. Routes following the southern bank of the Ganga would pass through Magadha towards Aṅga or north to Vaiśāli. This doubtless motivated the eventual conquest of Aṅga and Vaiśāli by Magadha. The northern route via the Gandak also terminated at the Ganga bordering on Magadha. In a sense the Vṛjji confederacy controlling the *uttarapatha* and Magadha controlling the southern route, facing each other across the Ganga, were natural enemies. The conquest of Vaiśāli gave Magadha control over the most extensive segments of the two trade routes.[205]

The political stability of Magadha was sought to be established by Ajātaśatru, the son of Bimbisāra. He came into conflict with Kośala, the main rival to the west and the conflict was closed by a marriage alliance in which Ajātaśatru, according to Buddhist sources, married his mother's brother's daughter, his mother being the sister of Pasenadi, the king of Kośala.[206] Eventually Kośala was annexed to Magadha. Ajātaśatru's major success was the destruction of the Vṛjji confederacy. After a protracted campaign of sixteen years in which the Vṛjjis managed to stave him off, he finally sent his minister to live among them sowing dissension, which broke the unity of the confederacy and it fell to Magadha.[207] The sowing of dissension disguises faintly the real cause of the decline

[204] Sabhā Parvan, II. 19.1ff.

[205] D.D. Kosambi, *The Culture and Civilisation of Ancient India in Historical Outline*, London, 1965, p. 122.

[206] *Thusa Jātaka* no. 338.

[207] *Dīg Nik.* II. 72 ff.

of the Vṛjjis which was the break-up of the clan system. Significantly the name of the minister was Vassakāra, the rain-maker. As a result the northern route fell into the hands of Magadha and the *gaṇa-saṅgha* system of the middle Ganga valley gradually disappered.

The importance of Ajātaśatru is reflected in the description of him as a pious Buddist in Buddhist sources despite his unsavoury reputation of being a parricide.[208] In the historiography of Buddhism he is associated with the summoning of the Council at Rajagṛha[209] after the death of the Buddha, when the first differences over doctrinal interpretation beset the Buddhist *saṅgha*. Ajātaśatru epitomized the powerful king presiding over a newly established state system. Magadha became the nucleus of political power and expansion for the next couple of centuries.

[208] Ibid., I. 85-6.
[209] *Cullavagga* VII. 2.1.5; VII. 2.3. 4 ff.; XI. 1.7.

IV. IDEOLOGY AND THE STATE

The state is distinct from society and from government; but the point at which the consciousness of a state comes into being and its functions are recognized, is the point when the nature of government and of society have also changed. Society sustains the form of the state, and government becomes the articulation of the state. The interrelation of these three facets is clearly set forth in the traditional theories on the origin of government in Vedic and Buddhist sources.

The evolution of government is ultimately traced to the appointment or election of one person in whom authority is vested and this also seems to be the point at which the idea of a state begins to germinate. In the brahmanical tradition the person assumes the office of a king. In the Buddhist tradition he is not actually referred to as a king but in effect rules as such, all authority being concentrated in the single person. This is in striking contrast to the many *rājā*s of the *gaṇa-sangha* societies which influenced the concepts of early Buddhism. Variations in forms of government are recognized both in the differentiation between monarchies and chiefdoms as also within the latter category. The possibilities of alternatives may account in part for the insistence on kingship as the legitimate form of government in the *rājadharma* sections of the Manu *Dharmaśāstra* and the *Mahābhārata* which date to the period after the establishment of the state. Kingship in itself does not constitute the arrival of the state for the latter required a number of other features of which kingship was only one aspect. Kingship seems to have been viewed as an intermediary position reflecting the tendency towards the increasing power of the chief in the lineage system as well as the emergence of a pivotal office integrating the requirements of a state.

Vedic sources reflect a society in which government played a minimal role. The major concern is with explaining the origins of the status of chief and later the elements of divinity which were invested in this office and helped to gradually convert it into kingship. In the *Ṛg Veda* and the *Atharvaveda* human chiefs are compared to Indra, the hero among the deities.[1] The association of

[1] *Ṛg.V.* VIII. 35.17, VIII. 86.10-11; *Atharvaveda,* IV. 22. 4-5; VI. 87

deities with kingship is explained invariably in the context of wars between the *devas* and the *asuras*, in which the latter were victorious and the *devas* in desperation agreed to Indra leading them in battle.[2] In a situation where cattle raids and inter-tribal conflicts were frequent there would inevitably be an emphasis on the chief being a successful leader in battle.

In the period during which the state was in the process of emerging there is a noticeable change in the explanation for the origin of government. In the later theories the contractual element becomes more evident following on from a situation in which society itself has undergone a change. The earliest society is described as a utopian remote past in which there were neither kings nor laws nor social distinctions. But gradually virtue declined and this made it necessary for laws to be instituted and for authority to be vested in the *rājā*. The description of the decline of virtue varies from brahmanical to Buddhist sources in accordance with the perspective of each on social change.

In the Sānti Parvan, Bhīṣma explains how the status of the *rājyam* came about.[3] In the Kṛta-yuga there was no *rājyam*, no king, no authority, because people protected each other out of righteousness. With the decline of righteousness people became covetous, lustful and wrathful although we are not told why this happened. Distinctions between clean and unclean food disappeared, as also between right and wrong. (The former was important to the hierarchy of purity and pollution in the *varṇa* system). Finally with the disappearance of Vedas the *devas* feared that all was lost and appealed to the god Brahma who in his infinite wisdom enunciated the concept of *puruṣārtha*, the balanced pursuit of *dharma*, *artha* and *kāma* leading to *mokṣa*. Brahma also expounded the concept of *rājadharma* or the law of government in which the notion of *daṇḍa*, authority backed by force, becomes important. The *devas* then asked Viṣṇu to select one among the mortals to wield authority and Viṣṇu created a son. But most of his descendants became *ṛṣis* until finally Veṇa ruled, but ruled so unrighteously that the *ṛṣis* had to slay him. From his body they first churned Niṣāda who was expelled to the forest and then they produced Pṛthu who venerated the *brāhmaṇs*, initiated agriculture and because he pleased the people he was called 'rājā'. (*ranjitāsca prajāḥ sarvāstena rājeti sabdyate* ...)

The 'disappearance of the Vedas' doubtless reflects the new ideas

[2] *Ait. Brāh.* I. 14; I. 24.

[3] *Mahābhārata,* Śānti Parvan, 59. 13 ff.

current in the middle Ganga valley and the falling off in the performance of ritual sacrifices. The expulsion of Niṣāda and the establishment of Pṛthu reflects the supersession of hunting and gathering by agriculture.[4] The etymology of *rājā* is generally unacceptable to scholars although it fits in with the story. Its purpose appears to be to explain the anomaly of power being concentrated in one person and carries an echo of the idea of the *rājā* being the most acceptable to all, a possible hint of earlier elections.

Further on in the text mention is made of the condition of *matsyānyaya*,[5] the law of the fishes when in a condition of drought the big fish eat the little fish, the analogy being to a condition of anarchy in human society which results from the absence of a king. Here the stress is placed on the king wielding the rod of authority, *daṇḍa*, with the power to punish offenders against social laws. It is then related that in times past when a condition of anarchy beset human society a few people assembled together and worked out a set of laws relating to mutual behaviour, respect for the family and protection of wealth. But eventually they appealed to the gods for a king and Manu was appointed. At first Manu was reluctant to take up this task of governance but eventually he agreed in return for receipt of one-tenth of the grain produced, one-fiftieth of the animal wealth, the most beautiful of the young women and a fourth part of the merit earned by his subjects. The condition of anarchy is characterized by an absence of family and property rights and the maintenance of law and order emerges from a contractual relationship between the king appointed by the gods and human society. Association with the gods is implicit in kingship.

On kingship itself perhaps the most explicit expression is to be found in the many versions of the story of Pṛthu (the son of the wicked Vena) who is remembered as the first righteous ruler.[6] Pṛthu is essentially the nourisher in the earlier versions of the story. Thus he pursues and milks the cow Virāj, provides grain and food for people and enables them to domesticate animals. He consolidates his domains and protects his subjects who in turn are so pleased with him that they call him *rājā*. His rule is characterized by uto-

[4] Romila Thapar, 'Origin Myths and the Early Indian Historical Tradition', in *AISH*, p. 294 ff.

[5] Śānti Parvan, 67.16; *Śat. Brāh*. XI. 1.6.24.

[6] *Atharvaveda* VIII. 10 ff; *Śat. Brāh*. V. 3.5.4; *Pañc. Brāh*. XIII.. 5.19. ff.; *Mahābhārata*, Drona Parvan, 69.

pian conditions; the earth yielded grain without cultivation, the cows gave milk, the trees bore luscious fruit and men were free from fear, old age, disease and calamities. Pṛthu ensured that the earth gave to each person whatever they required. Other versions of the story change the emphases and instead of the wealth going to whomsoever needs it, it is paid as tribute to Pṛthu.[7] It is also said that he was consecrated *rājā* by Viṣṇu, Indra and the *lokapāla*s (the guardian deities of the world) and Viṣṇu entered his body. A still later version has other details.[8] We are told that Veṇa obstructed the sacrifices and provoked the antagonism of the *ṛṣi*s, who in their wrath killed him with stalks of the sacred *kuśa* grass. But the absence of a *rājā* raised the threat of total anarchy. The *ṛṣis* churned the left thigh of Veṇa from which arose a dark, ugly short-statured man whom they called Niṣāda. Unhappy with what they had produced they banished him and he became the ancestor of the *mleccha*s and the wild tribes of the forest. The *ṛṣis* then churned the right arm of Veṇa and from this there appeared a handsome man whom they accepted as *rājā*. His rule was righteous and he provided prosperity for his people and even the earth Pṛthvī bestowed her name on him and he came to be called Pṛthu.

The incorporation of Viṣṇu into the body of Pṛthu marks a major change from the earlier divine appointment of the *rājā* to his now actually assuming divinity. Later brahmanical texts maintain that the *rājā* was created from the particles of the gods, frequently the eight *lokapāla*s. This association served to underline the *rājā*'s function as protector since the *lokapāla*s were the protectors *par excellence* of the eight quarters of the universe. Thus the link with protection as a function had been raised to divine status. Once the element of divinity entered the notion of kingship it became a special category. Nevertheless it is worth emphasizing that the implication of this is not that the king is of divine descent but that the office of the king is sacred and divinity enters when the *rājā* is consecrated. The interlocking of divinity and the state system in the monarchical form provides the king with powers qualitatively different from those of the lineage based *rājā*. In the version of the story which mentions Nisāda and Pṛthu, a distinction is sought to be made between the food-gathering tribes of the forest and the

[7] *Mahābhārata*, Śānti Parvan 29.131; 59.115 ff.
[8] *Viṣṇu Purāṇa* I. 13.

agriculturalists where the left side is associated with the former and the right with the latter. It is also stated that the *sūta* and the *māgadha* (bard and panegyrist) emerge out of the sacrificial fire of Pṛthu adding further legitimacy to his rule.

Predictably the emphases of the Buddhist explanation of the emergence of the state are different.[9] The story begins with a pristine utopia where food was not required since the physical body was luminescent. People were not divided into families, there were no individual or group possessions and consequently there was no need for social laws. But some among the people tasted the earth, found it delicious and greed and craving entered the being of man. Their luminance faded and their bodies became solid. They now required food to nourish them and therefore rice appeared in forest clearings. In spite of its plenitude they began hoarding it. Eventually this led to the demarcation of the clearings into fields and theft of one man's rice by another and appropriation of each other's fields by fraud. (The demarcation of fields and their allotment to individual families was contrary to the clan ownership of land and was therefore seen as a deterioration of society. It may well have reflected the association of better times with the earlier clan system prior to the emergence of individual holdings.) Lust and passion required the setting up of families and ultimately possession led to conflict and disharmony. Finally they decided to select one among them, the most qualified, to sit in judgement over them and have the right to censure and banish those who deserved to be so treated. In return for this they agreed to give him a share of their rice. Since the person chosen was elected by all he was known as the Mahā-sammata. He was given the title of *khattiya* because he was said to be the lord of the fields and was called *rājā* as he charmed everyone. Subsequent to this there followed the *varṇa*s: the *khattiya*s were the lords of the fields; the *brāhmaṇa*s were those who went into the forest to remain away from immoral customs or else spent their time in studying the *Veda*s and lived by alms collected from the village, town or royal city; the *vessa*s adopted the married state and took to various occupations; and the *sudda*s were those who remained and took to hunting and other low occupations. The *śramaṇa*s were ascetics who came from any of the four groups.

In this version the question of ownership of cultivated land is the crux of the issue which leads to the necessity of a government.

[9] *Dīg Nik*. III. 80-98.

Authority is vested in a person who is selected by others and no appeal is made to any divine agency. The function of the elected person is clearly stated as also the contract of a share of the produce. Division of society into recognized social groups comes after this stage which is essentially the recognition of inequality.

In these and other similar theories of explanation of the origins of government the main aim is to prevent the fission of society or to indicate that a segmenting off is no longer a solution to the problems of tension within a society and that the tensions arose because of individual demands on property and persons; to have a system of authority with the right to be coercive both physically and legally and to empower this authority to maintain law and order and to expect it to consolidate functioning by upholding the social laws. These functions required not merely an explanation of government but a much fuller definition of what constituted the state. This is first expressed in the Kauṭilya *Arthaśāstra* and is described as the seven elements (*prakṛtis*) which constitute the state.[10]

The seven items are listed as *svāmi, amātya, janapada/rāṣṭra, durga/pura, kośa, daṇḍa/bala* and *mitra*. *Svāmi* refers to the king or the ruler. It is significant that *rājā* or its synonyms such as *bhūpati, bhogtā, nṛpati,* etc. are not used, but *svāmi* which carries a much stronger meaning of possession and ownership. A distinct change in the power and status of the king is reflected in the use of this term. *Amātya* refers not merely to the body of ministers but to the structure of administration which they control and assumes a functional group with specific powers. The third constituent of *janapada* or territory is defined as being agriculturally fertile with mines and forests and pastures, with perennial sources of water for irrigation, traversed by routes and maintenance of trade in commodities, with dedicated farmers (*karṣaka*) who together with the traders are capable of bearing the burden of taxes, and a high percentage of inhabitants of the lower *varṇas*. The fort, *durga*,[11] is sometimes substituted by the fortified settlement, *pura*, but in both cases it comprises the royal capital together with sections of the city inhabited by artisans and guilds, clearly pointing to the major cities which have both a political and commercial base. It was around the king's palace and the treasury that the fortified capital was generally constructed. The treasury or *kośa* was where the revenue when

[10] VI. 1.

[11] Ibid; see also II.4.

collected was gathered and it was said that the *kośa* should be such that it should tide over periods of low revenue. *Daṇḍa* has been interpreted as the army or the access to legitimate physical force.[12] This is perhaps a somewhat narrow definition since in other texts it is treated more broadly as coercive power and relates even to the power of law and of authority. The definition of force would in itself have changed from the forays associated with cattle raids to the arbiter in social tensions among a more settled people. *Mitra* is the ally and is preferably one that has had a long tradition of alliance with the home state. These seven elements later come to be called the seven limbs, *saptāṅga*, of the body of the state.

The seven elements (*prakṛti*) or limbs (*anga*) can be recognized from the descriptions of governmental functioning in the texts. The *janapada* was no longer defined by the *jana* or clan land but by differentiated systems within the territory with the term *rāstra* coming into increasing use in preference to *janapada*. The inclusion of diverse clans, castes and languages pointing to an established heterogeneity required a controlling agency and the authority of the king (*svāmi*) was its symbol. *Rājyam* and *rāṣṭra* emphasized sovereign power rather than the control of clan lands. An important aspect of sovereignty was the claim to coercive legal authority which was required for the functions of government, namely, to prevent fission, to maintain law and order and to consolidate the claims to territory. The term *svāmi* should not be taken as referring to the divinity of kingship since the use of *svāmi* in the context of a deity is a late usage. The notion of divinity was not essential to kingship as such, but was an adjunct which in the western Ganga valley facilitated the trend from chiefship to kingship. Doubtless the consecratory rites were encouraged by the *brāhmaṇs* who might otherwise have been denied their *dāna* and *dakṣiṇā* with the decline of the lineage system. Dynasties of considerable power such as the Mauryas were not required to claim divine status. The existence of the state backing the king as its symbol was what enhanced the power of the king and divine kingship was not a precondition to the evolution of the state. However recourse to association with the deities was always a useful method of augmenting power.

The administrative framework, the rudiments of which were evident in the Vṛjji confederacy and in the kingdom of Magadha, now takes on major importance in the managerial and redistributive

12 Śānti Parvan XIV. 14; cf. *Manu* VII. 14.20.

function of government. The earlier assemblies of the clans declined, *gaṇa, vidatha* and *samiti* becoming something of the past. Others evolved into advisory bodies such as the *sabhā* and the *pariṣad*. Membership was not by kinship but by selection and was open to non-kinsmen of the king, although restricted to the upper castes.[13] The employment of *brāhmaṇs* in the higher grades of administration where literacy was at a premium increased the acceptability of the state system among *brāhmaṇs*. Their induction as advisors and ministers led to their validating the new system since the access to power and the redistribution of wealth was still within their reach. A gradually perceptible distinction arose between *brāhmaṇs* performing priestly functions and those in managerial office. The former were regarded as superior and helped eventually in reviving the major Vedic sacrifices as avenues of legitimizing kingship as well as providing genealogical links and *kṣatriya* status to newly established dynasties.

The state controlled access to resources, particularly the forests which permitted control of both timber and animal wealth as well as clearance of land for cultivation. A distinction was maintained between waste land, land owned by the state and communal and private land. State land (*sītā*) was cultivated by agriculturalists who cleared it and established villages[14] under the initiative of the state. The extent to which this occurred would depend on the surplus which the state accumulated to invest in the development of new areas. There was thus an extension of the tenurial system in which the land was owned by the state but cultivated by peasants on the basis of prevailing tenures. Such cultivation was not conditioned by (*viṣṭi*) forced labour, or labour in lieu of taxation, and at the time of the Mauryas when the extension of agriculture took place on a larger scale than before mention is made of a variety of tenures including, apart from *viṣṭi*, share-cropping and a range of taxes.[15] Communal land was largely village pastures (*vrāja*). Privately held land was either cultivated directly by the owners who had a peasant status or by tenants who gave a percentage of their produce to the owners.

Taxes — their source, nature and definition — become a matter of serious discussion from the Mauryan period onwards. It is then that the technical meaning of *bali, bhāga, śulka, kara,* etc is given

[13] *Arthaśāstra* I. 8.

[14] Ibid, II. 1. Cf. *Jayadissa Jātaka* no.513.

[15] Ibid, II. 24.16; J. Bloch, *Les Inscriptions d'Asoka* (Rummindei Inscription), Paris, 1950, p. 157; *Strabo* XV. 1.39-41; Arrian, *Indika,* XI.

currency and debated upon as part of the system of taxation and it is argued that revenue symbolized in the *kośa* is of the very essence of the state. Prior to that there is a groping towards an arrangement of taxes, since the principles of taxation are recognized. What earlier were prestations, shares and ritualized offerings are transformed into taxes. *Bali* and *bhāga* were now used to mean regular taxes. *Bhāga* is mentioned more frequently and as the share of the produce is computed at one-sixth. *Bali* may have been a nominal tax and *bhāga* the more substantial one.

The definition of *bali* as a tax, which has been variously interpreted, remains a little uncertain. Originally a voluntary offering of wealth, it may have retained its association with wealth and when wealth came to be linked with land, *bali* could have been used to mean a tax on land. It would thus relate to the area of land under cultivation whereas *bhāga* remained a share of the produce from land. *Bali* would be paid by all those who cultivated an area of land they owned. Thus when the Rummendei inscription comemoraitng the visit of Aśoka Maurya to the village of Lumbīnī where the Buddha was born,[16] records that Aśoka exempted the village from *bali* (*udbalika*) and reduced the amount of *bhāga*, the former would have affected only those who owned the land they cultivated, the latter would have applied to all cultivators. Alternatively *bali* could also have been a generalized tax on the area of land cultivated by each cultivator. This might have led to the confusion in the mind of Megasthenes, who states that the land belongs to the king because a tax is paid on it by those who cultivate it.[17] The payment of a land tax does not presuppose state ownership of land since it is in the nature of a tax on property. The measurement of land under cultivation as described in the *Jātaka*s would also suggest the prevalence of land tax.[18]

The *Dharma-sūtra* of Gautama states that the king can impose *bali* because he protects the people,[19] even though in the theoretical justification for the origin of government it is *bhāga* which is collected as a fee for protection. It is also argued elsewhere that taxes are the wages of the king as stipulated in the original contract drawn up with Manu when he agreed to become the first king.[20] Oppressive taxation is cautioned against in the advice frequently

[16] J. Bloch, *Les Inscriptions d'Asoka,* p. 157.

[17] Strabo XV. 1. 39-41; Arrian, *Indika,* XI. 1 ff

[18] *Kurudhamma Jāt.* no. 276.

[19] VIII. 39, X. 28.

[20] *Mahābhārata,* Śānti Parvan, 67 and 70 ; *Baudhāyana Dharma-sūtra* I. 10.1; *Arthaśāstra* I. 13;

given that taxes should not hurt those from who they are collected. It is suggested that wealth should be gathered in the manner of the bee taking honey from the flower.[21] It is also said that wisdom lies in placating the wealthy since the prosperity of the kingdom depends on the taxes which they provide,[22] an echo of the earlier statement of the *vaiśyas* being the *balihṛt*. The terminology need not change but the context and the connotation are different. *Bali* was no longer a prestation or oblation except on religious occasions; it was now used to finance the protection of the state and its well-being.

The production of commodities and the organization of their sale was also directed in part towards providing a tax to the state although this was not realized to the same extent as from agriculture in the initial stages. The use of non-kin labour, the *dāsa-bhṛtakas* and the *karmakaras*, was gradually being extended to centres of craft production and trade, and helped in furthering specialization. Since commerce was a lucrative source of revenue the state came to be associated with entrepreneurial activities as well, although this was not a state monopoly.

The managerial and redistributive functions of the administration were therefore largely those concerning the extension of agriculture and the collection of revenue from both agricultural and craft activities together with the maintenance of an army and public servants. The older system of tribute and prestations continued but became increasingly marginal to economic activity and took on the symbolic role which characterized such actions in later periods. The wealth expended on *yajñas* and *saṃskāras* became a smaller percentage of the wealth produced. The more substantial source of income was from the taxes, rents, tolls and customs dues collected from land and commerce, and directed towards the central treasury[23] (*kośa*). Those exempted from taxation[24] consisted of the learned *brāhmaṇ*, the ascetic, women, children, the sick and the infirm and the *śūdra* in the service of another person. In short, all those whose activities could not be regarded as directly economically productive. The treasury in turn became the hub of the redistributive function. The king and the ministers not only controlled this function but the channelizing of this income increased disparities in society. There is growing evidence of greater ap-

[21] *Mahābhārata,* Udyog Parvan, 34. 17-18.

[22] *Mahābhārata,* Śānti Parvan, 87. 25-33; 89. 25-6.

[23] *Āpastamba D.S.* II. 10.26.9.

[24] Ibid., II. 10.26. 10-17.

propriation by a smaller number. The capital city becomes the nucleus of redistribution. The existence of the *kośa* points to a changed attitude to wealth. It was not to be entirely consumed in prestations and rituals nor was it to be in substantial degree redistributed or even invested by the state in alternative entrepreneurial activities. Wealth was to be carefully accumulated and judiciously used for maintaining the state system. Should such maintenance coincide with entrepreneurial activities then these would be encouraged but a sizeable part of the revenue went into financing the administrative framework to ensure the flow of income, of goods and of services, and into the maintenance of a standing army (*bala/daṇḍa*) for the enforcement of claims to territory. The larger the claim the greater the force required to consolidate the claim.

The emergence of the state leads to the state taking over the function of integrating the ruler and the ruled and this gradually is extended to include all social relationships. This is done largely by the state monopolizing legal force through which it seeks to regulate social relations. In this sense *daṇḍa* can be rendered not merely as physical force but carries with it the sanction of coercion and authority. It is frequently translated as the rod of chastisement, punishment being an important aspect of *daṇḍa*. But the staff was also the symbol of the renouncer and the ascetic, the man whose authority may not have been tangible but was nevertheless effective enough to frighten even the rulers. The authority of the ascetic derived from his removing himself from society, even if notionally, and claiming immunity from social obligations and regulations. As such he could not only claim sanctions which were extra-societal, but could also become the source of a counter-culture.[25] Hence the fact that he was regarded with awe by those in political authority. Added to this was the popular image of the renouncer associating him with austerity, control over the physical body and the creation of energy or magical power. The symbiotic relationship between the renouncer and the community gave greater force to the image of the renouncer. The symbol of *daṇḍa* would therefore not have been restricted to coercion but would appear to represent all forms of authority.

Daṇḍa provides the support to the extension of *dharma*, the ordering of society in which caste as a theory of stratification

[25] Romila Thapar, 'Renunciation: the Making of a Counter-culture?' in *AISH*, p. 63 ff.

became one of the mechanisms by which the state was made acceptable in areas where no state had existed earlier: the state legitimizing the new society. The *Dharma-sūtras* formalized not only the laws of *varṇa* in stating the obligations of each *varṇa* to society and the regulations regarding practices but also formalizing those customary laws which could not be ignored. Custom (*ācāra*) became an important component of legal functioning and cut across any easy method of introducing a uniformity of laws for all. The concession to customary law did serve the purpose to begin with of preventing confrontations and fission since the emphasis was on consensus. One of the authors of a *Dharma-sūtra*, clearly an enthusiastic supporter of customary law, states that countries, castes, and families, together with cultivators, traders, herdsmen, money-lenders and artisans have the authority to formulate rules for themselves, provided such laws are not in opposition to those of the *Dharma-sūtras*.[26] Customary law would carry with it the use of ordeals, curses and analogous means as dispensers of law as well as the strength of supernatural sanctions in curbing conduct which met with social disapproval. In a society emphasizing ritual mores, actions resulting in ritual uncleanliness (as many socially disapproved actions were perceived to be) would require expiation rather than punishment — hence the increasing importance of *prāyaścitta*. In the early texts this was required of those who travelled to the *mleccha-deśa*, frequently places where the sacrificial ritual was on the decline or had not been introduced or where heterodoxy was in evidence. Even when legal institutions were recognized as the means of settling disputes, these were less often distinct bodies serving a legal function and more often existing bodies of deliberation which took on legal functions as well. Such a situation clearly militated against the over-despotic state. This doubtless changed as the state became more powerful and was able to impose impersonal laws through the efficacy of its right to *daṇḍa,* and to its being the chief arbiter. Compilation of the *Dharma-sūtras* would in itself indicate a society in which even custom come to require the backing of authority, although not necessarily political authority. It would also point to an inter-mixing of groups where norms for communities, professions and castes had to be stipulated. Such an attempt to regulate norms would be in keeping with the developing power of the state. Although the *Dharma-sūtra* literature was not

[26] *Gautama D.S.* XI. 20-2

seen as a system of civil laws *per se*, it did all the same reflect the views of those in authority.

That the notion of authority assumes considerable importance is in part a reflection of the tendency towards the centralization of power but also of the growing disparities of high and low in society. Disparities between the various *varṇa*s is strikingly noticeable in the *Dharma-sūtra*s.[27] Whereas in the *Ṛg Veda* there was a generalized payment or wergeld of a hundred cows (*śatadeya*) which was to be paid by one who killed another irrespective of their status, the *Dharma-sūtra*s maintain a hierarchy of payment in cows in accordance with the *varṇa* of the person killed.[28] Furthermore, the cows are not to be given to the kinsfolk of the dead man but to the king or to a *brāhmaṇ*. Punishments are also varied in accordance with *varṇa* status. In such a system *śūdra*s had the worst deal and paid the maximum penalty in most cases.[29] That the *Dharma-sūtra*s may have been prone to a little exaggeration in this matter, perhaps to make the point more strongly is suggested by Buddhist sources in which the *varṇa* disparities are not so sharp.[30] It may be argued that since Buddhism had less use for *varṇa* status it may have tended to be milder in making *varṇa* discriminations. Most sources are in agreement that the condition of the *dāsa*, even as a domestic slave, is not to be envied. *Dāsa*s are described as being afraid of their masters who took to beating them when angry.[31] References to kindliness and consideration towards slaves tend to be individualized and the Buddha expresses the need for this when he speaks of the duties of the *gahapati*.[32] The ill-treatment of slaves is a generalized description and is virtually taken for granted, in references to the beating, binding and even killing of slaves.[33] The *Dharma-sūtra*s seem to identify the *dāsa*s with the *śūdra*s on the question of disabilities of social groups and the real antagonism should perhaps be seen as between the *dāsa-bhṛtaka* and the *gahapati*, rather than the *brāhmaṇ* and the *śūdra*.

The last of the elements or limbs of the state was the ally (*mitra, suhṛta*) to which the *Arthaśāstra* adds as a corollary, *ari*, the enemy.[34] The need for an external policy involving either the con-

[27] R.S. Sharma, *Śūdras in Ancient India*, p. 122. ff.

[28] *Baudhāyana D.S.* I. 10. 19. 1-2; *Āpastamba D.S.* I. 9.24. 1-4.

[29] *Gautama D.S.* XXII. 14-16; *Āpastamba D.S.* I. 5.16.22; II. 10. 27.9.

[30] *Maj. Nik.* II. 88.

[31] *Maj. Nik.* I. 344; *Dīg. Nik.* I. 141; *Saṁ. Nik.* I. 76;

[32] *Aṅg. Nik.* II. 207-8; *Dīg. Nik.* III. 180-93.

[33] *Mahābhārata*, Śānti Parvan, 254, 38-9.

[34] VI. 1. 13-14

quest of the neighbour or a consciously worked out and carefully nurtured friendship became inevitable when the process of fission as the answer to internal tensions was no longer feasible. The breaking away of the segment of the clan was possible if there was enough land and other resources available in the vicinity. With the increase in numbers of *gaṇa-saṅgha*s and kingdoms this became more difficult since in the case of the latter erstwhile frontier zones would have been claimed, protected and defended. The need to expand access to resources both in terms of fertile land and busy trade routes encouraged the conquest of neighbours. But the conquest of neighbours was through a systematic campaign as that between Magadha and the Vṛjji confederacy, and not through sporadic raids. There is a noticeable decrease in cattle raids, except along frontier areas where such activities were to be continued and permitted as part of a buffer zone strategy.[35] Whereas the lineage system profited by intermittent raids and warfare the state system required a limitation on locations given to warfare — the fields of battles and of campaigns — with a substantial area of stability and peace. This was necessary to prevent the disruption of agriculture and trade. Neighbours were therefore envisaged in a network of either hostile or friendly alliances, sometimes expressed in the theory of *maṇḍala* — a construct of the state within a concentric series of states. Significantly, Kauṭilya includes this in the discussion on the seven elements of the state.[36]

The subjects of the king are referred to less as members of the same *janapada* (*sa-janapada*) and more as *prajā*, a word which originally meant progeny but eventually came to mean subjects and citizens as well. The notion of progeny carried over traces of kinship links but at the same time the paternal authority of the king was stressed. The duties of the king revolved around the protection of the *prajā* but this was seen not merely as protection from external danger; it was also the maintenance of the internal structure eventually symbolized in the expression, 'the upholding of the *varṇāśramadharma*.'

The preservation of internal order had its counterweight in attitudes to revolt and protest. The question of the legitimacy of revolt is discussed in sources of the post-Vedic period. The

[35] Romila Thapar, 'Death and the Hero', in S.C. Humphreys (ed.), *Mortality and Immortality: the Anthropology and Archaeology of Death,* London, 1982.

[36] *Arthaśāstra* VI. 1.

legitimacy of revolt is conceded should a king fail to protect his subjects.[37] However, with the growing association of divinity with the office of kingship the logical development of the alternative view gradually gained strength, that the killing of a king by his subjects was not to be permitted as he is the equivalent of a god.[38] It is further argued that the king's *karma* will take care of his unrighteousness and the subjects should not therefore take the law into in their own hands.[39] The fear of chaos in a situation where the king has been removed is held out as a threat against assassination.

The banishment of a king is alluded to.[40] Assassination is referred to symbolically in the *Mahābhārata*[41] and more realistically in the *Jātaka*s.[42] The actual act of killing is carried out either by *brāhman*s or by gods. In the case of Veṇa it was only the *ṛṣi*s who could kill him and that too with stalks of the sacred *kuśa* grass. At the same time kings are warned against oppression lest their subjects revolt and express their resentment in various ways. The migration of *brāhmaṇ*s brought humiliation but the migration of peasants was much more effective as it reduced the revenue and is therefore feared. Clearly the memory of groups migrating to ease tension was still fresh. Buddhist texts, needless to say, have a more matter of fact assessment of protest and revolt since the contractual basis of their theories on the origin of government provided a certain theoretical freedom for those contemplating the removal of the ruler.

The transition from lineage to state can be seen as a strand running through much of the literature which is included in the category of *itihāsa-purāṇa* and which is referred to as the ancient Indian historical tradition. Compiled by the *sūta* and the *māgadha* (bards and panegyrists) it grew out of the eulogies on heroes victorious in raids and the generous donors of wealth to the bards. Vedic literature has scattered fragments of a historical tradition in which the hero-lauds and narratives of the *nārāśaṃsī*s, *gāthā*s, *dāna-stuti*s and *ākhyāna*s,[43] were preserved partially because they are incor-

[37] *Mahābhārata,* Anuśāsana Parvan, 60. 18.20; Śānti Parvan, 79.42-3

[38] *Nārada* XVIII. 20-2.

[39] Manu VII. 19 ff.

[40] *Mahāsutasoma Jātaka* no. 537; *Khaṇḍahāla Jāt.* no. 542; *Mahābhārata,* Vana Parvan, 1; *Arthaśastra* I. 13; *AV* III. 3-5; *Tait. Sam.* II. 3.1.

[41] *Mahābhārata,* Śānti Parvan, 59. 100 ff; Udyog Parvan, 11.1 ff. 16.1 ff.

[42] *Saccamkira Jāt.* no. 73; *Manicora Jāt.* no. 194; *Padakusalamānava Jāt.* no. 432.

[43] *Vedic Index,* I, pp. 445, 350-1, 224, 52.

porated into the ritual of the *yajña*s. The *ākhyāna*s were the stories and ballads recited on ritual occasions incorporating some element perhaps of actual events, but substantially reflecting the assumptions of that society and the process by which these were established as social custom. Thus the story of Śunaḥśepa[44] is quoted as an *ākhyāna* and has as one of its elements, the adoption of a non-kinsman into the clan of Viśvamitra. These are essentially compositions eulogizing the prowess, valour, generosity of the hero, the chief of the clan. None of them depict the hero as the key person in a state system, nor for that matter is there a reference to what might be the background to a state.

Central to these early sections of the *itihāsa-purāṇa* tradition was the genealogical data. This was crucial in a society where kinship links determined status, land-rights, wealth, marriage relations and the preservation of tribal identity. The genealogies form the core of the tradition. It has been suggested that these as they appear in the *Purāṇa*s were originally recorded in Prākrit and were later rendered into Sanskrit[45] when the *brāhmaṇ* editors of what became the Purāṇic texts took over the tradition from the *sūta*s of earlier times. This would indicate the possible inclusion of both a pre-Vedic tradition (perhaps even going back to Harappan times and doubtless in a somewhat garbled fashion), as well as material conforming to contemporary needs, so that the texts could be used for contemporary purposes as well. A similar process can be suggested for the editing of the epics in their present form from earlier bardic sources. In memorizing the oral tradition various mnemonic devices would be used and legends commonly incorporated. Since the editing of the oral tradition in the form of the Purāṇic texts was done by *brāhmaṇ*s (probably the Bhṛgu *brāhmaṇ*s), the nature and function of the *Purāṇa*s would also have undergone a change. One of the more apparent functions of these texts would be to legitimize the *kṣatriya* status of non-*kṣatriya* families by linking them to the older established lineages,[46] through fabricated connections.

Of the descent lists as given in the Purāṇic texts, the depth is such that they can hardly be regarded as authentic. The artificial lengthening of genealogies is a frequently observed phenomenon by those working on genealogical data. This happens particularly

[44] *Ait. Brāh.* VII. 18.

[45] F.E. Pargiter, ...*Dynasties of the Kali Age*, p. 77 ff.

[46] Romila Thapar, 'Social Mobility in Ancient India with special reference to Elite Groups', in *AISH*, p. 122 ff.

when attempts are made to show a long-established settlement by a clan in an area. The occasional name may be remembered from the past but for the major part it is the pattern of the records which can reveal more than the actual lists.[47] The descent list is sought to be fleshed out occasionally by the inclusion of a myth involving one of the persons in the list. This can again act either as a mnemonic device or as stating certain assumptions about the lineage or can indicate the assimilation of a more recent tradition.

Apart from the Purāṇic texts, the *itihāsa-purāṇa* tradition includes the two epics, the *Mahābhārata* and the *Rāmāyaṇa*. The genealogical and mythical sections are not identical but similar and the epics probably contain the earlier versions of the edited material, before it was finalized into the form of the *Purāṇas*. The transition from non-state to state is indirectly represented in both epics. The earlier sections of both texts depict a society which is closer in spirit to the lineage system described here. The later additions would date to a period when the lineage system had declined and the state had emerged.[48] In so far as these are texts legitimizing a changed situation their analyses have generally been limited to viewing them as bardic literature converted to religious purposes. Yet this was neither accidental nor is it the sole aspect of the texts as sources of legitimation. That Kṛṣṇa and Rāma are *avatāras* of Viṣṇu has its own interest but they also represent other facets of society.

Many of the narrative sections[49] of the *Mahābhārata* represent the period just prior to the emergence of state systems. The structure of the Kuru *janapada* resembles the features which have been discussed here with reference to the western Ganga valley. Political institutions are as much kin-based as social relationships, the major ritual remains the *yajña* in various forms, and a pastoral-cum-agrarian economy is evident, with an emphasis on clan holdings rather than the breaking up of land into private holdings. The succession to the Kuru realm is among the *rājanya* lineages and this is firmly maintained even though neither of the contenders are actually related by blood to the Kuru lineage. The genealogical contortions necessary to establish the links and the recourse to divinity en-

[47] Romila Thapar, 'Genealogy as a Source of Social History,' in *AISH.*, p. 326 ff.

[48] Romila Thapar, 'The Historian and the Epic', *Annals of the Bhandarkar Oriental Research Institute,* 1979, LX, p. 199 ff; *Exile and the Kingdom: some thoughts on the Rāmāyaṇa,* Bangalore, 1978.

[49] As for example, the Sabhā Parvan and the Āranya Parvan.

courages the suspicion that this segment was artificially added onto the lineage which strictly terminates with Bhīsma.[50] Even if this was the case it is important that such lineage links were regarded as essential to the narrative. The activities of the Yādava tribe are even further away from a state system. The Andhaka-Vṛṣṇi were the ruling clan among them and Kṛṣṇa a prominent chief within the group. As the incarnation of Viṣṇu, Kṛṣṇa is outside the struggle for succession, and plays the role of the sympathetic kinsman. Śiśupāla has to be killed because he objects to clan connections determining status. The role of Kṛṣṇa as the charioteer in the battle, apart from its complex symbolism, and the frequency of face-to-face combat among the protagonists, is more suggestive of the earlier system than are the complicated battle formations. Post-Vedic society is clearly depicted in the didactic sections of the text[51] where the existence of the state is taken for granted. This is in itself a subtle endorsement of the state since monarchy is described as the ideal system and is axiomatic to the major didactic tracts such as the *rāja-dharma* and *mokṣa-dharma* sections. A characteristic of lineage society which is noticeable in the *Mahābhārata* is the resort to migration to ease tension and conflict, particularly in relation to political power. Thus the Pāṇḍavas build a new capital at Indraprastha and a segment of the Andhaka-Vṛṣṇis migrates from Mathurā to Dvārkā. In a sense the frequency of exile is also partially associated with fission since the need for exile arises out of crises concerning legitimacy and power both in the *Mahābhārata* and the *Rāmāyaṇa*.

In terms of the confrontation between non-state and state systems, the *Rāmāyaṇa* encapsulates the conflict more clearly and is essentially a statement in favour of the monarchical state.[52] Viṣṇu is reborn as the heir-apparent and ultimately becomes the initiator of the epitome of the monarchical state in the concept of *rāma-rājya*. Rāma's greatest virtue is that he upholds the duties of the king. Kośala is the ideal monarchical state and the descriptions are such that they could only have been based on Kośala in the post-Vedic period. The houses of the citizens of Ayodhyā are well-stocked with rice.[53] Families are said to be wealthy in cattle, horses

[50] Romila Thapar, 'The Historian and the Epic', *ABORI* 1979, x, p. 199 ff.

[51] As for example, the Śānti Parvan.

[52] Romila Thapar, *Exile and the Kingdom : some thoughts on the Rāmāyaṇa.*

[53] I. 5.17. It is stated that the rice was the excellent *śāli* quality.

and grain.[54] Rāma questioning Bharata on his governing of Kośala reiterates some of the requirements of the *saptānga* theory.[55] The descriptions of the city of Ayodhyā in the *Bāla-kāṇḍa* seem to refer to the city after the mid-first millennium B.C.[56] There is a concentration of power in the king, an administrative hierarchy, a clearly defined territory with some notion of boundaries, a capital in which the main action of the earlier section of the epic takes place, a treasury, a regularly constituted army and a range of allies and foes. Kośala and Videha are treated sympathetically by the author and represent a society conforming to the mores of a transition to monarchical culture.

The contrast between state and non-state is most effectively shown in the deliniation of the *rākṣasa*s. They are not bound to any territory, roam where they will and are present in virtually every area mentioned in the story. Rāvaṇa is more a chief than a king and is constantly advised by his kinsmen. There is no administrative hierarchy in Laṅkā and again the decisions are taken largely by the kinsmen of the chief. Laṅkā is the capital and although it is described as encrusted with gold and gems and boasting of considerable wealth none of these come through any system of taxation or revenue. The army of Rāvaṇa consists more of terrifying figures than of a well-trained professional force and his friends and foes are individuals whose relationship with Rāvaṇa is determined largely by goodwill and marriage alliances. Whereas Ayodhyā is described as replete with rice there is little mention of grain in Laṅkā.[57] Kośala is dotted with gardens and fields, only gardens are mentioned in the description of Laṅkā. The contrast between the two societies is highlighted by the confrontation. Whatever the original kernal of the epic events may have been, by the time it was rewritten as a *kāvya*, the differences between the state and the non-state were implicit in the rewriting.

The *Rāmāyaṇa* therefore became among other things an epic legitimizing the monarchical state. This is in part indicated by the many versions and adaptations of the *Rāmāyaṇa* in various languages in the Indian sub-continent and in south-east Asia. The adaptation frequently coincides with the establishment of monarchies based on indigenous power. The variants on the original text often relate to the particulars of the local situation in terms of kin-

[54] I. 6.7. [55] II. 94. [56] I. 5, 6 and 7.
[57] D.R. Chanana, *The Spread of Agriculture in Northern India*, New Delhi, 1963.

ship, economy and religion, all of which tend to strengthen the idea that the text as such validated the monarchical state. Whereas in the *Rāmāyaṇa* the difference is projected in the depiction of two entirely different societies, in the *Mahābhārata* the change is interpolated into the same society but is evident in the difference between the narrative and didactic sections. In the *Rāmāyaṇa* the epic hero becomes the archetypal figure representing the past and changes which may have occurred gradually over time are consolidated and attributed to him.

The transition from one sytem to another is demonstrated, apart from the epics, in some of the Purāṇic texts as becomes evident from a careful analysis of the *vaṃśānucarita* (genealogical) tradition contained in the major *Purāṇa*s. The *Viṣṇu Purāṇa* is often described as the exemplar among these texts since it is characterized by the five standard components (*pañca-lakṣana*) of the genre. These are described as *sarga,* the evolution of the universe from a first cause, *pratisarga,* the recreation of the universe at the end of each *kalpa* or cycle of time, *vaṃśa,* the genealogies of gods and *ṛṣi*s, *mānavāntara,* the cycles of aeons in which mankind is created afresh from the ancestral Manu, and *vaṃśānucarita,* the descent lists of those who are said to have ruled from earliest times. The structure is that of a book of genesis describing in an orderly fashion the view on the past. The genealogical section setting out the genealogical history of early times is contained in Book IV. An attempt is made to construct the past in terms of the history of lineages. The question of whether or not the reconstruction is historically authentic is not central to our argument. In the past genealogical lists have been used for calculating chronology on the basis of collating the diverse lists and attempting to assign a regnal period to each generation.[58] This is almost an exercise in futility. Such genealogies are notorious for not being exact since chronological exactitude is not their function. It would seem more purposeful to derive a different type of information from this data which would be more enlightening on lineage forms, geographical distribution and to some extent political perspective. What is important is to analyse why the information was put together in this particular way. The *Purāṇa* was probably composed sometime in

[58] S.N. Pradhan, *Chronology of Ancient India,* Calcutta, 1927; R. Morton Smith, *Dates and Dynasties in Earliest India,* Delhi, 1975. For an analytical study of this question see D.P. Henige, *The Chronology of Oral Tradition,* Oxford, 1974.

the Gupta period since the 'prophecies' regarding the dynasties ruling in Jambudvīpa terminate at this point. This was a period of considerable historical change in northern India and as such the *Purāṇa* represents a looking back on the past to construct an image of the past, of providing the past with a framework and at the same time preparing for the past to be used as a legal charter for contemporary and successor political systems. The *vaṃśānucarita* section therefore becomes a book of origins to be used by those seeking political legitimacy.

The authorship of the *itihāsa-purāṇa* tradition as collated in the *Purāṇa*s has some bearing on its function. It is said to have been compiled and edited by Vyāsa,[59] thus in a sense giving it the status of the Vedic texts and the *Mahābhārata*. It is in fact sometimes referred to as the fifth *Veda*. There was however a crucial difference in that the *itihāsa-purāṇa* tradition was taught by Vyāsa to his fifth disciple, the *sūta* (bard) Lomaharṣana who was of course not a *brāhmaṇ*. The latter divided the tradition into six parts each of which he taught to his six disciples who were all *brāhmaṇ*s. In addition, Lomaharṣana also taught the tradition to his son, Ugraśravasa who, being a bard, recited it for a living. Clearly there is an ambivalence on whether the tradition should be ascribed to *brāhmaṇ* authorship or to the bards and chroniclers. It is also suggestive of a shift in the maintenance of the tradition from bards to *brāhmaṇ*s. Most existing *Purāṇa*s claim the stereotype origin common to many *itihāsa* texts that they were revealed by a god to a *ṛṣi* who then recited the text at a sacrifice. Status is conferred on the tradition by linking it to a ritual event, and *brāhmaṇ* connections doubtless grew when the tradition was required for legitimation. The shift in status would also be indicated by the suggestion that the tradition was originally oral and probably composed in Prākrit but was converted to Sanskrit when it came to be maintained by the *brāhmaṇ*s and was recorded in writing.

As an oral tradition it would have been kept initially by the *sūta* and the *māgadha*. *The sūta* as a professional person was of high status and close to the chief. In later Vedic literature the *sūta* is one of the eight *vīras* (heroes) and one of the eleven or twelve *ratnin*s (jewels) and therefore associated with the *rājā* on ritual occasions.[60] In order of precedence the *sūta* follows the *mahiṣi* (chief queen) and precedes the *grāmaṇī*. He is described as being *ahantya* (inviolable)

[59] Pargiter, *Ancient Indian Historical Tradition,* p. 21 ff.

[60] Ibid., p. 16 ff

which may indicate that he was also the emissary. The origin of the *sūta* and the *māgadha* is linked to the consecration of Pṛthu when the two emerged out of the sacrificial fire and immediately began reciting the lineage of Pṛthu and a eulogy on his activities (*praśasti*). Pṛthu thereupon appointed them hereditary chroniclers to the eastern lands including Magadha. The link with Magadha and Aṅga is again curious and reflects either a late origin for the story or an association with the people of the middle Ganga valley, an association which would indicate a low status since these were *mleccha* lands. The hint of low status is suggested by the connection between the *māgadha* and the *vrātya* made in the *Atharvaveda*.[61] To this may be added the strange etymology of the word *sūta*. If it derives from the root **su* as is generally believed, then it can mean, 'to impel' or 'to give birth to'. That this refers to the sacrifice and the emergence of the *sūta* is to stretch the etymology; similarly to explain it on the basis that the *sūta* gave birth, metaphorically, to genealogies and lineage records is far-fetched. It might be more appropriate to consider the possibility of deriving it as a Prākrit form from either *sūtra* or *śruti*: the former meaning a thread would symbolize descent as a thread running through lineage and the latter referring to that which is heard or the oral tradition. If either of these derivations are feasible they would support the idea of the original record being in Prākrit. The meaning of *sūta* as a charioteer, would indicate a function which placed him close to the chief and consequently to the activities of ruling families.

The value of the *Purāṇa*s as historical records is circumscribed by their having been rewritten or edited at a period subsequent to that of the events described and that the rewriting was done not by the earlier custodians of the tradition but by *brāhmaṇ*s whose perspective would be very different from that of the *sūta*. Nevertheless their value lies in the fact that they did become the texts of a certain perception of the past in which a particular world view is articulated. As such they are important documents to the historiography of the tradition. Further, the perception of the past was linked to contemporary needs and the *vaṃśānucarita* section recording descent lists of lineages came to be regarded as especially significant.

[61] xv. 2. 1-4.

The structure of this section has its own interest. We are told that originally the world was ruled by a succession of Manus[62] and during the period of the seventh Manu there was a devastating flood created by the gods to punish man. This is described in some detail in the *Matsya Purāṇa*[63] since it is Viṣṇu in his *matsya-avatāra* (fish incarnation) who saves Manu and the seven *ṛṣi*s, by advising Manu to seek refuge in a boat which he ties to his horn and swimming through the deluge lodges it safely on a mountain until the flood subsides. Manu returns home and performs sacrifices to obtain sons and continue the lineage. His many sons become the founding fathers of various lineages. The eldest Ikṣvāku, founds the Sūryavaṃśa or Solar lineage and it is this lineage which is eulogized in the *Rāmāyaṇa*. Manu's youngest child, occasionally described as a hermaphrodite or else as one who takes a male and female form alternately, becomes in its female form, Ilā, the ancestress of the Candravaṃśa or Lunar lineage whose members are the protagonists of the events described in the *Mahābhārata*. A substantial part of the *vaṃśānucarita* section lists the descendants of the various lineages covering geographically the whole of northern India. All the surviving lineages participate in the Mahābhārata war, after which the text takes on the future tense, speaking as if prophecying the events to come.[64] Mention is now made of dynasties and there is a concentration on the dynasty at Magadha which is clearly regarded as the most important and continues to be until well into historical times when other dynasties are also mentioned. Whereas for the earlier period the descent lists merely gave the succession of *rājā*s there is now a significant change in that the regnal years, no matter how exaggerated in some cases, are given for each ruler and the total length of reign of a dynasty is also mentioned. There is clearly a historical change which is sought to be recorded.

That genealogies were maintained is evident from the statement of Megasthenes[65] that there was a count of one hundred and fifty-three/four kings prior to the coming of Alexander to India, and their reigns covered a period of six thousand four hundred and fifty-one years. As with most genealogical records the process of 'telescoping' events and generations must certainly have resulted in some confusion and deviation from an authentic record of events. Telescoping is in effect the pruning of the list in order to make its

[62] *Viṣṇu Purāṇa* III. 1.
[63] *Matsya Purāṇa* I. 10-33; II. 1-9.
[64] *Viṣṇu Purāna* IV. 21; F.E. Pargiter, *Dynasties of the Kali Age*, p. 14.
[65] Frag. L.C., Pliny, *Historia Naturalis*, VI. 21.4-5; Solin 52.5

preservation more manageable. Nevertheless the structure of the genealogy has its own importance.

The reference to the earliest Manus is the most vague and would suggest a period of remote antiquity or even mythical kings. The Flood acts as the first time-marker since floods symbolize the washing away of what went before and a new beginning with the receding of the flood and 'the abolition of profane time'.[66] The break is not complete since the lineages of the second period are the progeny of the Manu who survived the flood, via their eponymous ancestors. These lineage lists are said to be the *kṣatriya*s in power at the time. The form which they take are suggestive of their being the clans or the chiefships of the period prior to the emergence of the state. In some cases the names in the descent lists are identical with the names of the *jana*s or tribes as given in other sources which develop into territorial names, such as the five sons of Bali—Aṅga, Vaṅga, Kaliṅga, Puṇḍra and Śuhma. In other cases they are individual names of chiefs. The genealogies from the *Purāṇa*s do not necessarily always tally with those from the epics or from Vedic literature. Genealogical depth in Vedic literature tends to be shallow in comparison with the epics and even more so when compared to the Purāṇic lists. But some of the names do get repeated in the later sources although their place in the descent may differ.[67] Nor should the number of generations listed in the *Purāṇas* be taken too literally since lists can be conflated merely to emphasize a longer period of time. It is a moot point whether synchronization of the texts was really important to the compilers. Had it been so then an effort would have been made to rewrite these sections in conformity with the data in the epics or vice versa. Considering that the original compilers, the *sūta*s and the *māgadha*s, as well as the later editors, were the same for each category of text, such a synchronism would not have been difficult. It might be more apposite to view these descent lists as indicators of social forms rather than as factual records.

The two major lineages are constructed on two differing principles. The senior lineage descended from the eldest son of Manu, Ikṣvāku, records only the senior line of descent in each generation, among the descendants of Iksvāku. The Kośala lineage is regarded

[66] M. Eliade, *Cosmos and History*, New York, 1959, p. 5ff.

[67] F.E. Pargiter, *The Ancient Indian Historical Tradition*. Pargiter has attempted some comparative study both between the *Purāṇa*s and with the epics in an effort to establish synchronisms, but the variants are too many.

as the most important and is given in the greatest detail. The emphasis is on primogeniture, an issue which is of the utmost importance to the narrative of the *Rāmāyaṇa* as well. The descendants of the youngest child of Manu, the Ailas, are recorded as a series of segmenting lineages. The seniormost lineage, that of the Yādavas, is exiled to western India; *madhya deśa* (essentially the Ganga-Yamuna *doāb* and its fringes) is inherited by the juniormost, that of Puru, the disruption of primogeniture being explained by the famous story of Yayāti postponing his old age.[68] The descendants of the intermediate sons of Yayāti are listed up to a point but soon these lists peter out and ultimately the Candravaṃśa is the record of the Pūru and Yādava lineages.[69] The segments are obviously not all related by blood and the record includes those who were assimilated into the lineage through conquest and through marriage alliances. The lineage lists are therefore also documents recording migrations, the assimilation of other groups and alliances. The emphasis is on legitimacy through claiming lineage links and hereditary sucession is not crucial, as is demonstrated in the links sought to be made between the Puru lineage and the Kauravas and the Pāṇḍavas. The importance of lineage links was both to claim *kṣatriya* status as well as to assert rights over territory and land. In the more settled agricultural society of the middle Ganga valley inheritance would have been an important issue from an early period with clearly defined rules for succession; but in the less hospitable areas of western and central India with large groups of pastoral-cum-agricultural peoples, rights to succession would still have been aspired to and fought over by the senior lineages.

The Mahābhārata war can be seen as the second time-marker in the structure of the *vamśānucarita* section. Virtually all the major *kṣatriya*s of the Candravaṃśa and many others gather together to take part in the war. What might have been an inter-tribal conflict

[68] *Viṣṇu Purāṇa* IV. 10.

[69] The lineage is essentially concerned with the Pūrus and their descendents in the watershed area and the upper Doāb and with the Yādavas in western India. I have made an attempt to discuss the possible archaeological identity of these two descent groups by comparing their settlements with those of the Painted Grey Ware and the Black-and-red Ware, but the identification remains very tentative and uncertain. 'Purānic Lineages and Archaeological Cultures', in *AISH,* p. 240 ff. Curiously the two regions which became the geographical focus of these two groups were the areas where the Late Harappan developed and overlapped with post-Harappan cultures. This makes it feasible to argue that some of the material included in the tradition may go back to Harappan times.

over succession takes on the dimensions of the end of an epoch. This is precisely what it is; the end of the epoch of *kṣatriya* chiefships and in a sense the war clears away this system as the dominant political system and makes way for the monarchical state of the middle Ganga valley. That the latter clings to some aspects of the earlier system is evident from the insistence that ideally kings should be of the *kṣatriya varṇa*; however, in fact many were not and some sought a *kṣatriya* status through a fabricated genealogy. Significantly, the location of the battle is associated with the pre-eminent among the *kṣatriya*s—the land of the Kurus. It is also significant that the battle occurs in the western Ganga valley and not in the middle Ganga valley since the latter area was to witness an easier transition to state formation. The intrinsic sorrow of the battle at Kurukṣetra is not merely at the death of kinsmen but also at the dying of a society, a style, a political form. The concept of the present as Kali-yuga combines a romanticization of the earlier society with the sense of insecurity born of a changing system and every fresh change of a major kind leads to the reiteration of the fears of the Kali-yuga.

The transition to a monarchical state in Kośala is reflected not only in the form in which the lineage is recorded in the *Purāṇa*s but also and more so in the *Rāmāyaṇa* itself. The same transition in Magadha remains without an epic to eulogize it. This may in part be due to the inclination of the rulers of Magadha towards the heterodox sects, where, in the chronicles of early Buddhism, the epic as it were, of the rulers of Magadha is to be found in the *Dīpavamsa* and the *Mahāvamsa*, chronicles of the early history of Sri Lanka. It may also be because the central core of the *vaṃśānucarita* tradition becomes in fact the dynastic history of Magadha.[70] In any case the eulogy of the emergent state required a form different from the epic.

After the rise of Bṛhadratha the rulers of Magadha are listed together with their regnal years and the focus is on the succession in this region.[71] This is particularly stressed since the form of this record is prophetic and the intention is clearly to suggest that Magadha was the most important state to emerge after the *Mahābhārata* war. With the establishment of the monarchical state, these alone are considered worthy of record, even when the dynasties are not of *ksatriya* origin and are as low as *śūdra* as in the case of the

[70] *Visnu Purāna* IV. 23.

[71] Ibid., IV. 23-4.

Nandas.[72] References to chiefships are excluded in these lists, the *gaṇa-saṅgha*s of the middle Ganga valley being either ignored or referred to obliquely by the inclusion of some names in a descent list. Thus Śākya is a name in the Ikṣvāku genealogy, whose son is Śuddhodhana and his son Rāhula is the father of a Praśenajīt — a good example of telescoping![73] The exclusion of the *gaṇa-saṅgha*s of this period is in contrast to their being mentioned where they existed in northern and western India in the period prior to the war, and serves to emphasize the significance of the monarchical state in the eyes of the compilers of the *Purāṇas*.

The *vaṃśānucarita* section was not merely an attempt to record the past, it was also the clearing house of the genealogical material for contemporary political use. In the continual process of state formation which was accelerated with the establishment of new settlements serving both to extend agriculture and subsequently often also to encourage trade, new rulers had to be legitimized and this was frequently done by providing lineage links with earlier lineages recorded in the Purāṇic tradition. In the transition from *jana* to *jāti,* families of chiefs would often claim *kṣatriya* status. This was not only an expression of sanskritization and acculturation but was also an effective means of demarcating those families which could claim rights over land (the equivalent of the earlier *rāja-kula*s) and those who gradually subsided into the lesser categories of the *vaiśya* and *śūdra varṇa*s. That succession lists are crucial to all those claiming status and property is evident not only from these lineages but also from the succession lists of teachers maintained by the Buddhist monasteries which could on occasion be substantial property holders.[74].

The Purāṇic evidence suggests, if looked at analytically, that prior to the rise of the dynasties, the recording of *kṣatriya* descent groups was important since power resided in the lineages. The system came to an end in the western Ganga valley and this termination was represented in the description of the Kurukṣetra war. The emergence of dynasties which was a major change in the socio-political form, took place in the middle Ganga valley and doubtless posed a threat to the lineage system. Thus Jarāsandha is the natural enemy of the Vṛṣṇis since he portends the birth of the new state and they represent the continuance of the *gaṇa-saṅgha* system.

[72] Ibid., IV. 24.

[73] Ibid., IV. 22.

[74] This is demonstrated in R.A.L.H. Gunawardana, *The Robe and Plough*, (Arizona, 1979), describing the process for the monasteries of Sri Lanka.

If the above analysis is acceptable then it suggests that the *itihāsa-purāṇa* tradition in some of its facets does make an attempt to represent a semblance of the past, if not as authentic history then at least as an authentic pattern of changing social relations. The same tradition is picked up by Buddhist authors and more fully developed in a Buddhist context. This in itself makes a worthwhile point of contrast.

The seeds of the Buddhist historical tradition may be located in the *itihāsa-samvāda,* the dialogues incorporating stories reminiscent of the dialogue hymns of Vedic literature but formulated in a recognizably Buddhist context and included in the *Sutta Piṭaka*[75]. Some of the *sutta*s are similar to the *ākhyāna*s but are used to illustrate Buddhist doctrine and often focus on an event connected with a well-known person. There is also reference to the legend of the life of the Buddha and his more important disciples. In the early texts the distinction between the biography of the Buddha and the history of the religion tends to merge. The *Sutta Nipāta* contains elements of the biography of the Buddha[76] and the *Jātaka* stories soak up a floating tradition, some of which is found in the *Rāmāyaṇa* and the *Mahābhārata* as well. The *Jātaka* stories echo the revised versions of the epics where frequently stories illustrate a moral, except that the *Jātaka* stories do so more invariably. The opening of the story carries a distinct historical flavour in that it often refers to a place, a period of time and a person. Those with an *itihāsa-purāṇa* connection are usually associated with the *Rāma-kathā* and the *Bharata-kathā* or else with themes from the epics such as the exile theme used so effectively in the *Vessantara Jātaka*.

Links with the *itihāsa-purāṇa* tradition are more evident in the two chronicles the *Dīpavamsa* and the *Mahāvamsa*, in the sections dealing with the history of Sri Lanka prior to the coming of Buddhism. There are lengthy lineage lists of Indian ancestors extending over many centuries and covering practically all the then known geographical regions. Vijaya and his entourage are the first humans to settle on the island and although their ancestry is from eastern India they sail from a port in western India.[77] Since Vijaya has no son his brother's son, Pāṇḍuvāsudeva is sent for. The name is almost archetypal and obviously suggests a

[75] M. Winternitz, *History of Indian Literature,* vol. II Calcutta, 1933, p. 34.
[76] Nalaka sutta III. 11; Pabbajja sutta III. 1; Padhana sutta III. 2.
[77] *Mahāvamsa* VI.

Pāṇḍava-Kṛṣṇa connection, perhaps an attempt to find links with the pre-eminent clans of the Yādavas. The link is further underlined by the story of Pāṇḍukabhaya the grandson of Pāṇḍuvāsudeva whose early life resembles that of Vāsudeva Kṛṣṇa to such a degree that it could not have been coincidental. The child is hidden at birth and brought up by relatives. There is also a conflict with the maternal uncle whom he destroys. It may be argued along the lines of Otto Rank that this story carries the stereotype myth of the birth of the hero[78] but the incidents are too similar for the similarity to have been accidental. Evidently the story was not only popular but carried some status. The frequency with which the Yādava lineage crops up along the west coast and in the peninsula would suggest that in the proximity of Sri Lanka it was the most respected lineage.[79] As if the Yādava status was not sufficient the wife of Pāṇḍuvāsudeva was said to have been a Śākya princess. Thus the ancestry of the earliest rulers of the island is traced back to or associated with the highest antecedents — the Śākya family to appease Buddhist sentiment and the Yādavas as part of the Candravaṃśa lineage of the *itihāsa-purāṇa* tradition.

The Buddhist Pāli canon was put together some centuries after the events which it records. The two main themes of Buddhist historiography can both be traced to these texts : the life of the Buddha and other important members of the *saṅgha* which was to become the nucleus of the *carita* or biographical tradition and the need to record the history of the *saṅgha* together with the sectarian conflicts and differentiations which emerged in time. The *Vinaya Piṭaka*, among other things, describes the formation of the Buddhist community and attempts a chronological narrative of these events. Commentaries on this text discussed the various sectarian differences. Another text, the *Kathāvatthu* of the *Abhidhamma Piṭaka* claimed by the Theravāda sect as a history of the *saṅgha* is not acceptable to some other sects, a difference of opinion which is of considerable historical significance. The historical material was built into the Canon almost accidentally through the sheer necessity of maintaining a record of the controversies and disputations.

The concern with historicity (whether factual or not) is a striking feature of the Buddhist historical tradition. The need to maintain a

[78] O. Rank, *The Myth of the Birth of the Hero,* New York, 1959.

[79] Romila Thapar, 'Purānic Lineages and Archaeological Cultures', in *AISH*, p. 240.

record of sectarian changes was doubtless due to control over property through monastic establishments and donations to the *sangha*. Close association with royal patronage made these records more imperative. Added to this was the fact that from the third century B.C., after the Council at Pāṭaliputra, the proselytizing mission of Buddhism was actively propagated with a number of missions being sent to various parts of the subcontinent and beyond. A record of these had to be maintained, particularly when in later periods the increasing sectarian rivalries sought sanction from the past. That the tradition took a systematic form may have originated in its hinging around a precise point in time and space, the historic person of the Buddha. This was also to provide the chronological starting point in the date of the Buddha's *parinirvāna,* a date which even though under dispute is nevertheless the commencing date in Buddhist history. At a wider level there were other factors which encouraged a more historical perception: the monks maintained a literate tradition in which the maintenance of records was a normal activity and the initial establishment and expansion of Buddhism was related to an urban context and was closely associated with the founding of the major state of Magadha.

The history of Magadha is narrated in some detail in the Buddhist Chronicles particularly the *Dīpavaṃsa* and the *Mahāvaṃsa.* This was both because it was the most powerful state and its kings were therefore the most prestigious, and because it was the crucible of the Theravāda/Sthaviravāda sect and therefore its history became a part of the sacred history of this sect. Linked to this was the fact that the first missionary to Sri Lanka, Mahinda, the son of Aśoka Maurya, was sent on his mission after the Council at Pāṭaliputra. It is possible that the events as narrated are correct but it is also plausible that the link with the Mauryas was an afterthought to enhance the prestige of the Theravāda sect. These histories were essentially accounts of the evolution of certain doctrines and the growth of particular monasteries, in well-defined kingdoms. The *Dīpavaṃsa* is the history of Buddhism in the island and the *Mahāvaṃsa*, the history of the major monastery, the Mahāvihāra. Interest lies in the manner in which the narrative brings into play the political authority at the time with the sacred history. These are not necessarily contemporary records and are frequently reflections on potential connections in a period after the arrival of Buddhism. Thus the *Dīpavamsa* and the *Mahāvaṃsa* were compiled in their present form in the mid-first millennium A.D. which allowed the idea of seeking to link the *saṅgha* with the state to mature.

The *Dīpavaṃsa*, the more archaic of the two texts demonstrates many of these facets of Buddhist historiography. It drew on various oral traditions[80] and among these were the *Sīhalaṭṭhakathāmahāvaṃsa* and the *Porāṇā*. The Buddha not only visits Sri Lanka but also predicts the coming of Buddhism to the island, thus sanctifying the history of Buddhism in that area.[81] Another section, the *rāja vaṃsa,* traces the descent of *rājā*s and *khattiya*s from Mahāsammata which is here taken as the name of the first ruler. This extensive descent list borrows names from both the Ikṣvāku and Aila lineages, but is substantially a different list.[82] (Elsewhere, the Buddha's family is said to be of the Ikṣvāku *vaṃsa*.) The list continues down to Rāhula the son of Siddhartha. The last few verses mention the kings Bimbisāra and Ajātsatru as contemporaries of the Buddha.[83] The two councils at Rājagṛha and Vaiśāli are described and the seccessionist sects resulting from these are listed. This is followed by a succession list of the Theras of the *saṅgha,* the chronology of which is related to the succession of ruling monarchs at Magadha, a useful method of associating chronological information with reigning kings.[84] Since the age and years of ordination of the Theras is given[85] the cross-reference to kings seems unnecessary and suggests a conscious attempt at bringing in a political focus. Aśoka Maurya's biography though brief is embellished with details since he was the father of Mahinda.[86] Events leading up to the calling of the Third Council at Pāṭaliputra after the dissident monks have been expelled are narrated and this is attributed to the initiative of Aśoka.[87] It is of great importance since the pre-eminence of the Theravāda sect (dominant in Sri Lanka) was established at this council. The subsequent chapter deals with the various missions which were sent out as a result of this council, including Mahinda's mission to Sri Lanka.[88] The identity of the mission having been invested with the highest religious

[80] F. Perera, *The Early Buddhist Historiography of Ceylon,* unpublished Ph.D. thesis, Gottingen, 1976.

[81] *Dīp.* I and II. [82] *Dīp.* III. [83] III. 55-59.

[84] IV. 55-7. [85] IV. 83-96. [86] VI. 1 ff.

[87] *Dīp.* VII. This is made even more explicit in the *Samantapasādikā* 47-62, and the *Vaṃsatthapakāsinī*. G.P. Malalasekara, *Vaṃsatthapakāsinī*, London 1935.

[88] *Dīp.* VIII.

and political credentials, there follows then the history of Buddhism in the island. The narrative has occasional flashes of similarity with the Purāṇic tradition as for example in some of the echoes of stories associated with the Yādava lineage[89] and the chronological co-relation of events in Sri Lanka with the rulers of Magadha continues, though briefly. The final few references are incidental, embedded in what is essentially the history of Sri Lanka in the latter half of the text.[90]

The transition from the lineage system to the state is reflected in the narrative of these Chronicles as well as in other Buddhist sources on which the narrative draws.[91] The Śākyas for example bear all the marks of a lineage society. Their ancestry goes back to the Ikṣvāku line or Okkāka as it is called in Pāli sources. They originate in the exile of the four sons and five daughters of Okkāka who settle in the Himalayan foothills near the hermitage of Kapila where they build their city of Kapilavastu. Four brothers marry four sisters and become the progenitors of the Śākyas by giving birth to sixteen pairs of twins. The origin myth of the Kolya clan links them to the Śākyas stating that the Kolyas married the Śākya women who were their maternal uncles' daughters. The new group in each case migrates away from the old and establishes its own *janapada* with its capital. The name of the clan provokes the etymological imagination as in deriving Śākya from *śaknoti* (to be able) or the *śaka* tree. The insistence on sibling twins as the procreators of the *jana* has to do with maintaining the purity of the lineage and tracing lineage origins back to those of identical blood. There is also a deliberate attempt to associate cross-cousin marriage with elite groups which also emphasizes kinship links among the *gaṇa-saṅgha* clans of the middle Ganga valley. The bearing of sixteen pairs of twins seems indicative of the *rāja-kula*, a symbolic diffusion of power into a small but effective social group. The *kṣatriya* status of the clan is evident from the Ikṣvāku connection which was high even by Purāṇic standards. Curiously the Purāṇic sources are either silent about these clans or cursorily mention a few names. Clearly Purāṇic authors did not approve of them, probably because they maintained a non-monarchic system.

Many of these elements are carried over in the *Mahāvaṃsa* as

89 *Dīp.* X, XI. 1-4.

90 *Dīp.* XI. 8-40; XII. 1-8, 50 ff; XV. 6-7, 83-94; XVI. 1-23; XVII. 81-6.

91 Romila Thapar, 'Origin Myths and the Early Indian Historical Tradition', in *AISH*, p. 309 ff.

noticed earlier in the descriptions of the origins of Vijaya who first colonizes Sri Lanka.[92] The transition to the state system is again associated with the region of Magadha, and by the time of the Mauryas when the major events take place in relation to the arrival of Buddhism in Sri Lanka, the state is well-established in Magadha. At an underlying level the linkage is also sought through maintaining that the Maurya clan was an off-shoot of the Śākyas. However with the introduction of the Mauryas the vestiges of lineage society tend to be shed and the *saṅgha* has to face the emergent state.

The Buddhist endorsement of the state was in some ways a contradiction. The organization of the *saṅgha* borrowed its form from the *gaṇa-saṅgha* system and led the *saṅgha* to see itself as a contrast to monarchy and insisted on a separate identity. Perhaps its success in setting up a parallel system drew it towards the idea of further strengthening its position by accepting royal patronage and ultimately moving towards a close association with political authority. Thus in some areas it becomes the source of legitimizing the state, as is evident from the history of Buddhism in Sri Lanka. Association with political authority also had the advantage of the *saṅgha* reflecting in the 'glory' of 'great kings' as the association of Aśoka with the despatch of Buddhist missions would suggest.[93] Such an association is also important in ousting dissidents and here the *saṅgha* borrows the wielder of the *daṇḍa* to perform this role. The expulsion of dissidents is sought to be justified in terms of keeping the *saṅgha* pure, but it is in effect the underlining of authority. The first council is appropriately held at Rājagṛha, the capital of a powerful kingdom with its king, Ajātaśatru extending his patronage. The breakaway group of the Vajjiputtaka monks was established at the Council at Vaiśāli, the capital of the Vṛjjis. These monks were regarded as dissidents,[94] a curious parallel to the political relationship between Magadha and the Vṛjjis. The Theravāda sect which claims to represent the original teaching of the Buddha is associated with the Mauryan state through the statement that Aśoka was instrumental in calling the Council at Pāṭaliputra, (Even the later Sarvāstivāda sect associated with the northern school of Buddhism links itself with the Kuṣāṇa state through the tradition of the Council held at Kashmir to establish its status.) The

[92] *Mahāvaṃsa* VI.

[93] E. Frauwallner, *The Earliest Vinaya and the Beginnings of Buddhist Literature*, Rome, 1956.

[94] *Mahāvaṃsa* IV. 9 ff; *Cullavagga*, VII. 4.1 ff; XII. 1.1. ff.

association of Aśoka with the Buddhist *sangha* as described in the Ceylon Chronicles can be seen as the *saṅgha* conceding that Aśoka had authority over its activities. Aśoka at the same time claimed the right to adjudicate in the ecclesiastical matters of the *saṅgha*. This is clearly stated in the famous Schism Edict inscribed at various centres of Buddhist importance such as the monasteries at Kauśāmbi, Sārnāth and Sanchi in which he calls for dissident monks and nuns to be expelled from the monastic centres.[95] Such a concession to political authority by the *sangha* was the logical culmination of its connection with political power. The need to hold councils was also a pointer to the entry of secular power into the calculations of the *saṅgha* since controls of various kinds had now to be adjusted and balanced. That the role of Aśoka was viewed differently in the later and northern Buddhist tradition which did not share the historiography of the Theravāda sect, is apparent from the *Aśokāvadāna*.[96] Here the ruler is depicted largely as an enthusiastic royal patron of Buddhism who expresses his enthusiasm through magnanimous donations, some of which are on such a scale as would embarrass any government. He is also shown as suffering in the end for his support of the *saṅgha* since he is deprived by his ministers and successors of the power to give this support. The intention of the *Aśokāvadāna* may well have been moralistic, that even rulers have their time of troubles or that donations are not conditioned by the wealth of the donor and that the truly generous man gives even if he has only half a mango to give; but perhaps the moral is more subtle and relates to the problems of religious sects becoming enmeshed in politics.

The Buddhist *saṅgha* supporting the state system was useful to early states in that it provided an ideological framework for the integration of diverse groups. The network of monasteries could become either a series of supporting institutions backing the state, or alternatively, there was equal danger of their becoming a network of opposition. Initially monasteries were established in the vicinity of towns and large villages since the monks were dependant for alms on the lay community. Later when endowments of land were made to the monasteries then these institutions would act as centres of agrarian activity in areas newly opened up by the state. It was probably at this stage that the link with political authority

[95] Bloch, *Les Inscriptions d'Asoka*, p. 152 ff.
[96] J. Przyluski, *La Legende de l'Empereur Açoka*, Paris. 1923.

became a factor of consequence to the Buddhist tradition. At a wider level the universalistic ethics of Buddhism would appeal to a variety of social groups cutting across lineage and caste ties. This was more evident in the membership of the *saṅgha*. Concessions to political authority were however made, as for instance in the rule that slaves and debtors were not to be recruited as monks,[97] since many of them would have treated the monastery as a refuge from the inequities of society. At the ideological level the Buddhist concern with a transient universe justifies the propagation of change. The doctrines of *karma* and *saṃsāra* (actions and transmigration) as doctrines of retribution in which the cycle of rebirth accounts for social injustices had their use in weakening protest.[98]

With the break-up of the lineage society new alignments were sought. For the monk the *sangha* provided a changed set of relations and a different identity. The initial schism of the Mahāsaṅghikas came from the Vajjiputtakas, those monks who had been associated with the Vṛjji *gaṇa-sangha*, and therefore different from the system prevalent in Rājagṛha or Śrāvasti. Doubtless some older ties of kinship and political associations persisted in the sects of the *saṅgha* which took on the character of local factions. Interestingly the central problem at the Council of Vaiśāli was whether or not the monks were to be permitted to accept monetary donations as alms on which there was a sharp difference of opinion. The monks of Vaiśāli who supported the acceptance of donations of money were defeated and broke away. Other questions related to the kind of food which could be accepted as alms, seating arrangements and procedure in discussion within the monastery. These were questions relating to protocol, hierarchy and property.

The Buddhist support for the new order did not arise merely out of the wish to associate with authority. The egalitarian society of the *saṅgha* was possible only when the state system came into being and monastic institutions could be maintained. A parallel monastic society can only survive when there is a well-ordered agrarian system and trade to provide the surplus since the monastery for its daily needs has a parasitical relationship with society. Hence the statement of the Buddha that good government requires the invest-

97 *Mahāvagga*, I. 40.1 ff.

98 Romila Thapar, 'Ethics, Religion and Social Protest in the first millennium B.C. in Northern India', in *AISH*, p. 40 ff.

ment of seed to the cultivators, of capital to the traders and of food and wages to those who work for the government.[99] The insistence on *ahimsā* would also be endorsed by groups such as peasants or traders who required peace and stability for purposes of production. Recurring violence was inimical to the interests of societies in a state system. The harshness of the state was ameliorated in the concept of the *cakkavati/cakravartin*, the universal ruler whose reign is synonymous with law, order and justice. Significantly it is the wheel of law which rolls across his domains and not the *daṇḍa* of chastizement.

The Buddhist view of this dual relationship also revolves around the role of the king and the *bhikkhu*. The king provides law and order, the *bhikkhu* breaks away from law and order and enters a new domain with its own rules and which is in theory at least beyond society, although in practice it has a close link with society. The *bhikkhu* therefore is in a middle position between the two polarities of the king and the ascetic. The king is in origin the Mahāsammata and aspires to be a *chakkavati* : the aim being the universality of law and order. The *bhikkhu* emulates the Buddha and supports the universality of the doctrine and the ethic. The king has to be seen as the hub of society, the *bhikkhu* of the *saṅgha*. Society moves from a pristine, casteless, egalitarian body to a stratified caste society. The *sangha* excludes stratified caste society and tries to recapture the pristine, egalitarian society.[100] The dual relationship between the *saṅgha* and the state is captured in a later phase of Buddhism in the mirror image of the *bodhisatta* and the *cakkavati*, where the *bodhisatta* is either an earlier incarnation of the Buddha or works towards this through his concern for the welfare of people.

The importance of the *bhikkhu* was not merely in terms of his relationship with the king, but even more so with the lay community. The *bhikkhu* ideal lay not in the monkhood or priesthood but in the mendicant wanderer who had renounced the world but was not cut off from the community. The etymology of *bhikṣu* from the root **bhaj* suggests asking for alms in the sense of sharing: presumably the sharing of the householder's wealth. To this extent the *bhikṣu* was still adhering to the ideals of the earlier system of sharing wealth. The definition of *bhikkhu* in the later Pāli sources

[99] *Dīg. Nik.* I. 135.

[100] S.J. Tambiah, *World Conqueror and World Renouncer*, p. 15 ff, Cambridge, 1976. See also *Dīg. Nik.* III. 101; *Suttanipāta,* 554.

changes noticeably where it refers to one who has cleansed himself of the stains of worldly existence and who is apprised of the horrors of rebirth.[101] That the notion of the *bhikkhu* was initially rooted in renunciation and mendicancy is apparent from the link between the *bhikkhu* and the *śramaṇa/samana*. The mendicant aspect of the *bhikkhu* which is emphasized in the code of behaviour enunciated for Bhuddhist *bhikkhus* requires that he lives off the alms collected from the lay community. This presupposes the proximity of a lay community willing and able to give alms and also a constant interaction with the lay community. The *śramaṇa* was more of a recluse and an ascetic who had the option either of being a mendicant or living in isolation in the same way as the *saṃnyāsins*.

The proximity to or distance from the lay community remains an essential feature of the religious sects of this time and goes back to the dichotomy between the *brāhmaṇs* and the *śramaṇas*, a dichotomy which was so sharp that Patañjali refers to it as synonymous with the relationship of the snake to the mongoose or the cat to the rat.[102] It is reiterated by Megasthenes who divides the caste of philosophers into Brachmanes and Sarmanes and also by Asoka who calls for the honouring of *bammana* and *samana*.[103] The *brāhmaṇs* are deeply embedded in the community and cannot exist as a category outside it. The *śramaṇas* and *samnyāsins* deliberately opted out of society as is reflected in the *Upaniṣads* and the *Āranyakas* where their main intention was to think and act away from social obligations. Distance was further maintained by restricting the membership of such groups by and large to the upper castes and by taxing the mind with enigmatic discourses.

The renouncers of the middle Ganga valley — the Nirgranthas, Ājīvikas, Buddhists and other sectarian groups preferred a middle course in this dichotomy. At one level they were renouncers but at another level they returned to society and were dependent on the lay community.[104] In fact the lay follower (*upāsaka*) in the Buddhist scheme of things played a major role both in supporting the *saṅgha* and in return being ministered to by the *bhikkhus*. The need for an institutional base, the monastery, made the dependence on the lay community even greater and in this there was competition

[101] *Visuddhi-magga* 3.16; *Vibhaṅga* 245–6.

[102] *Vyākaraṇa Mahābhāṣyam* II. 4.9, I. 476.

[103] Bloch, *Les Inscriptions d'Asoka*, p. 126.

[104] Romila Thapar, 'Renunciation: The Making of a Counter-culture?', in *AISH*,

among the various new sects as well as between them and the *brāhmaṇ*s. The antagonism was both at the ideological level as for instance in the sarcasm with which the Buddha treats the views of other sects[105] as well as at the more mundane level of competing for patronage. The ire of most was directed against the Cārvāka and the Lokāyata sects since they mocked even the efficacy of monkhood and sought to question the entire structure of explanation.

These sects are generally located in the cities of the middle Ganga valley suggesting that even the capitals of the *janapada*s of the western Ganga valley were an insufficient background to such movements. The qualitative difference can be seen in the *Dharmasūtra* instructions to include dicing in the assembly hall,[106] whereas in the middle Ganga valley there were *kutūhala-sāla*s or places for relaxation and debate. These were not merely shelters for the peripatetic teacher during the rainy season, for they attracted an audience of citizens. Urban life released a degree of curiosity and free thinking which was made use of by some of these *śramaṇa*s, and far from isolating themselves in the wilderness they were anxious to address large audiences. The teaching was open to everyone and because it was aimed at a large audience was perhaps less esoteric than the discourses of the forest dwellers. The importance of a teacher was recognized by the size of his following as much as by the theories which he expounded. Such sizeable followings were more available on the fringes of large urban centres. The subjects debated were varied but the basic questions centred on the universality of human experience, knowledge and intuition. The halls were often located in parks and were demarcated by rows of trees, reminiscent of the forest. The *kutūhala-sāla*s were the successors to the forest retreats.

The *kutūhala-sāla*s were maintained by wealthy citizens or through royal patronage and were clearly important locations for debating a variety of doctrines. Most references to them mention discourses on matters of religious and ethical importance but inevitably the discussion must also have included other concerns. Apart from the general interest in the new religious sects the encouragement of such discussion would also arise from the changed historical situation. It is repeatedly said that many of those who

p. 63 ff.

[105] *Dīg. Nik.* I. 27; I. 55.

[106] Āpastamba, II. 10.25.12.

frequented the *kutūhala-sālas* whether *brāhmaṇs* or *śramaṇas* were highly respected and had large followings.[107] Their popularity would lead those in power to treat them with respect. The gatherings at the *kutūhala-sālas* were doubtless also one avenue of assessing which sects should receive patronage. This is not to suggest that those with large followings were the leaders of popular opposition. There is in fact a remarkable lack of direct political statement on the increasing power of the state. Whatever questioning there was, has to be culled from the cynicism and satire of the wanderers. Nevertheless ethical systems are not constructed in a social vacuum and the questioning of existing mores by the Cārvāka and Lokayata teachers for example, could have been taken to a logical conclusion, namely, the direct questioning of the new political order. It is perhaps as well to keep in mind that the only evidence on revolts in the literature of this period comes from Buddhist sources and is generally in the form of citizens in the capital overthrowing the king or expressing their discontent with the oppression of the officials. The *Jātaka* literature has generalized references to such occurences.[108] In another text the revolt of the citizens of Taxila against Mauryan officials is described more than once.[109]

The centrality of philosophical disputation and the appeal to analytical thinking is at the ideological level reflective of a shift away from the security of the group towards the cutting edge of individual intellectual endeavour. Doubtless the *kutūhala-sālas* encouraged the group audience in that rhetoric, oratory and sophistry were all at a premium. But in effect it was the force of an individual's conviction and power of argument which drew the audience and eventually the following. The argument may not have been entirely logical but claimed frequently to be so and the theory propounded may well have been, as the descriptions suggest, often an attempt at an ambitious *tour de force*. Nevertheless, the appeal to the individual at an impersonal level was an important contribution and tied to similar changes in other spheres of life.

[107] *Dīg. Nik.* I. 179; *Maj. Nik.* II. 2; *Saṁ. Nik.* IV. 398.

[108] *Khaṇḍahāla Jātaka* no. 542; *Maniçora Jātaka* no. 194; *Padakusalamānava Jātaka* no. 432.; Romila Thapar, 'Dissent and Protest in the Early Indian Tradition', in *Studies in History*, 1979 vol. I, no. 2, p. 177. ff.

[109] *Divyāvadāna* C. 372, p. 234; C. 407, p. 262.

V. ERGO

An attempt has been made in the previous chapters to trace the gradual movement from a lineage based society to the emergence of a state system in the mid-first millennium B.C. The awareness of change is amply reflected in the texts of the period, where there is a recognition of the absence of a state for the earlier beginnings. Thus the Śānti Parvan declares:[1]

> *naiva rājyam na rājāsīnna daḍo na ca dāṇḍikaḥ dharmenaiva prajāḥ sarvā rakṣanti ca parasparam*
>
> (Once there was no ruling authority, no king, no coercion and no coercer, for people took care of each other out of a sense of righteousness).

The same sentiment is echoed in Buddhist texts. Some of this sentiment arose from locating a utopia in the past and therefore regarding antiquity as an ideal society not requiring the discipline of a state. The transition was from chiefships to kingships and inevitably with a considerable overlap between the two.

In suggesting the need for pointing to the differentiation it has been argued that although the terminology may not have changed, its connotation underwent substantial changes: thus *rājā* in Ṛg Vedic society had a different meaning from its use in the Kuru-Pañcāla period or from the *gaṇa-saṅgha* use of the term or for that matter its meaning in Buddhist sources. The definition in the *Sutta Nipāta*[2] that ' he who enjoys an income from land or from a village is a *rājā* ', would have been unrecognizable to the cattle-raiding *rājā*s of the Purus and Bharatas. Many of the terms discussed are carried over from the one society to the other, since there are rarely any sharp breaks in such change. But their connotation has to be viewed in the context of the change. There have been many reasons for the extrapolation back of the meanings of these terms from later sources to earlier periods. Often the reason was historiographical, especially when nationalism demanded that a supposedly more sophisticated society be presented for Vedic beginnings. But equally often it was the relative fullness of the

[1] *Mahābhārata*, Sānti Parvan, 59.14.

[2] *Sutta Nipāta*, Vaseṭṭhasutta, 26.

evidence from later sources and paucity from earlier ones which encouraged the assumption that the meaning of the term had not undergone any substantial change.

A further aspect is the examination of traditional concepts in relation to their own evolution. Thus the constituents of the *Saptāṅga* theory are noticeably absent in the earlier society. Of the seven elements, the *rājā* and *janapada/rāṣṭra* are referred to although the concentration of power in the office of the *rājā* and the notion of a defined territory remain vague. There is in Vedic literature little reference to the capitals of the *janapada*s and had the towns of Hastināpura, Ahicchatra and Kāmpilya, not to mention others, been the nucleii of power at this time they would surely have featured more prominently. The concept of a treasury, a standing army as well as a body of ministers appears to be altogether absent. Nor is there much evidence to suggest the awareness of the *maṇḍala* theory with its almost mathematically balanced diplomacy. Here again it would be incorrect to pose an insurmountable dichotomy between lineage and state since this would be unreal. There is a considerable shading off from one to the other. There were intermediate positions and one among these was undoubtedly the slow transformation of the chief into the king. These positions have also to be seen in the totality of a changing situation.

The movement from lineage to state registers changes at many levels. One among them is reflected in the *itihāsa-purāṇa* tradition. In trying to demonstrate the relevance of the tradition to these changes and the form given to the tradition by these changes, there is an implicit suggestion that the historical interpretation of early Indian society could now move away from the preoccupations of the historiography of the colonial period and seek an analysis which might take into consideration, at least in broad outline, the *itihāsa-purāṇa* view of the early Indian past. Such a view may not record factual history but may well provide pointers to historical actuality. The pattern of change reflected in the *itihāsa-purāṇa* tradition seems to synchronize with the argument supporting a change from a lineage society to a state system in the middle Ganga valley; a system which later evolved into a variety of states, each deriving its form from the region where it took shape and the degree to which it incorporated facets of the earlier lineage society. This would inevitably lead to a review of some of the theories which have been used to describe the early Indian past.

It would be impossible to pinpoint any single factor as crucial to the evolution of the state in the middle Ganga valley. The ecological niches of Ṛg Vedic times did not develop into a state system since there was less of confrontation and more of symbiosis. The resolution of conflict arising through stratification or demographic increase was not achieved by changing the system but by the migration of people which eased the tension, with migrating groups reproducing the structure and organization of the earlier society. The absence of geographical barriers encouraged this process. Land was available in the western Ganga valley and was more easily settled than in the marshlands and the monsoon forests of the middle Ganga valley. The need to defend the settlement was constant but external conflict did not require major changes in the administration of resources, since it was limited by and large to skirmishes, cattle-raids and the defence of fortified settlements. Pitched battles were not of frequent occurrence and when they did take place they were regarded as special events. In the middle Ganga valley rice agriculture and irrigation were initially important but probably were not sufficient causes. However they sharpened stratification between those who owned the land and those who laboured on it. The imminence of internal tension made the possibility of control through a state system feasible. The recognizable state emerges when the stratification is much more widespread both socially and geographically. This takes the form of the transformation of the *gahapati/gṛhapati* from a household head within a clan system to a landowner, and subsequent to this, as a participant in trading activities and in its counterpoise in the transformation of the *śūdra* into the peasant cultivator and the artisan.

These changes were by no means universal but were large enough to affect the overall system. Settlements were nucleated and became the foci of political power and exchange, some eventually developing into towns. Because of the greater concentration of wealth and power in such settlements they were required to be defended. External conflict was no longer a cattle-raid but a calculated campaign for acquisition of territories and towns. The concentration of wealth at the court and in the commercial towns is qualitatively different from the wealth obtained by chiefs and distributed as booty or as sacrificial offerings. Under the impact of trade the item which was a gift in the lineage system became a commodity when exchanged.[3] Whereas earlier the *kṣatriya* gave gifts to the *brāhmaṇ*s in exchange for the abstract notion of status and legitimacy, in the new system the gift included immovable property. Thus the gift was transmuted into property and the concept of exchange also underwent a transformation.

In some areas the ethnos is replaced by the polis. The pivot of the community shifts from the clan to the town. The *janapada* is the territory of the clan and is identified as such but the concept of the *paurajanapada* introduces the urban settlement. The slow change to *rāṣṭra* is self-explanatory since the term *rāṣṭra* is said to derive from **rāj*, to rule. *Rāṣṭra* would therefore suggest territory in the political sense and not in the tribal sense as would *janapada*. Although again *rāṣṭra* manifests a difference of nuance from the Vedic to the later period. The importance of the town is also evident in the new category of *nāgarika*, the townsman, often used in the sense of citizen. Qualifications for citizenship which in the *gaṇa-saṅgha* system required high descent and claim to ownership of land through descent, were gradually eroded and by the time that the state is well established, the *nāgarika* includes all town dwellers although by implication the more influential are those who are highly placed by birth and by wealth.

These changes were more evident in urban society which was in any case a small percentage of the whole. Nor was the distinction between urban and rural a sharp divide. Yet rural society carried a larger component of lineage forms than did urban society. Land and produce changed from usage to property rights. Pasture land hardly required demarcation and was commonly owned. Cultivated land changed from clan ownership where it was worked by household units to ownership by the *gṛhapati* as the head of the household. Whether the *gṛhapati* was a *kṣatriya* or a *vaiśya,* lineage connections would have provided lateral links especially where ownership was vested in the family. The *kṣatriya* links being those of the senior lineages were the more effective and lasting. The *viś* as the lesser lineages would tend to disintegrate faster.

The question of class antagonism in relation to the lineage system[4] has produced a lively discussion. It has been argued that the distinction between senior and junior lineages where the latter pro-

[3] C. Meillassoux, 'The Social Organisation of the Peasantry: the economic basis of kinship', in D. Seddon (ed.), *Modes of Production*, London, 1978, pp. 159 ff.

[4] Ibid; G. Duprée and P.P. Rey, 'Reflections on the Relevance of a Theory of the History of Exchange', in Seddon (ed.), *Modes of Production*, pp. 171-208; P.P.

vided the prestations and the former asserted authority and presided over the redistribution processes, was sufficient to result in class antagonism. The senior lineages also controlled marriage relations, demographic reproduction, the induction of slaves and the exchange of élite goods. Neverthless it is probably more correct to maintain as it-has been said, that all this indicates at most a class function rather than an actual class. Since the major source of power was control over kinship (actual or fictive) it is difficult to accept the emergence of class at this stage. In the evidence considered here it was the gradual evolution of private ownership of land and the possibility of the alienation of land as well as the trend towards a commercial economy which encouraged the decline of the lineage system in the area under discussion. This released the *gahapati* into the ranks of landowners and traders and *śūdra* labour moved from the confines of service inherent in the householding system to a slow crystalizing into artisan professions and tenurial peasants. The *gahapati* may be said to approximate a class since the *gahapati* could be from any of the *dvija varṇa*s. The counterpart to the *gahapati* was, at the narrowest level, the *dāsa-bhṛtaka* and at the wider level the more dependant sections among *śūdra* peasants and artisans. At this point incipient classes become feasible.

The pattern of state formation and the particular factors which went into its making influenced the specific form it was to take. But even the evolved state was not frozen and in turn underwent substantial changes reflecting wider historical change. A distinction may be made not only between primary and secondary states but between varieties of states. Magadha is an example of a primary state and it has been argued that secondary states are formed by primary states conquering non-states.[5] This may not be an automatic sequence. What is crucial is that the area conquered must be economically restructured and integrated into the conquering state. In the case of Magadha, even after conquering a wide area including the Ganga valley there were substantial parts which were not integrated. Some of the Magadhan conquests included existing primary states but elsewhere the territory brought under control did not have a state system. Hegemony was extended over a range of differentiated systems — hunter-gatherers, chiefships, a variety of peasant tenures and exchange relationships extending

Rey, 'Class Contradiction in Lineage Societies', in *Critique of Anthropology*, 1979, 4, nos. 13 and 14, pp. 41-60.

[5] Cohen and Service (eds.), *Origin of the State*, p. 6 ff.

from barter to nascent market systems. Many of these survived the conquest and continued as before. Even after the conquest by the Nandas and Mauryas which included central India and Rajasthan, the *gaṇa-saṅghas* of these areas seem to have continued. Despite its size and administrative control, the Mauryan state does not appear to have attempted a restructuring of all the areas under its control. Possibly a distinction has to be maintained between what might be called the metropolitan state in such a system which would be the core region or the area which initiates conquest and control of the peripheral regions subservient to the metropolitan state but substantially continuing much as before.[6] The metropolitan state would be organized on a unitary, centralized basis. Its control over the peripheral areas would be through administration, the upper levels under central authority and the lower levels under local authority. This bifurcation would be possible if the major concern of the metropolitan state was to collect tax and tribute and even plunder during campaigns but not to restructure the economy of the peripheral areas in an attempt to integrate it and bring it into a uniform pattern. Tax and tribute would be collected not only from cultivators but from a variety of professions utilizing a range of resources : in fact from every conceivable human activity with which the state could be associated, as seems apparent from the *Arthaśāstra*. Major economic change would then be limited by and large to the metropolitan state and to potentially rich areas likely to provide a sizeable revenue. But the maximum development of the latter areas was not envisaged at this stage. The decline of states would be related among other things to the availability of finance to support the state structure. If the metropolitan state was in the main collecting revenue without extending, on a large scale, the activities leading to revenue then its income would hardly meet the expenses of such a structure. (Incidentally this might also help explain the remarkable paucity of monuments from the Mauryan period. Apart from the buildings at the site of Kumrahar there is little else to prove the grandeur of an empire. This is particularly noticeable when compared to the monuments of the Achaemenids or even to those of a single ruler, Shi Huang Ti.) Here might also be an explanation of why the *Arthaśāstra* tradition, even though it had known an empire as extensive as that of the Mauryas, visualizes a

[6] Romila Thapar, 'The State as Empire: the Mauryan case', in H. Claessen and P. Skalnik (eds.), *The Study of the State*, The Hague, 1901, p. 409 ff.

relatively small state in its discussion on how a state is to be administered. Or why Aśoka takes no grandiloquent titles and on occasion even confines himself to the simple title of *rājā māgadhe* (*rājā* of Magadha).[7] There is no reference, neither in his own edicts nor in the descriptions of the Mauryan state in the Ceylon Chronicles, to an empire as a new and distinctive category in the state system. This is not to suggest that there was no empire but rather that the control was flexible and that the metropolitan state was seen to be the most important element. The *itihāsa-purāṇa* tradition also maintains that the Mauryas ruled a kingdom but no distinction is made in terms of its being an empire.[8] What the tradition records in each case are the dynasties which ruled the metropolitan states. The concept of the *cakravartin* however does suggest control over a vast territory although it has been suggested[9] that the concept is not so much that of ruling a geographically vast territory as of centring control, as it were, firmly and securely in a hub of power. The symbolism of the wheel does suggest a differentiation between power at the centre of the circle and at the rim. The domain need not be restricted to the political for in the Buddhist concept the spiritual domain is also open to the *cakkavatti*. The *maṇḍala* theory may also have had its origins in a kaleidoscopic relationship between the metropolitan state and the peripheral areas, a relationship which would be characterized by concerns of friendship and hostility with the metropolitan state playing the role of the *vijigīṣu*.

Restructuring of the economy seems more evident in the post-Gupta period when there are many more nucleii of metropolitan states and when areas of land previously regarded as waste and isolated were brought under cultivation. There was then either a smaller range of differentiated systems or alternatively a condition where the less developed systems were more marginal to a larger component of complex agrarian structures and commercial networks. The metropolitan area tends to invest in the more complex systems often by encouraging their expansion, not directly, but through intermediaries. The question of restructuring the economy hinges on the wider question of landownership which has remained controversial in the context of early India.

The question of the ownership of land by the state cannot be

[7] J. Bloch, *Les Inscriptions d'Asoka*, p. 154.

[8] Pargiter, *The Purāna Text of the Dynasties of the Kali Age*, pp. 26-7.

[9] Gonda, *Ancient Indian Kingship*, p. 123 ff.

answered with a clear negative or affirmative, since ownership patterns changed over time and varied in different regions. For the early period of Indian history there cannot be an all-inclusive answer which would be applicable to the entire subcontinent. Even during the Mauryan period there was no uniformity in landownership. There are references to state-owned lands (*sīta*) as well as to the private ownership of land and its alienation by the owners. With the decline of clan ownership and of the householding economy there was a change to a tenurial system and the gradual emergence of a peasant economy. This was not based on cultivation through forced labour. The state did collect revenue from the cultivators and various supplementary taxes, of which only one is listed as *viṣṭi*. It is mentioned in the *Arthaśāstra*[10] in connection with those villages, among a large category of others, that provide *viṣṭi* in lieu of taxes. Evidently the state's claim to *viṣṭi* was not universal. New land was brought under cultivation and deserted areas resettled through the agency of the state; mention is made in the Mauryan period to the settling of agriculturalists and the deportation of prisoners-of-war to such areas. The *Arthaśāstra* clearly states that families of *śūdra* agriculturalists should be drafted from overpopulated areas or induced to migrate from foreign *janapadas*.[11] This suggests a very different scene from the enslavement of clans and their employment in cultivation through a system of forced labour. One of the edicts of the Mauryan king Aśoka speaks of the deportation of prisoners of war after the campaign in Kalinga,[12] and it is presumed that they were used in establishing new agricultural settlements.[13] If this was the case then they were removed from their homelands and taken as colonists to new areas. In each of these cases, where the changed situation is brought about by the state, it results not in transforming agrarian relations in the existing settlements but in creating fresh settlements where the cultivators are in a direct relation with the state. These activities on the part of the state did not eliminate the independent owners and peasants. The question of which type of cultivation predominated remains without a conclusive answer, but possibly the short duration of large-scale state systems and the continued availability of new lands until recent centuries would suggest that forced settlements by the

[10] *Arthaśāstra*, II. 35.1. [11] Ibid; II. 1.1.

[12] J. Bloch, *Les Inscriptions d'Asoka*, p. 125 ff.

[13] D.D. Kosambi, *Introduction to the Study of Indian History*, Bombay, 1956, p. 189 ff.

state were not the predominant system. The evidence on state enterprise in irrigation works is also limited. There are so far only the single examples of the Nandas building a canal in Kalinga and the Mauryas constructing a dam in Saurashtra. The *Arthaśāstra* provides no details for such state supervised irrigation systems. It suggests the abolition of the water cess on those who provide their own irrigation facilities and strongly urges the encouragement of such private enterprise.[14] This would amount to a fairly limited effort by the state at restructuring the economy. The location of the two irrigation works are in areas geographically peripheral but agriculturally rich and this would point to some state initiative. However, the evidence of only two examples is not very impressive or extensive in terms of the area covered by the Mauryan empire.

The major form of peasant protest against oppressive taxes was not revolt but migration to new lands outside the control of the state to which the peasants belonged.[15] There are enough authors who warn the king against oppressive taxation lest the peasants migrate,[16] as there are also instances of such migrations. This would again point to the availability of access to land for fresh settlements. Such protestors were doubtless welcome in neighbouring kingdoms for their migration would have meant additional revenue to the states where they settled. Possibly this is what Kauṭilya was referring to in his advice that *śūdra* agriculturalists should be induced to come from foreign kingdoms or that deserted lands should be resettled. It is more than likely, however, that peasant protesters would settle in forested areas or take to brigandage. The continuation of independent clan systems juxtaposed with areas of peasant economies would also suggest that state entrepreneurship in agriculture was not a uniform system throughout the territory held by a particular state.

A recent suggestion that the model of the segmentary state as developed for the Alur in Africa might be more purposeful for the Indian state would also posit a situation very different from that described in earlier models.[17] Perhaps the most positive contribution of this theory is the notion of territorial sovereignty being recognized by degree in various zones of control. Areas under direct

[14] *Arthaśāstra*, II. 1. 20-4; II. 24. 18; III. 9. 32-8; III. 10. 1-2.

[15] E.g. *Gaṇḍatiṇḍu Jātaka*, no. 520.

[16] *Manu* VII. 111; *Artha*, XIII. 1. 20-1; VII. 5; *Mahābhārata*, Śānti Parvan, 88. 35-8.

[17] A. Southall, *Alur Society*, Cambridge, 1956, p. 248 ff; B. Stein, *Peasant State and Society in Medieval South India*, Delhi, 1980.

state control were differentiated from peripheral areas of limited control and from spheres of influence. The form of administration at the centre tended to be repeated in miniature at the periphery. However the monopoly of force at the centre was restricted at the periphery. Peripheral units therefore have the flexibility to change allegiances. Political sovereignty and ritual sovereignty was kept distinct with the latter relating to the process of legitimization. Although the theory of the segmentary state may not be largely acceptable in the context of the early Indian situation, there are, nevertheless, elements of the system which can be noticed from time to time, particularly in areas and periods where lineage systems were moving over to state systems. The theory also raises the question of the possible variation on the unitary state which has long been the model for early Indian society.

The discussion on ownership of land has tended to cloud the reality of the early Indian state as one essentially interested in revenue collecting functions and less concerned with claims to ownership as is indicated in the *Arthaśāstra* of Kauṭilya. It would therefore be more meaningful to inquire into the range and variation of peasant tenures. This would require some discussion of the concepts of the village community and the peasant economy as developed for the colonial period of Indian history and their application to the early period.

The village community was believed to be a community of equals and economically self-sufficient. However, as we have seen, from the earliest period for which there is evidence, stratification is noticeable in the village community. The tension between the *rājanya* and the *viś* from the Vedic period becomes more acute in the hierarchy of the *Ksatriya*, the *gahapati* and the *śūdra* in the subsequent period. Sharper stratification emerges with the breaking up of the clan system and landownership taking the form of private holdings with grants to religious beneficiaries and peasant tenures that included independent cultivators, tenants and sharecroppers. The closed economy of the village community has been over-emphasized for it is observable only in those areas and those periods of Indian history in which the *jajmāni* system based on service relationships rather than on payment for services was the norm.[18] This varied in time and place. Artisans central to the village

[18] T.O. Beidelman, *A Comparative Analysis of the Jajmani System*, New York, 1959; W.H. Wiser, *The Hindu Jajmani System*, Lucknow,1958; S. Epstein, 'Productive Efficiency and Customary Systems of Rewards in Rural South India', in

economy such as carpenters are said to be working on daily wages.[19] Wages could be in kind or in cash and monetary salaries are mentioned in the *Arthaśāstra* and the *Jātaka*s. Nevertheless at this time too there is a variation,for in those areas where the use of coined metallic money had not been introduced or there was an absence of market centres, there service relationships and exchanges in kind would have persisted. Service relations or *jajmāni* relations reflecting a system of exchange of services in accordance with a recognized hierarchy could have had their genesis in a householding economy. The ritual status of the *yajamāna* in such a system would extend to mundane matters as well. The function of the *śūdra* to serve the higher *varṇa*s is explicit in the theory of *varṇa* and such service was not defined as based on wages. Service relations are distinct from the *jajmāni* system as such and the existence of the former does not necessarily imply the presence of the latter. However the *jajmāni* system would have evolved historically from *jajmāni* relations. It was supported by the hierarchy of ritual status and in turn reinforced it. This was not an idyllic, mutually supportive system but was based on power deriving from ownership of land and expressed economic disparities. The self-sufficiency of the village in the early period was encroached upon by itinerant professionals and by villages providing for merchants and markets outside the village. Even for later periods the degree to which self-sufficiency may have been eroded by horizontal links through local markets and fairs, networks of religious centres playing an economic role as well and trade in essential items brought by itinerant herders, artisans and traders, remains to be examined with greater precision.

The constituents of a peasant economy (as distinct from the existence of peasants as cultivators), are that roughly half the total population should be engaged in agriculture and that this should form approximately half the working population; that there should be a state and a ruling hierarchy, a separation of town and country, and that the unit of production and consumption should in the main comprise of peasant households.[20] Of the seven categories listed by Megasthenes in his description of Indian society,

Themes in Economic Anthropology, ASA 6, London, 1967.

[19] V.S. Agrawala, *India as Known to Panini*, pp. 236-7.

[20] D. Thorner, 'Peasant Economy as a Category in Economic History', in T. Shanin (ed.), *Peasants and Peasant Society*, Harmondsworth, 1971, p. 202 ff.

he writes that the cultivators are the largest in number and considering the small size of at least three, the philosophers, overseers and councillors, out of the seven, they were evidently above half of the working population.[21] The presence of towns as commercial centres is evident from Buddhist sources. The peasant household has been defined as one that cultivates its own allotment of land with or without slaves and wage-labourers, includes some production of handicrafts and indulges in petty trade. These characteristics were present in the peasant households of this period. As units of consumption the peasant households function without the mediation of markets,but presumably where markets exist even marginally some production would be geared towards these markets. The state and the ruling hierarchy control the administration of revenue. On the basis of this definition it can be argued that a peasant economy emerged with the establishment of the state in the Ganga valley.

Changes in the perception of society are reflected in the post-Vedic sources. The economic categories are however more easily distinguishable in the Buddhist texts since they reflect a wider social reality than the brahmanical literature of the time. Social categories even in Pāṇini are more often discussed in terms of *jāti* rather than *varṇa*, the currency of the former being in any case post-Vedic. The etymology of the two terms are distinct and separate and *jāti*s are described as having evolved out of the common bonds of mutual kinship.[22] Buddhist sources rank *jāti*s into a high and a low category, a dual division which is commonly adopted in Buddhist classifications. The frequency of reference to *jāti* as compared to *varṇa* would suggest that the *jāti* became the more evident category of social perception and *varṇa* the more theoretical. As an endogamous group *jāti* conserved elements of the lineage system. It is interesting that Megasthenes uses the term *genos*, in referring to caste and states that its essential characteristics are endogamy and hereditary occupation. He does however exclude the philosophers (Brachmanes and Sarmanes) from having to conform to endogamy, perhaps a reference to *gotra* exogamy.

[21] Diodorus II. 40.

[22] PED, p. 281 Pāṇini, V. 4.9; cf. VI. 3.85; II. 4.6. S.C. Vasu mentions that the term *jāti* is used to mean genus in Indian logic, *The Aṣṭādhyāyi of Pāṇini*, Delhi, 1962, I. p. 310. This has a significance for the use of the term as a social category. V.S. Agrawala, *India as Known to Panini*, p. 93, quotes the Kāśikā as saying that *jāti* is in itself an invisible entity which achieves concrete form only through its component parts or *bandhus* (kinsmen).

In the transition from lineage to monarchical states, *varṇa* as a theory assisting this process gradually becomes evident over time. The *brahmaṇ* legitmizes the new political roles in the monarchical state and provides those in high office with religious sanctions and appropriate genealogical connections. In return for this the *brāhmaṇ* not only retained the highest ritual status but also had access to prime economic resources through the grants of land and other wealth. Gradations both ritual and economic within the *varṇa* were however apparent as only a few *brāhmaṇ*s could aspire to these benefits, many being content with lesser prestations as village priests and performers of ceremonies. Not all rituals drew sanction from Vedic or Purānic sources; some were survivals of indigenous, local forms and were to be maintained by non-*brāhmaṇ* castes acting as *pujāri*s and performers of rituals. A distinction was to develop between those who were of high social status and ministrants to the high gods via the high culture and those who were of low social status and were the practitioners of cults dedicated to local deities. One of the avenues of upward mobility relates to the rise of such local cults to high status, often through their patrons becoming politically powerful.

The *kṣatriya varṇa* was reserved for those who had earlier been ruling clans and were converted into the royal families of the monarchical state, or else were those of obscure origin who, having come to power required the appropriate connections, the latter being acquired often through latching onto the ancient established lineages such as the Sūryavamśa and Candravamśa. The extended kin groups would also acquire status and become landowners, the economic rank depending on the amount of land owned. *Kṣatriya* status was important in the early stage of the transition from lineage to state. With the establishment of the latter, political power became more open and even *śūdra*s were recognized (although grudgingly) as kings, after the advent of the Nanda dynasty. The bi-polarity between the lineage and the state system is perhaps expressed in the harking back to facets of the lineage system by those who performed Vedic sacrifices to acquire legitimacy and who claimed *kṣatriya* status as against others such as the Mauryas who ignored Vedic rituals, supported the 'heterodox' sects and were relegated to the status of *śūdra*s and described as *adharmaḥ*. The continuance of the former into the centuries A.D. would indicate attempts to seek connections with the traditional sources of validation.

The status of the *vaisya* although ritually lower varied in accordance with economic actuality. The *sreṣṭhin*s and the *jyeṣṭha*s of the *śreni*s commanded respect whereas others had a lower status. The *śūdra*s and the *caṇḍāla*s had less access to resources and at this level lowness of ritual status tended to conform to a low economic status as well. There was, it would seem, some flexibility in the *śudra* ranks, some of which as *jatis* were added on when professions became more specialized and the existing stratification became inadequate. References to *śūdra*s as artisans and peasants increase when craftsmen and cultivators began to get separated from clan holdings and the householding economy. In the classification of the *śūdra*, the *jāti*s are usually associated with an occupation, locality, cult or tribe. The occupational aspect was clearly more important than in the case of the *dvija varṇa*s where the occupation is defined briefly and in a more generalized fashion. For the *śūdra*s and lesser groups, occupation was more central to status than lineage. By the same token new social groups identified by occupation were often accorded a *varṇa* status of *śūdra* even when they became affluent.

With the proliferation of lower caste groups the extremes of pollution also get extended further from *śūdra*s to *caṇḍāla*s and various other similar groups. Separation is not limited to a general bifurcation. There develop degrees of separation on the axis of purity-pollution with an eventual demarcation even between clean *śūdra*s, unclean *śūdra*s and untouchables together with a hierarchy within each of these. Thus the notion becomes embedded in every sizeable group. Pollution as a concept is not discussed in any of the sources, only its observances are listed. Pollution in theory relates to moments of contact with bodily discharges and dead bodies, and those constantly in contact with these were permanently polluted. Participation in rituals requires a state of purity and those professionally involved in rituals would tend to be regarded as purer than others. Segregation became essential for those who were performing rituals and the counter-weight to them had to be a group regarded as impure. Ritual segregation became a useful mechanism for keeping certain socially low status groups permanently servile. This may also have been a counterpoint to the heterodox theories of the fundamental ethical equality of all.

In the late-first millennium B.C. there was therefore no exact corelation between *varṇa* status and economic status. The *varṇa* hierarchy arose in and related to a lineage-based society but was adapted to a state system. Within each *varṇa* there were recognized gradations, some of an economic nature but not excluding ritual functions or even ethnic distinctions. The gradation within each *varṇa* was in accordance with access to resources as well as a traditional sanction which was slowly built up and which facilitated this access using among other things the notion of hereditary occupations and insisting on a close control over expertise. The importance of *varṇa* as ritual status had primacy where the *yajña* and *gṛhya* rituals were of central importance. Where they had ceased to play a central role the hierarchy of the *varṇa*s changed, as in the middle Ganga valley in Buddhist and Jaina sources. The building of institutional bases in the form of monasteries for these religious sects required a far greater economic outlay and the interlinkage of politics and religion, which is one aspect of the spread of these sects, takes on a new dimension. If *varṇa* is not to be defined as a system of economic status then it takes on the characteristics of a theory not entirely divorced from reality but at the same time not mirroring reality. For purposes of historical analyses each group has to be located both in terms of ritual rank and economic status although the two points need not necessarily have coincided. However, correspondence was frequent among some groups of high ritual status and virtually predictable among those of the lowest strata. Middle-level groups remained ambiguous and were probably the most mobile in terms of actual status; a movement which nevertheless would have had some restrictions emanating from ritual ranking. As a theory epitomizing a social form the continuity of *varṇa* had to be adhered to and this might explain the relative lack of major change in the theoretical formulations on the functioning of *varṇa*. Because of the centrality of marriage and kinship rules such a society carried along with it one of the essentials of the lineage system, thus ensuring the survival of some elements of lineage society even in a situation where much had changed. To this was added the concept of segmentation. The proliferation of a caste was either through fission where a new caste emerged on migrating away from an established caste or from taking on a new profession or from the assimilation of a new segment. Ethnic coherence therefore became less reliable within the *varṇa* although it was possibly retained to a greater degree in the *jāti*. Sometimes the ethnic coherence was claimed irrespective of the reality: a convenient fiction to establish a niche in the local hierarchy. Historically it would be worthwhile to locate and identify the hierarchy of economic status as a parallel system and investigate whether at some points in history the two systems would either cohere or modify each other; or for that matter consider the possibility that in the actual working of a caste society the role of *varṇa* is less important than has been made out so far.

The theory of *varṇa* furthered horizontal networks reminiscent of the lineage system. This was expressed through ritual ranking and identities which acted as links across territory. To some extent this modified the more vertical dimensions of the *jāti* framework. Like lineage, *varṇa* was a mechanism for assimilation and arises with stratification but pre-dates the conditions conducive to a possible class society. It may therefore be said to have an intermediate position between stratified and class societies. The assimilation is frequently through fission: a segment is recognized as breaking off from the existing *varṇa* (often because of changes in occupation), it claims higher status and if it can defend its claims or has adequate patronage, it moves into higher status, a process reminiscent of lineage systems. This appears to have been the case with some at least of those who became members of the ruling class and then claimed *kṣatriya* status.[23] Those who were economically well off but failed in their claim to high status asserted that they had belonged to a *dvija varṇa,* but because of the non-observance of some ritual taboo had been demoted. Ritual categories remain static even though the occupations carried out by their members may change. Thus *brāhmaṇs* could be priests and at a later period administrators or even horse-dealers.[24] Kṣatriyas moved from being warriors to becoming landowners or religious teachers. *Varṇa* therefore acts as a bridge between lineage systems and society under a state. The continuity of *varṇa*, would partially account for the contours of the state in the Indian polity being sometimes dimly perceived by those participating in its functions. This further permitted brahmanical sources to emphasize the greater relevance of *varṇa* as they saw it and to project it as the reality of Indian society, a viewpoint which seems partial and requires correction. As a corollary to this it becomes necessary to examine the changes which caste itself

[23] B.D. Chattopadhyaya, 'Origin of the Rajputs...' *IHR*, July 1976, III. 1, pp. 59-82.

[24] G. Bühler, 'The Peheva Inscription from the Temple of Garibnath', *Epigraphia Indica*, I. pp. 184-90.

underwent and which were occasioned by wider historical change. Thus even though the *varna* terminology is retained, the composition, role and function of members of a *varṇa* is seen to differ in time. The history of *varṇa* is not static. The four orders of the *varṇa* remained constant and represented an idealized theory of social functioning but the actual functioning of their members could deviate from the theory.

The articulation of economic status followed on the emergence of two changes, the peasant economy and the rise of towns and commerce. Both these changes in the mid-first millennium B.C. helped in weakening the lineage system and consequently the importance of ritual status in societies dominated by brahmanical values as well as in the static power of the ruling clans in the *gaṇa-saṅgha* system. The commercial economy in a sense prised economic status out of the earlier system. Trade and urbanization were not the sole causative factors in the emergence of the state but were of significance in changing the social structure of the time. Theories of state formation applied to India, such as that of the Asiatic Mode of Production and the segmentary state, tend either to ignore or underplay the importance of the commercial economy as a factor in historical change.

The lineage system did not die out with the emergence of the state. Population pressure was concentrated on areas of optimum economic activity so large tracts of less than optimum areas retained a *gaṇa-saṅgha* or a clan system for many centuries. Such areas did not change even under Mauryan hegemony and as late as the Gupta period Samudragupta boasts of uprooting various ruling clans.[25] The extension of intensive agriculture in the post-Gupta period through a system of land grants and the frequency of fresh states being consolidated in new areas was often as the result of the conversion of clan systems into the state system. The juxtaposition of the two remains therefore a continual feature of Indian history until well into the second millennium A.D.

Even where the lineage system was absorbed into the state its identity was not entirely eliminated. Administration, except at the higher levels, remained a local concern and the absence of impersonal recruitment to office meant that kinship ties were still effec-

[25] Allahabad Posthumous Pillar inscription of Samudragupta; J.F. Fleet, 'Inscriptions of the Early Gupta Kings and their Successors', *Corpus Inscriptionum Indicarum*, III., Varanasi 1970 (reprint), p. 6 ff.

tive. Legal codes drew substantially on customary law and incorporated local practices. Legitimacy was frequently expressed through rituals pertaining to the lineage system such as the Vedic sacrifices of the *aśvamedha, vājapeya, rājasūya* and *abhiśeka,* or through conversion of clan deities and their rituals into the religious expression of the state, where the domain of the deity and its clientele would be fused into equivalent loyalty to the new state.[26] These became increasingly symbolic in the post-Gupta period but nevertheless acted as a link with the lineage system. Various lineage forms were reflected in the functions of *jāti.* Although occupation on occasion contradicted *varṇa* rules, nevertheless it would be worth investigating whether there was a weakening of the notion of the state where *varṇa* cohered with economic status. Thus it was not so much that the state was a segmentary system with a concentration of power at the centre shading off into ritual hegemony at the periphery as that the state system in itself was not a unitary, monolithic system restructuring the entire territory under its control but rather that it had a margin for flexibility in relation to peripheral areas.

The continuation of some aspects of the lineage system also required the continuation of the records of its history as well. Thus the *itihāsa-purāṇa* tradition remained the constant source of the earliest history. Nor is it strange that much of the tradition was preserved in the Purāṇic texts since these were also the sources which were drawn upon for validating *varṇa* status in the form of fabricated lineage links and myths of origin. Such validation was especially pertinent to the *kṣatriya varṇa.* The recourse to the *itihāsa-purāṇa* tradition as an introduction to a history was in part the usual search for legitimacy in tradition as well as the attempt to use tradition to disguise innovations. This technique was widely used in literature with a historical purpose. The genealogical material was central to the tracing of genealogical relationships irrespective of whether they were real or fictional and genealogical relationships were indicators of power. The persistence of some aspects of lineage society in many areas made the record of genealogical data an essential part of any process of political legitimation. The transition of royal status in a state system required genealogical support which could ultimately be provided by the *itihāsa-purāṇa* tradition.

Even when the *itihāsa-purāṇa* tradition gave rise to some new forms such as historical biographies and regional histories (as for

[26] H. Kulke, *Jagannātha-Kult und Gajapati-Königtum*, Weisbaden, 1979, p. 223 ff.

example, Bāṇa's *Harṣacarita*, Bilhaṇa's *Vikramānkadevacarita* and Kalhaṇa's *Rājataraṅginī*), it had its roots in the earlier tradition and some of the texts of this tradition were re-edited but not superseded. The rise of these new forms of the *itihāsa-purāṇa* tradition is linked to the establishment of states whose legitimacy was centred on brahmanical ideology. The state system itself underwent a change in that the states of the late first millennium A.D. registered a more pervasive activity on the part of the state and the monarch even if through intermediaries. The monarch was the symbol of the state and his biography became part of historical legitimation. The culmination of this process was the recognition of territory within which the restructuring had occurred as crucial to the definition of the state and in this context regional histories began to be written.

An analysis of state formation in early Indian history can be seen as a process of change from social formations which may broadly be classified as lineage systems to those dominated by a state system, but the nature of the domination does not fall easily into any of the existing models and its dynamics require a fresh-reworking. Nor is the change from one social formation to the other a clear-cut transformation for there is much that survives from the earlier to the later and many overlaps. Apart from the interpretational preconceptions of many theorists on pre-modern India, it is also these overlapping forms which have often helped to maintain the inter-links between ritual and economic status, leading to the clouding over of the one by the other and thus effectively hiding both the essential points of historical change and the complexities of Indian society in its early history.

BIBLIOGRAPHY

Adams, R.McC., *The Evolution of Urban Society*, Chicago, 1966.

Agrawal, D.P., and S. Kusumgar, *Prehistoric Chronology and Radio-Carbon Dating in India*, New Delhi, 1974.

Agrawal, V.S., *India as Known to Panini*, Varanasi, 1963 (revised ed.)

Aitareya Brāhmaṇa, ed. K.S. Agashe, Poona 1896, tr. A.B. Keith, H.O.S. XXV, Cambridge, Mass., 1920.

Allan, J., *A Catalogue of the Coins of Ancient India*, London, 1967.

Allchin, B. and R., *The Birth of Indian Civilization*, Harmondsworth, 1968.

Altekar, A.S., *State and Government in Ancient India*, Banaras, 1949.

Altekar, A.S., and V. Misra, *Report on the Kumrahar Excavations, 1951-55*, Patna, 1959.

Andersen, P., *Lineages of the Absolutist State*, London, 1974.

Aṅguttara Nikāya, ed. R. Morris and E. Hardy, P.T.S., London, 1885-1900; tr. F.L. Hare, 'The Book of Gradual Saying', P.T.S., London, 1932-6.

Āpastamba Dharmasūtra, ed. G. Bühler, Bombay 1894; tr. G. Bühler, SBE, vol. II. O.U.P., 1879.

Āpastamba Gṛhya Sūtra, ed. Chinnaswami Shastri, Benaras, 1928.

Āpastamba Śrauta Sūtra, ed. R. Garbe, Calcutta, 1882-1902.

Apte, V.M., *Social and Religious Life in the Grihya Sūtras*, Bombay, 1954.

ASA Monographs 2, *Political Systems and Distribution of power*, London, 1965.

ASA Monographs 6, *Themes in Economic Anthropology*, London, 1967.

Āśvālayana Gṛhya Sūtra, ed. A.G. Steuzler, Leipzig, 1864.

Āśvalāyana Śrauta-Sūtra, ed. Ganesh Shastri, Anandasrama, Poona, 1917.

Atharvaveda, ed. R. Roth and W.D. Whitney, Berlin, 1856; *Atharvaveda-Saṃhita* tr. W.D. Whitney, H.O.S. VII., Delhi, 1971 (2nd rpt).

Baden-Powell, B.H., *The Indian Village Community* (London, 1896), New Haven, 1957 (rpt).

Banerji, S.C., *Dharma-sūtras, A Study in their Origin and Development*, Calcutta, 1962.

Bareau, A., *Les Sectes Boudhiques du Petit Vehicule*, Saigon, 1955.

Barua, B.M., *Pre-Buddhistic Indian Philosophy*, Calcutta, 1921.

Basham, A.L., *The History and Doctrine of the Ājivikas*, London, 1951.

Baudhāyana Dharma-Sūtra, ed. E. Hultsch, Leipzig, 1884; tr. G. Bühler, SBE, vol. XIV., Oxford, 1882.

Beal, S., *Romantic History of Buddha*, London, 1907.

Bechert, H., 'Beginnings of Buddhist Historiography', Ceylon Studies Seminar, 1974, series no. 2 (mimeographed).

Beidelman, T.O., *A Comparative Analysis of the Jajmani System*, New York, 1959.

Belshaw, Cyril S., *Traditional Exchange and Modern Markets*, New Delhi, 1969.

Benveniste, E., *Indo-European Language and Society*, London, 1973.

Bhāgavata Puraṇa, ed. V.L. Pansikar, Bombay, 1920; tr. M.N. Dutt, Calcutta, 1895.

Bloch, J., *Les Inscriptions d' Asoka*, Paris, 1950.
Bose, A., *Social and Rural Economy of India*, Calcutta, 1942-5.
Boserup, E., *The Conditions of Agricultural Growth*, London, 1965.
Bougle, C., *Essays on the Caste System*, tr. D. Pocock, Cambridge, 1971.
Bṛhad-Devatā, ed. A.A. MacDonell (pts I and II), HOS V, Delhi, 1965 (rpt).
Brohier, R.L., *Ancient Irrigation works in Ceylon*, Colombo, 1934.
Brough, J., *The Early Brahmanical System of Gotra and Pravara*, Cambridge, 1953.
Buddhaghoṣa, *Visuddhi-Magga*, ed. Dharmananda Kosambi, Bombay, 1940.
Buitenan, J.A.B. van, *The Mahabharata*, vols. I, II, III, IV, Chicago, 1973; 1975.
Burrow, T., *The Sanskrit Language*, London, 1965.
Burrow, T. and M.B. Emeneau, *Dravidian Etymological Dictionary*, Oxford, 1961.

Cardona, G., *et al.* (ed), *Indo-European and Indo-Europeans*, Philadelphia, 1970.
Carneiro, R.L., 'A Theory of the Origin of the State', *Science*, 1970, 169, pp. 733-8.
Chakrabarty, D.K., 'The Beginning of Iron in India', *Antiquity*, 1976, 50, pp. 114-24.
Chakrabarty, D.K., 'Distribution of Iron Ores and Archaeological Evidence of Early Iron in India', *JESHO*, 1977, XX, pt. 2, pp. 166-85.
Chanana, *Slavery in Ancient India*, New Delhi, 1960.
Chāndogya Upaniṣad, ed. & tr. O. Bohtlingk, Leipzig, 1889.
Chaudhuri, K.A., *Ancient Agriculture and Forestry in Northern India*, Bombay 1977.
Claessen, H.J.M. and P. Skalnik, *The Early State*, The Hague, 1978.
Cohen, R., and E.R. Service (eds.), *Origins of the State*, Philadelphia, 1978.
Coulanges, Fustel de, *The Ancient City*, New York.
Cullavagga, qv. *Vinaya Piṭaka*.

Dalton, G. (ed.), *Primitive, Archaic and Modern Economics: the Essays of Karl Polanyi*, New York, 1968.
Damle, Y.B., *Caste: A Review of the Literature on Caste*, M.I.T., 1961.
Deshpande, M.M., and P.E. Hook, *Aryan and Non-Aryan in India* (Michigan Papers on South and South East Asia, no. 14, 1978), Ann Arbor, 1979.
Dhammapada, ed. S.S. Thera, P.T.S., London, 1914; ed. & tr. Mrs. Rhys Davids, SBB, London, 1931.
Dīgha Nikāya, ed. T.W. Rhys Davids and J.E. Carpentier, P.T.S., London, 1890-1911; tr. T.W. Rhys Davids, 'Dialogues of the Buddha', SBB, London 1899, 1910, 1921.
Dikshit, K.N., 'Exploration along the Right Bank of River Sutlej in Punjal *Journal of History*, 1967, 45, pt II, pp. 561-68
Dīpavaṃsa, ed. and tr. H. Oldenberg, London, 1879; ed. B.C. Law, *The Ceylon Historical Journal*, VII, 1959, nos. 1-4.
Divyāvadāna, ed. E.B. Cowell and R.A. Neil, Cambridge, 1886.
Drekmeier, C., *Kingship and Community in Early India*, Bombay, 1962.
Dumezil, G., *Flamen-Brahman*, Paris, 1935.
Dumezil, G., *Mythe et Epopée*, vols. I, II, Paris, 1968, 1971.

Dumont, L., *Homo Hierarchicus*, Paris, 1966; trans., London, 1972.
Dutt, N., *Early History of the Spread of Buddhism and Buddhist Schools*, London, 1925.
Dutt, N., *Early Monastic Buddhism*, Calcutta, 1973.
Dutt, S., *Early Buddhist Monachism*, London, 1924.
Eliade, M., *Cosmos and History*, Paris, 1949; New York, 1959.
Eliade, M., *Shamanism*, Princeton, 1974.
Engels, F., *The Origin of the Family, Private Property, and the State*, London, 1940.
Fick, R., *The Social Organisation in North East India in Buddha's Time*, trans. S.K. Mitra, Calcutta University, 1920.
Finley, M.I., *Ancient Slavery and Modern Ideology*, London, 1980.
Flannery, K.V., 'The Cultural Evolution of Civilisations', *Annual Review of Ecology & Systematics*, 1972, 3, pp. 399-426.
Fleet, J.F., *Inscriptions of the Early Gupta Kings and their successors*, Corpus Inscriptionum Indicarum, vol. III., Varanasi, 1970.
Fortes, M., *Kinship and the Social Order*, Chicago, 1969.
Frauwallner, E., *The Earliest Vinaya and the Beginnings of Buddhist Literature*, Rome, 1956.
Fried, Morton H., *The Evolution of Political Society*, New York, 1967.
Fuchs, S., *The Children of Hari*, Vienna, 1949.
Garaudy, R., *Sur le 'Mode de Production Asiatique'*, Paris, 1969.
Gautama Dharma-Sūtra, ed. ASS, Poona; tr. G. Bühler, SBE, vol. II, Oxford, 1897.
Geiger, W., *The Dipavamsa and Mahavamsa and their Historical Development in Ceylon*, Colombo, 1908.
Gerth H.H. and C.W. Mills, *From Max Weber*, London, 1947.
Ghosh, A., and D.P. Agrawal (eds.), *Radio-Carbon and Indian Archaeology*, Bombay, 1972.
Ghosh, A., *The City in Early Historical India*, Simla, 1973.
Ghoshal, U.N., *A History of Hindu Political Theories*, Calcutta, 1923.
Ghoshal, U.N., *The Agrarian System in Ancient India*, Calcutta, 1930.
Ghose, B., Amalkar and Z. Hussain, 'The lost courses of the Sarasvati river in the Great Indian Desert: new evidence from Landstat Imagery', *The Geographical Journal*, 1979, 145, pt 3, pp. 446-51.
Ghose, B., Amalkar and Z. Hussain, 'Comparative Role of the Aravalli and Himalayan River Systems in the Fluvial Sedimentation of the Rajasthan Desert', *Man and Environment*, 1980, IV., pp. 8-12.
Ghose, R.L.M., *et al.*, *Rice in India*, ICAR, New Delhi, 1960.
Gobhila Gṛhya Sūtra, ed. Chintamani Bhattacharya, Cal. Sans. Series, Calcutta, 1936; tr. H. Oldenberg, S.B.E., vol. XXX, Oxford, 1892.
Godakumbara, C.E., *Sinhalese Literature*, Colombo, 1955.
Godelier, M., *Perspectives in Marxist Anthropology*, Cambridge, 1977.
Goldman, I., *Ancient Polynesian Society*, Chicago, 1970.
Gonda, J., *Ancient Indian Kingship from the Religious Point of View*, Leiden, 1969.
Gonda, J., *Selected Studies*, IV. Leiden, 1975.
Goody, J., *Comparative Studies in Kinship*, London, 1969.
Gunawardana, R.A.L.H., 'The Analysis of Pre-Colonial Social Formations in Asia

in the writings of Karl Marx', *Indian Historical Review*, 1976, II, no. 2, p. 365 ff.

Gurdip Singh, 'The Indus Valley Culture', *Archaeology and Physical Anthropology in Oceania*, 1971, vol. 6, no. 2, pp. 177-89.

Gurdip Singh, *et al.*, 'Late Quarternary History of Vegetation and Climate of the Rajasthan Desert, India', *Philosophical Transactions of the Royal Society of London*, 1974, 267, pp. 467-501.

Hara, M., 'A Note on the Sanskrit Word *Jana*', *Pratidānam*, p. 256 ff, The Hague, 1968.

Haswell, M.R., *The Economics of Subsistence Agriculture*, London, 1967.

Heesterman, J.C., *The Ancient Indian Royal Consecration*, The Hague, 1957.

Held, G.J., *The Mahabharata: An Ethnological Study*, Amsterdam, 1935.

Henige, D.P., *The Chronology of Oral Tradition*, Oxford, 1974.

Hiraṇyakeśin Gṛhya-sūtra, ed. J. Kirste, Vienna, 1889; tr. H. Oldenberg, SBE, XXX, Oxford, 1982.

Hopkins, E.W., 'Pragathikani', *JAOS*, 1896, 17, p. 84.

Horton, R., and R. Finnegan, (eds.), *Modes of Thought*, London, 1973.

Humphreys, S.C. (ed.), *Mortality and Immortality: the anthropology and archaeology of death*, London, 1982.

Jain, J., *Life in Ancient India as depicted in the Jain Canons*, Bombay, 1947.

Jayaswal, K.P., *Hindu Polity*, Bangalore, 1943 (first ed. 1924).

Jātaka ed. V. Fausboll, London, 1877-97; tr. E.B. Cowell, vols. I-VII., Cambridge, 1895-1907.

Jayatilleke, K.N., *Early Buddhist Theory of Knowledge*, London, 1963.

Jha, H.N., *The Licchavis*, Varanasi, 1970.

Joshi, J.P., 'Interlocking of Late Harappan Culture and Painted Grey Ware Culture in the Light of Recent Excavations', *Man and Environment*, 1978, vol. II, pp. 100-3.

Kane, P.V., *History of Dharmaśāstra*, Poona, 1943 ff.

Kangle, R.P., *The Kauṭilya Arthaśāstra*, Bombay, 1965.

Kāṭhaka Samhitā, ed. Von Schroeder, Leipzig, 1900-11.

Kātyāṇa Śrauta-sūtra, ed. Vidyadhara Sharma, Benaras, 1933-7.

Kauṭilya, *Arthaśāstra*, qv. Kangle.

Kosambi, D.D., 'Brahman Clans', *JAOS*, 1953, 73, pp. 202-8.

Kosambi, D.D., *Introduction to the Study of Indian History*, Bombay, 1956.

Kosambi, D.D., *The Culture and Civilisation of Ancient India in Historical Outline*, London, 1965.

Kosambi, D.D., 'The Vedic "Five Tribes" ', *JAOS*, 1967, 87 pp. 33-9.

Kosambi, D.D., *Indian Numismatics*, New Delhi, 1981.

Krader, L., *Formation of the State*, New Jersey, 1968.

Krader, L., *The Ethnological Notebooks of Karl Marx*, Assen, 1972.

Krader, L., *The Asiatic Mode of Production*, Assen, 1975.

Krishna Deva and V. Mishra, *Vaiśāli Excavations, 1950*, Vaisali, 1961.

Kulke, H., *Jagannātha-kult und Gajapati Königtum*, Weisbaden, 1979.

Kunāla Jātaka, ed. W.B. Bollee, London, 1970.

Lakatos, I., and A. Musgrave (eds.), *Criticism and the Growth of Knowledge*, Cambridge, 1970.

Lambrick, H.T., *Sind: A General Introduction*, Hyderabad, 1964.

Law, B.C., *Kṣatriya Clans in Buddhist India*, Calcutta, 1922.
Law, B.C., *A History of Pali Literature*, 2 vols., London, 1933.
Law, N.N., *Aspects of Ancient Indian Polity*, Oxford, 1921.
Lloyd, G.E.R., *Magic, Reason and Experience*, Cambridge, 1979.
Lowie, R.H., *Primitive Society*, New York, 1920.
Lakṣman Sarup, *Nighantu tathā Nirukta*, Delhi, 1967.
Macdonnel, A.A., and A.B. Keith, *Vedic Index of Names and Subjects*, vols. I and II, Delhi, 1967.
Mahābhārata (Critical Edition), Ādi Parvan, ed. V.S. Sukthankar, Poona, 1927-33.
Mahābhārata, Sabhā Parvan, ed. F. Edgerton, Poona, 1943-4.
Mahābhārata, Udyog Parvan, ed. S.K. De, Poona, 1937-40/47
Mahāvagga, qv. *Vinaya Piṭaka*.
Mahāvaṃsa, ed. W. Geiger, London, 1908; tr. W. Geiger, London, 1912.
Maitrāyanī Saṃhitā, ed. Von Schroeder, Leipzig, 1881-6.
Majjhima Nikāya, ed. V. Trenckner and R. Chalmers, 3 vols., London, 1887-1902; I.B. Horner, 'The Middle Length Sayings', P.T.S. London 1954.
Malalasekara, G.P., *The Pali Literature of Ceylon*, London, 1928.
Mānava Dharmaśāstra, ed. J.R. Gharpure, Bombay, 1920.
Mānava Dharmāsastra/Manu Smṛti, G. Bühler, *The Laws of Manu*, SBE, XXV, Oxford, 1886.
Mankad, D.R., *Puranic Chronology*, Anand, 1951.
Marshall, J., *Taxila*, Cambridge, 1951
Marx, K. and F. Engels, *On Colonialism*, Moscow, 1968.
Matsya Purāṇa, ed. ASS, Poona, 1907.
Mauss, M., *The Gift*, London, 1954.
Megasthenes, J.W. McCrindle, *Ancient India as described by Megasthenes and Arrian*, London, 1877.
Mehta, R.L., *Pre-Buddhist India*, Bombay, 1939.
Meillassoux, C., 'From Reproduction to Production', *Economy and Society*, 1972, I, no. 1, pp. 93-105.
Meillassoux, C., 'Historical Modalities of the Exploitation and Over-exploitation of Labour, *Critique of Anthropology*, 1979, 4, nos. 13 and 14, pp. 7-16.
Middleton, J. and D. Tait, *Tribes without Rulers*, London, 1958.
Morton-Smith, R., *Dates and Dynasties in Earliest India*, Delhi, 1975.
Mukherji, P.C., *Antiquities of Kapilavastu*, no. XXVI, pt 1, Calcutta, 1901 (rpt, Delhi, 1969).

Nadel, S.F., *A Black Byzantium*, London, 1942.
Narain, A.K. (ed.), *Local Coins of Northern India, c. 300 B.C. to 300 A.D.*, Varanasi, 1966.
Narain, A.K. and L. Gopal (eds.), *Seminar Papers on the Chronology of the Punch-Marked Coins*, Varanasi, 1966.
Narain, A.K., and T.N. Roy, *The Excavations of Prahladpur*, Benaras, 1968.
Narain, A.K. and T.N. Roy, *Excavations at Rajghat*, Benaras, 1976.
Naroll, R. and R. Cohen, *A Handbook of Method in Cultural Anthropology*, New York, 1970.
O'Callaghan, M., *Sociological Theories: Race and Colonialism*, UNESCO, 1980.
Oppenheimer, F., *The State*, New York, 1975 (rpt).
Pāli-English Dictionary, ed. by T.W. Rhys Davids and W. Stede, London, 1966.

Pañcaviṃsa Brāhmaṇa, ed. A. Vedantavagisa, Calcutta, 1869-74.
Pande, G.C., *Studies in the Origins of Buddhism*, Allahabad, 1957.
Pāṇini, *Aṣṭādhyāyī*, ed. S.C. Vasu, Delhi, 1962.
Pargiter, F.E., *The Purana Texts of the Dynasties of the Kali Age*, Oxford, 1913.
Pargiter, F.E., *Ancient Indian Historical Tradition*, London, 1922.
Patañjali, *Vyākaraṇa Mahābhāṣyam*, ed. F. Kielhorn, vols. 1 and 2, Poona, 1962.
Patañjali, *Vyākaraṇa Mahābhaṣya*, ed. S.D. Joshi, Poona, 1968.
Pleiner, R., 'The Problems of the Beginning Iron Age in India', *Acta Praehistorica et Archaeologica*, 1971, 2, pp. 5-36.
Polanyi, K., *The Great Transformation*, Boston, 1957.
Polanyi, K., *Trade and Markets in the Early Empires*, Glencoe, 1957.
Polanyi, K., *Dahomey and the Slave Trade*, Seattle, 1966.
Pradhan, S.N., *Chronology of Ancient India*, Calcutta, 1927.
Pusalkar, A.D., *Studies in the Epics and the Puranas*, Bombay, 1955.

Raikes, R.C., 'Kalibangan: death from natural causes', *Antiquity*, 1968, pp. 286-91.
Ramaswamy, C., 'Monsoon over the Indus Valley during the Harappan Period', *Nature*. 1968, 217, pp. 628-9.
Rāmāyaṇa, Bālakāṇḍa, ed. G.H. Bhatt, Baroda, 1960.
Ramāyaṇa, Ayodhyakāṇḍa, ed. P.L. Vaidya, Baroda, 1962.
Rank, O., *The Myth of the Birth of a Hero*, New York, 1959.
Rey, P.P., 'The Lineage Mode of Production', *Critique of Anthropology*, Spring 1975, no. 3, pp. 27-29.
Rey, P.P., 'Class Contradiction in Lineage Societies', *Critique of Anthropology*, 1971, 4, nos. 13 and 14, pp. 41-60.
Rg Veda, ed. F. Max Müller, Oxford, 1890-2; tr. R.T.H. Griffith, 2 vols., Varanasi, 1963.
Rhys Davids, T.W., *Buddhist India*, London, 1903.
Rockhill, W.W., *Life of Buddha*, London, 1907.
Samantapāsādikā, ed. N.A. Jayawickrama, London, 1962.
Samyutta Nikāya, ed. L. Freer, 5 vols., PTS, London, 1884-98; tr. Mrs Rhys Davids and F.L. Woodward, 'Book of Kindred Sayings', PTS, London, 1913.
Sankalia, H.D., *Prehistory and Protohistory of India and Pakistan*, Poona, 1974.
Sānkhāyana Gṛhya Sūtra, tr. H. Oldenberg, SBE, XXIX, Oxford.
Śatpatha Brāhmaṇa, ed. A. Weber, London, 1885; tr. J. Eggeling, pts. I-V, SBE, Oxford, 1882.
Scott Littleton, C., *The New Comparative Mythology*, Berkeley, 1972.
Seddon, D. (ed.), *Relations of Production*, London, 1978.
Senart, E., *Le Mahāvastu*, Paris, 1882-97.
Senart, E., *Caste in India: The Facts and the System*, tr. D. Ross, London, 1930.
Service, E.R., *Origins of the State and Civilization: The Process of Cultural Evolution*, New York, 1975.
Shanin, T. (ed), *Peasants and Peasant Society*, Harmondsworth, 1971.
Sharma, A., 'An Analysis of the Epithets applied to the Śūdras in Aitareya Brāhmaṇa', XVIII, pt 3, pp. 300-18
Sharma, G.R., *The Excavations at Kauśāmbi*, 1957-59, Allahabad, 1960.
Sharma, G.R., *The Beginnings of Agriculture*, Allahabad, 1980.
Sharma, J.P., *Republics in Ancient India*, Leiden, 1968.

Sharma, R.S., *Light on Early Indian Society and Economy*, Bombay, 1966.
Sharma, R.S., *Aspects of Political Ideas and Institutions in Ancient India*, Delhi 1959/1968.
Sharma, R.S., 'Forms of Property in the Early Portions of the Ṛg Veda,' Essays in Honour of Prof. S.C. Sarkar, New Delhi, 1976, pp. 39-50.
Sharma, R.S., 'Class Formation and its Material Basis in the upper Gangetic Basin', c. 1000-500 B.C., *IHR*, July 1975, II, no. 1, p. 1 ff.
Sharma, R.S., *Śūdras in Ancient India*, Delhi, 1980.
Singh, R.L., *Regional Geography*, Varanasi, 1971.
Sinha, B.P., and B.S. Verma, 'Preliminary Report of Chirand Excavations for the year 1969', *Patna University Journal*, July 1978, 23, no. 3, p. 97 ff.
Southall, A.W., *Alur Society*, Cambridge, 1956.
Spate, O.H.K., *India and Pakistan*, London, 1964.
Spooner, B., 'Politics, Kinship and Ecology in S.E. Persia', *Ethnology*, 1969, I, pp. 139-52.
Spooner, B. (ed)., *Population Growth*, Cambridge, Mass, 1972.
Srinivasan, D., *Concept of Cow in the Rig Veda*, Delhi, 1979.
Srivastava, B., *Trade and Commerce in Ancient India*, Varanasi, 1968.
Stein, B., *Essays on South India*, New Delhi, 1976.
Stein, B., *Peasant State and Society in Medieval South India*, Delhi, 1980.
Steward, J.H.. *Theory of Culture Change*, Urbana, 1955.
Sumaṅgala Vilāsinī, ed. T.W. Rhys Davids, P.T.S., London, 1886.
Suraj Bhan, 'Excavation at Mithathal 1968 (Hissar)', *Journal of Haryana Studies*, 1969, I, no. 1, pp. 1-15.
Suraj Bhan, and J.G. Shaffer, 'New Discoveries in Northern Haryana', *Man and Environment*, 1978, II, pp. 59-68.
Suraj Bhan, *Excavation at Mithathal (1980) and other Explorations in the Sutlej-Yamuna Divide*, Kurukshetra, 1975.
Taittirīya Brāhmana, ed. R. Mitra, Calcutta, 1855-70.
Tambiah, S.J., *World Conqueror and World Renouncer*, Cambridge, 1976.
Terray, E., *Marxism and 'Primitive' Societies*, New York, 1975.
Thapar, Romila, *The Past and Prejudice*, New Delhi, 1975.
Thapar, Romila,. 'A Possible Identification of Meluhha, Dilmun and Makan', *JESHO*, 1975, XVIII, pt 1, p. 30 ff.
Thapar, Romila, *Ancient Indian Social History: Some Interpretations*, New Delhi, 1978.
Thapar, Romila, *Exile and the Kingdom: Some thoughts on the Rāmāyaṇa*, Bangalore, 1978.
Thapar, Romila, 'The Historian and the Epic', *Annals of the Bhandarkar Oriental Research Institute*, 1979, LX, pp. 199-213.
Thorner, D., 'Peasant Economy as a Category in Economic History', *Deuxieme Conference Internationale de' Histoire Economique*, Aix-en-Provence, 1962, vol. 2, pp. 287-300, Mouton; rptd. T. Shanin (ed.), *Peasants and Peasant Societies*, pp. 202-18.
Thorner, D., 'Marx on India and the Asiatic Mode of Production', *Contributions to Indian Sociology*, 1966, no. 9, pp. 33-66.
Trautmann, T.R., *Kauṭilya and the Arthaśāstra*, Leiden, 1971.
Trautmann, T.R. (ed.), *Kinship and History in South Asia*, Michigan, 1974.

Tripathi, V., *The Painted Grey Ware, An Iron Age Culture of Northern India*, Delhi, 1976.

Upaniṣads, ed. and tr. S. Radhakrishnan, *The Principal Upanisads*, London, 1953.

Uvāsaga Dasāo, ed. R. Hoernle, Calcutta, 1980.

Vājasaneyi Saṃhitā, ed. A. Weber, London, 1935.

Vamsatthapakāsinī, ed. G.P. Malalasekara, London, 1935.

Varma, S., *The Etymologies of Yāska*, Hoshiarpur, 1953.

Varma, V.P., *Early Buddhism and its Origins*, Delhi, 1972.

Vasiṣṭha Dharma-sūtra, ed. A.A. Führer, Bombay, 1916; tr. G. Bühler, SBE, vol. XIV, Oxford, 1892.

Vāyu Purāṇa, ed. R. Mitra, 2 vols., Calcutta, 1880-8.

Vibhaṅga, ed. Mrs Rhys Davids, P.T.S., 1904.

Vinaya Piṭaka, ed. H. Oldenberg, P.T.S., London, 1879-83; tr. T.W. Rhys Davids and H. Oldenberg, SBE, Oxford, 1881-5.

Viṣṇu Purāṇa, ed. J. Vidyasagara, Calcutta, 1882, tr. H.H. Wilson, 5 vols., London, 1864-70.

Wagle, N., *Society at the Time of the Buddha*, Bombay, 1966.

Watters, T., *On Yuan Chwang's Travels in India*, New Delhi, 1973 (rpt).

Wilhelmy, H., 'Das Urstromtal an Ostrand der Indusebens und dar Saraswati Problem', *Zeitschrift fur Geomorphologie*, Supplement Band, 1969, 8, pp. 76-93.

Wittfogel, K., *Oriental Despotism*, New Haven, 1957.

E.V. Winans, *Shambala*, Berkeley, 1962.

W.H. Wiser, *The Hindu Jajmani System*, Lucknow, 1958.

Yadav, B.N.S., 'The Kali Age and the Social Transition', *IHR*, 1978-9, V, nos. 1 and 2, pp. 37-8.

Yajñavalkya Smṛti, ed. ASS, Poona, 1903-4; tr. G.R. Gharpure, Bombay, 1936.

INDEX